IN
SENSORIUM

BOOKS BY TANAÏS

In Sensorium: Notes for My People

Bright Lines

IN SENSORIUM

NOTES FOR MY PEOPLE

TANAÏS

HARPER

An Imprint of HarperCollins*Publishers*

HarperCollins books may be purchased for educational, business, or sales promotional use. For information, please email the Special Markets Department at SPsales@harpercollins.com.

Original line breaks not observed in *Seam* epigraph on page 165.

FIRST EDITION

Designed by Chloe Foster

Library of Congress Cataloging-in-Publication Data has been applied for.

ISBN 978-0-358-38170-9

1 2022

For Mojo

CONTENTS

III. HEAD NOTES

AUTHOR'S NOTE

PORTALS • PERFUME AS PORTAL

Let us begin — at the end of the world —
I sheltered in place in New York City, where tens of thousands of my fellow city dwellers died of a virus, and in mid-April of the year 2020 I, too, became sick. For two weeks, I was immobile from fatigue and headaches, everything I ate came out of me as liquid, and my sense of smell grew faint. My illness began around midnight, when I received news from Dhaka — my maternal grandmother, Nanu, had a fever and seemed to be nearing her end.

Her breathing, her cries for her son who died, her sleeplessness, her prayer, and, of course, her will that we should practice Islam, were as familiar to me as the scent of her body, one of the first sensuous cartographies in my memory — jasmine attar, violet talcum, *paan* juice, crushed rose powder, coconut oil, Pond's cream, Tabasco sauce, canola oil. Nanu's tastes were village girl through and through: she loved a bright red lip and attar of jasmine, a narcotic floral with an animal stink. After each meal, we watched her methodically prepare her *paan,* filling the betel leaf with contents she kept in a metal tiffin. First, she stroked the leaf with white limestone paste, then filled it with names I read off the bottles in Bangla: *supari, chaman bahar, jorda.* I later learned the words in English: areca nut, rose powder, tobacco. Carcinogens be damned — and she went on to survive cancer twice — this ritual brought her so much pleasure.

As a Bangladeshi Muslim raised in the United States, I am still just two generations out of the village. I've felt called to do right, to write, because of my grandmothers, both child brides, who lived as British, Indian, and Pakistani, and never had a say in shaping the world outside of their homes. My paternal grandmother did not live long enough to witness the birth of Bangladesh, a fifty-year-old country at the time of this book's writing. Whereas a body cannot escape circumstance — in my grandmother's case, she married at thirteen, did not finish school, lost her son and husband at a young age — a perfume allows us to, if only for a moment.

When I heard news of Nanu's imminent death, I prayed for her to feel peace, to feel my love across the ocean. She lay alone in a hospital room, facing the indignity of her last moments on Earth without any of the children she'd raised beside her. I sprayed myself with one of my perfumes, Night Blossom, an ode to the jasmine attar she wore. But I couldn't smell the jasmine notes in the perfume. I sprayed my wrists, my neck — nothing. I started hyperventilating, spraying perfume, and spiraling. *I can't smell, I can't smell, babe, she's gonna die alone, I'm gonna die alone, I can't smell,* I cried, waking up my husband, Mustapha, who held me in his arms, guiding me through deep pranayamic breaths to calm me down. Holding the pain of the world, of New York, felt unbearable. For the next two weeks, I became so exhausted I could barely get up from the couch. I would stare at my ceiling, unable to sleep, smell, or catch my breath.

Finally, a sharp malodor pierced through my olfactory numbness: a dead mouse in our walls. Mustapha and I guessed that since all of the restaurants in our neighborhood had closed, critters needed our haven, but their appearance felt like more signs of plague: roaches, ants, millipedes. The sickly sweet scent of decomposition permeated the walls, growing sharper at night. As I faced the possibility of my own death, I understood the profound significance of perfume in times of plague.

Perfume, in Latin, means *through smoke,* a reference to the sacred burning of incense, resin, and woods that have defined spiritual practice since ancient times. Perfume is a smoke signal worn on the body, a way to convey who we are, while drawing a protective border between our self and the outside. Perfume is an object of immanence, rooted in our physical world of raw materials, used to transcend this world for the Divine. Ancients incensed their clothes with the smoke of burned frankincense, embalmed the dead in oils of cedar and pine, wore garlands of jasmine and rose in *gandharva* love ceremonies, where there were no witnesses besides the lovers themselves. During the plague, pomanders of clove-studded oranges or herbal concoctions of saffron, turmeric, rose, and orange water were thought to stave off sickness. During my illness, the necessity of perfume became clear. I understood why humans *needed* the fragrant to survive the stench of our own filth, in life and in death. I understood why mass death made us yearn for beauty; after a genocide, beauty revives a possibility of survival.

Throughout history, humans have divided themselves by odor, what they found putrescent versus pleasant — between the sick and the healthy, the poor and the rich, the polluted and the pure, the slave and the master, the Dalit and the Brahmin.

I lit the scented candles and perfumes that I make and sell as another hustle besides writing — if I could smell these, I would know that I did not still have the virus. But everything continued to smell faint, save for the dead mouse at night. After being unable to eat or keep anything inside my body for more than fifteen days, I received a distant drop-off of home-cooked food from my Ma, whom I waved to from six feet away for the first time in six months. Her food healed the last traces of illness, which made sense, since our mothers nurture our gut biome. The next day, I woke up at dawn for *sehri* to begin my first fast for Ramadan in almost twenty years. I sipped water, slowly, but not wanting to push my luck, I didn't eat. I didn't read the Quran; this time around, I would only have spiritual notes by Kazim Ali, an Indian-Canadian Muslim author whose book *Fasting for Ramadan* — in addition to our daily email correspondence — would be my guide as I reclaimed a religious tradition I'd shed as a young person.

Being attuned to my body felt like communion with my grandmother, a thread between her, me, and all other Muslims observing Ramadan who empathize with those suffering from hunger and poverty. Rituals are how the sediments of faith are laid down, banded, formed. I feel most at home in syncretic religious traditions, a bit of every faith, a personal spirituality that holds the infinite — the cosmic, the natural, the unknowable — at its center. During my fast, I began to understand why Islam shifted the history of my ancestors, who experienced caste oppression, conquest, colonialism, floods, famine, and mass death. I began to think of fasting as a portal, a connective hunger, a preparation for what might come after catastrophe. I read once that during the month of Ramadan, the gates of heaven are wide open, and anyone who dies during the holy month is permitted to ascend. But I'm not sure my grandmother ever worried, since she performed the Hajj. Her two pilgrimages to Mecca would surely secure her place in heaven. For the first time in decades, it gave me peace to believe this, too. I didn't know if I would ever see her again.

I weep seeing the images of India, mass pyres in New Delhi, where I once lived, millions of people dying of the virus and a lack of precious oxygen. A year before India's burning, isolated and ill at home, I watched a brilliant conversation between Arundhati Roy and Imani Perry, hosted by Haymarket Books on YouTube. Their mutual affection and expansive intellect lightened my mood. Roy's essay "The Pandemic Is a Portal" illuminated the intense planetary shift we are living through, this period of mass illness and death, of vast migrations of refugees and laborers fleeing wars and gangs and climate change to make passage to new homes.

People think the realm of the imagination is not material, but everything is material, said Perry, and I thought about how my connection to my ancestors continues through material culture — textiles, jewelry, photographs, perfumes — remembrances that have been spared despite war and migration. *Everything I write and say comes from communal wisdom,* said Roy. I felt those words deeply; gathering the knowledge for this book has felt like weaving eons of such wisdom into a massive textile. I grabbed her essay collection *The End of Imagination,* wanting to reread the title essay, remembering the solace I found in her image of another world being possible, one that we could hear breathing, waiting for us.

I wanted this relief, as I struggled to catch my own breath.

I opened Roy's book, and immediately I noticed the Void.

On the map of India, every single Indian state and South Asian country is named — but not Bangladesh. There is just an open, blank space, a niche. Bangladesh is a ten-letter word, too long for its own borders on this map that made sure we knew it was *not to scale* but didn't even bother to name my motherland. For most of my childhood in the 1980s, no one had even heard of Bangladesh. The erasure brought up an old feeling of being illegible. Invisible.

Maps make borders real. On this map, Bangladesh didn't matter. As if generations of our people — who lived as Indian, British, Pakistani — didn't fight or die for India's Independence. As if they had not labored to build India's economy and wealth for centuries. As if this land where India's rivers end can be separated from the rivers and dams that Roy has written so fiercely about. As if the women-led garment workforce and rural microfinancing have not shaped modern South Asia's feminist future. As if the soil of East Bengal did not birth ways of divine feminine worship. As if we have not always been despised, maligned, and erased by upper-caste Brahmins as the *mleccha,* low caste, Dalit, Muslim, barbarians. As if the Liberation War of 1971 — or genocide and rape by the Pakistan Army — never happened. As if the rise of fascism and communal violence against minorities does not turn people into refugees. As if the cyclones, floods, and famines do not come for Bangladesh first.

Borders are rife with violence, but also longing. As we move through this portal, we face the truth that the cracks and lies in our systems are being exposed. This is the endgame of late capitalism. No greater myth than the free market built on racist legacies of slavery, sexual violence, police brutality, fascism, and war — once fueled by the European colonial quest for fragrant spices. Would I ever find my people's histories if I kept looking for them in upper-caste Indian narratives? As Imani Perry sagely observed: *Stepping through the portal is releasing one's attachment to that which dominates.*

This book reimagines a release from that which dominates. I write this book into the Void on that map, holding at its center the frontier that my people hail from, long considered profane by Brahmin priests and Mughal conquerors, a land where Buddhist and Hindu kingdoms once flourished before Islam became the dominant faith, a land that holds memories of ancient opulence, the ancestral feminine and revolutionary history of India, a land severed by multiple Partitions and renamings: East Bengal, East Pakistan, and as of fifty years ago, since 1971, Bangladesh. My grandmother had been a citizen of them all.

On the seventh day of my fast, I pulled Tarot and got Death. In that moment, I knew.

Before I went to bed that night, I held my arms around my shoulders, embracing myself as though I were embracing Nanu. I repeated the words: *I love you, I release you, release if you have to, shanti te thaken, shanti te jao, be at peace, leave in peace.* I pictured her serene, enveloped in a soft wave of white light, from my apartment across ocean and land and air and the melted core of this Earth. I touched my skin, pictured the softness of her old, barely wrinkled brown skin, her thick arms. The next morning, I woke up faint of my sense of smell; within an hour, my sister called with news of her death.

I assembled an altar, something I'm sure she'd disapprove of, since candles, crystals, and Kali were decidedly not Islamic, but Nanu understood how beautiful objects bring comfort. Tiger-eye mala for supplications — *la illaha illallah* — counted on one hundred and eight beads. I lit three tapers in the white and pink of her widow's clothes, and draped one of her soft hand-stitched *kantha* quilts around me. I would never see her again.

On Day Seven in *Fasting for Ramadan,* Kazim Ali writes, *What will happen to our bodies — our own human, individual bodies: touch yours now, right now, touch the skin, it is real — what happens to our bodies next?*

I see my Nanu, still young, stepping down into the dirt grave where her son lay, his body no longer bound to his spirit. She is sobbing, screaming, shaking his body, unable to leave him in the ground, unable to believe he is gone. This memory isn't mine, but I've heard it enough that it feels like my own.

Ancient perfumes exist as fragments in texts, but what if we ourselves don't appear in texts? The dominant culture version of our histories becomes the Record of Power, where lies, misrepresentations, and erasures abound. I call these the *patramyth* — foundational lies and mythologies recorded in history to protect the powerful. There are multiple etymologies in the word *patramyth,* which shares the Greek root *patria,* or lineage, with *patriarchy; patra* is a written document in Sanskrit, a language wielded by the powerful in India for a couple thousand years. *Myth* is an origin story, but in my mother tongue, Bengali, *mithya* is a lie. Patramyths have justified grave violence by way of religion, science, philosophy, literature, anthropology, books, and laws that deemed brown-skinned, Black, and Indigenous people smelly, savage, slave, prostitute, deviant — deserving of exploitation until death. Learning to see ourselves outside of the specter of the dominant culture's

patramyths — decolonizing   ourselves — means   recognizing
true knowledge from that which seeks to uphold domination.

Scent is a savior for people in exile and diaspora, said my friend
Dana El Masri, an Egyptian-Lebanese perfumer living in Mon-
treal. I make perfume to encapsulate the notes of *desh,* homeland that has never been my home. Perfume would be the
shortest route to my grandmother after her death. *Gandha* is
a perfume, aroma, or a stink, *gandha* is my pilgrimage through
the vast, syncretic lineage I've inherited: Dravidian, Sufi, Muslim, Hindu, Buddhist, Persian, Afghan, Turkish, Indian, Pakistani, snake-goddess worshipper. As Western modern thought
and whiteness evolved during European colonization, the sense
of sight ascended to prominence. Smell became associated with
primitive and barbaric people. They imagined man as separate
from nature, severing the connection to the feminine and the
sacred. A perfume collects these fragmented histories into a
single borderless substance, a seamless composition of oils and
resins distilled from plants that might be strangers in nature,
from countries with a violent colonial relationship, like French
lavender and Haitian vetiver. By collecting fragrant materials,
what Saidiya Hartman calls *degraded material of the archive,*
and transforming them into new compositions, I have found
a way to wrest back our memories, bodies, stories, and smells
from the hard damage of colonization. This book is shaped like
a perfume, built from the perspective of a perfumer. First, I lay
down the patramyths, the heavy base notes of history, of South
Asia and my childhood; a foundation for the heart notes, col-

lected stories about the women in my family, feminine love and desire, the unimaginable violence imprinted on survivors; all the way to the top notes, the invitation to a fragrance, touch-points akin to sites of pilgrimage, psychedelic experience, and spiritual awakening, as evocative as they are fleeting.

Using this degraded material, a perfume emerges as a sensuous act of resistance.

When my grandmother fell ill, her youngest son drove her around for eight hours, just to find a hospital that would admit her. Roads, hospitals, futures, nothing had ever been guaranteed. When Nanu passed, she died without being touched, loved, soothed. Alone. Without her children or grandchildren near her. All of her kin scattered across the world — the meaning of diaspora is a scattering, like seeds — we were so far from her when she left us. I fasted for Ramadan as she ascended to Ancestor. Hunger radiated through my body, every sensation became strangely heightened — the longing, sorrow, lust, and fear for where our world was headed. I was separated from my family; we were unable to mourn Nanu's passing together, unable to console my mother as she grieved. Nanu crossed oceans throughout her life to see us in the States, but she had never set foot on the silvery waters of the Bay of Bengal, at the edge of her own homeland. Her body is buried next to my grandfather, in his ancestral village. She was a portal between this world and an older world I am descended from, a world that I feel in my bones, but will never know.

I
BASE NOTES

Mojave

Invisible Indians

Romantic Scientist

~~Orientals~~

Beloved

Mojave — Perfume Interlude

HEAD

Black Copal

Wild White Sage

Blue Eucalyptus

Juniper Leaf

HEART

Palo Santo

Linden Blossom

Honey

BASE

Mitti Attar

Sandalwood

Leather

Norlimbanol

My path to the Native history of this land is through per-maculture, the indigenous plants, the native plants, the soil, where the water runs — I am learning to read the land. In Sufi mysticism, to experience an ascent on the spiritual path, one has to feel and cycle back to a spiritual poverty, a place where there is nothing. From that place, the longing for the Divine starts. Where being starts. Where you listen. The more I get to know the desert, the emptier it becomes.

— Fariba Salma Alam,
American Bangladeshi artist, in an interview

Joshua Tree, January 2020. In the morning, I meditated, wrote by hand, and did yoga asanas in the backyard, beside the lone Joshua tree in the yard, its wayward branches casting a shadow like an arboreal Durga. I spent the rest of the day making myself simple lunches, quesadillas or pasta, comfort I craved because I knew that what I'd be reading for research would hurt. In the afternoon, I would drive to the park to take a hike and record what I saw and smelled. Juniper needles I cracked between my fingers, the scent of wet clay from the remnants of snowfall in the shadows between boulders, untouched by the sun.

I found a spot near the Oasis of Mara, and watched the sunset bathe the desert pink. I stayed until the full moonrise above the peaks that formed over two billion years ago. Darkness settled. I surrendered to silence, as stars populated the night sky. As I beheld this immense expanse, I recalled my grim morning reading, about a colonial-era famine in Bengal. Death disguised as exploration, expansion, natural selection, manifest destiny, white supremacy, industrialization, and innovation. This land, where the Mojave and Sonoran deserts meet, once belonged to the Serrano, Cahuilla, Chemehuevi, and Mojave tribes. The presence of water in a desert is a gift, and once they lived near this oasis, until white settlers descended with violence. Where I sat in a rented jeep, hemmed in by the park, had been land they'd lived on for thousands of years. Their descendants live on in Twenty-Nine Palms and Coachella, far from their ancestral oasis.

After two weeks of intense work in the desert, I noticed that my scalp had started to feel tender, that I was losing clumps of hair each day. I discovered a bald ring, just as my grandmother had first discovered my alopecia years ago, when she'd been braiding my hair. Alopecia returned whenever I felt heartbroken, usually over a person, not history. Reading these narratives produced stress in my body, triggering an autoimmune response. Research suggests trauma is recorded in our genes, but some scientists argue this is circumstantial, and that encoding trauma as something we inherit in our bodies would be undesirable. I believe in science, but I believe in the unknowable, too.

I lost my hair, my sleep, my desire to eat, sick to my stomach as I've absorbed these stories.

Do we need scientific evidence to prove that the violence against our ancestors affects us, too?

We cannot turn back time and resurrect the world before genocide. I made a perfume called Mojave, to honor the First People of this land. Sacred notes of palo santo, wild white sage, and black copal are the incenses of the Americas, burned in ceremony for protection and clarity; as oils they smell as cool as a desert night.

One morning after meditation, I tripped and dropped a crystal, a smooth white sphere of selenite that I keep on my writing desk. This reminded me of the splitting of the moon, a miracle in Islam — one that has multiple interpretations; that Muhammad is a true prophet, that the day of judgment will split believers and infidels. From Surah Al-Qamar, The Moon: *the hour has come near / the moon has split in two / they see a miracle / they turn away and say / this is passing magic* — I prefer my own interpretations. The moon's dark side is unseen, but we know it's there. The splitting of the moon, my body's unraveling, a portent of everything to come.

Invisible Indians

Perfume as Erotics & Past Lives

NOTES

Musk & Choya Nakh

Like the snake, I am my own future.

— Natalie Diaz, "Snake-Light," *Postcolonial Love Poem*

Language is a skin: I rub my language against the
Other . . . my language trembles with desire —
— Roland Barthes, *A Lover's Discourse*

MEMORY

Will we be ruined? This is the first thing I wonder, when we begin our — *affair* — if loving without touch counts as one. *What do you mean, ruin?* you write back. I imagine you whispering the word, *ruin,* wondering how a fantasy has that sort of power. I mean a love that ruins us because we have to hide. Love doomed by repression and secrecy. Love bound by a lust insatiable as it is impossible, we are fucked, fucked over, in its aftermath. The ruins of a lover, their imprint on us — *vasana* — their skin, their scent, and traces fixed in our mind. Ruins of femmes you've loved in secret before me, the ruins of those we will hurt to have each other, the ruins of women you are bound to by duty — wife, child, mother, sister. Love as duty, burdened by the crushing weight of another's need. I have loved Indian men before, but none ever chose me as their mate. Each time, their love became an extraction, ultimately, a rejection. I'm not sure you understand what it feels like to be from a people who are considered backwards by other people who look just like them. I suppose what I'm asking you: *Will you ruin me?*

My birth name sounds like the word for water in Tamil, the mother tongue that you cannot speak. *Vacanai* is the Tamil word for perfume, perhaps a loanword from the Sanskrit, *vasana*. Given how ancient Dravidian language is, and still spoken by millions today, I wonder if it's possible that language flowed in the opposite direction, from Tamil to Sanskrit, which evolved in the second millennium BCE, entombed as the liturgical language of scripture, governance, literary arts, the realm of the so-called twice-born, men who've been initiated into Vedic rituals, Brahmins, like you; forbidden for women or lower-caste people, long before femmes like me converted to Islam or called themselves Dalit. Of course, they knew these rituals, because they are a part of them, mala makers stringing flower garlands, makers of incense and *tilak* paste and sacred fires, right there, as high-caste men chanted and performed their purification rituals. Outsider means that you are invisible until you provoke or bother the social order — then you become hypervisible — being excluded makes you keenly aware of your oppressor. As a youth, I felt enthralled by the pantheon of female deities, the *pujas*, the mantras, that belonged to my Indian Bengali Hindu family friends, even though I'd never be invited to take part in their prayers. Only years later, as an adult, living in India, would I partake in *puja,* but I suppose I was passing as a Hindu.

Vasana is a karmic memory, traces of a former life carried into the next; an imprint of a person or a place you once knew. These are the perfumes we know from other lifetimes, in the Hindu tradition a sense of cosmic déjà vu, a scent that we've encountered before. As with most words in Sanskrit, there are double, multiple, sometimes opposing meanings. *Vasana* also means a perfume enfleurage, pressing flowers into fat, so that a fragrance is transferred into a new medium. In the medieval Indian process, described in the perfumery treatise *Gandhasara,* the perfumer placed flowers with sesame seeds in a scented cloth. The sesame seeds were crushed, as the scent of the flowers diffused into the oil, becoming the perfumed *vasana.* Flowers that don't want to express their oils easily, like jasmine or tuberose, too delicate for the stress of steam distillation, are well-suited for *vasana.* Thousands of flowers are steeped and replenished and steeped, until their fragrance is imprinted into the fat, like a memory. In my mother's village dialect, *bashna* is a pleasant odor, whereas *bashona* in Bengali, or *vasana* in Hindi, means desire. Impressions processed in our brain's olfactory bulb move onward to the ancient almond in our brain, the amygdala. Memory, scent, desire — an archetypal trine. Laced throughout this text are *vasanas* that live in my body, my own, those of my family, those of my people. They're not precise recordings, just what I remember. When we know a person's body, as we inhale them, our mind forms a memory, a *vasana* of their scent into our own body. Their molecules imprinted into our minds. Medieval Indian perfumers named the blending of wet substances *vedha,* piercing. We are activated by different senses, me, smell, you, sound, my voice aspirated with pleasure an erotic jolt for you, and the scent of my perfume on another person's skin does the same for me.

You and I study each other's faces in photographs, little art videos of me gazing and spinning and filtered and dreamy, soft smoky voice notes, voyeur to my orgasm. I don't yet know what you smell like. I never want to be seen too close. I want to be a fantasy, I'm not at home in my body as much as I project this on the Internet, filters let me hide myself, the parts that I'm half a generation too old to love fully, the folds of my belly, the black brush of pubes, calloused feet, nipples only drawn out by teeth, useless to feed the baby that I'll never have, the shyest part of my body. If we knew each other in a past life, did I have these same eyes that you love to gaze into through the little portal in your hand? These eyes that are near-sightless without my glasses. In another life, when I felt you inside of me, were you just a blur?

Can I be your muse? We ask this of each other, as if we needed permission to be inspired by desire. Art is where our longing must go, how this distance disappears, a sublimation of sex into text. I'm not sure you know what you're asking, though, to be a writer's muse is to surrender the boundary of a secret for the story. We always choose the story; I cannot be kept a secret. Men like you have always loved femmes like me. We have always been your muses, we know all the sordid details — the cheating on your wives, the brokenness, the lies — that are written out of the patramyths you tell the world. All of the great Indian epics depict low-caste women as smelly, filthy, destructive. We know too much, so you have to disassociate from us, the shamed woman, the woman who talks too much, the femme who doesn't give a fuck. We are inherently ruinous for powerful men.

Love feels like a visit to another country, love infatuates new language, I begin making up words to describe this feeling, one that I've never quite had as an adult: loving an Indian man, and being loved in return. Sliding into a chat is nothing new, from my first moment online, in an AOL chatroom, I was furiously cybersexing Indian boys, who may have been pedophilic men in their thirties for all I know. Meeting Indian boys on the Internet let them lust after a girl who would likely scandalize their mothers. In the closed box of the chat, we found a safe space for filth, our little wet dreams came alive. When I got older, dates with *desi* guys in finance became more about scoring a fancy dinner to escape the drudgery of grad school, my diet of a pizza slice or truck burritos. Hooking up led to nowhere, I couldn't fake the wifey shit. You remind me of the thrill of the secret of my first crushes, my first loves and heartbreaks in high school, the delicious sensation of a secret blooming inside of me. I had long given up on this sort of connection happening ever again — the Indian men I've loved always ended up dating or marrying professional women of their own caste or religion, their same class status, skyrocketing to wealth. Or they ended up with white women. Bangladeshi men never even considered a bad femme like me an option, their mothers never sent over biodatas — you can't spin a respectable lover résumé out of me. The sorrow that this sentiment brings up in me is old, a wound that I want to heal with you.

Apocalypsexual, that's my word for longing for someone at the end of the world, love in exile, eleven miles — lifetimes — apart. Our conversations are at turns dissertations and psychosexual revelations and confessions, an archive of deep secrets, intellectual, spiritual, lucid, unfiltered thoughts, we begin to name our traumas and our families' traumas, our shame. We experience a free range of feelings with each other, knowing full well that our fantasy is a fiction that might turn true if we choose. The inexplicable part of all of this is that I've known you before, in a past life, a belief that I didn't grow up with, nor am I supposed to believe. Our kink, our karma, the actions we've carried from one life to the next that have brought us to this erotic encounter, one that feels much older than we can understand. *Do you believe in gods?* I wonder, as I have reconnected to my belief in All — h, just as I begin to know you.

What does sacred mean to you? You asked me this once, and I want to answer: *Everything.* I sense mysticynicism in you; you are a natural skeptic, or maybe just discerning. I wonder if you've numbed the part of you that trusts the sacred. Do you feel deadened by the very systems designed to kill us? You want to know what I find sacred? That you make music, reach for transcendence, for you and for your listener, a gift that connects you to something vaster than sound. I consider this sacred.

Each night this week I've sat on the stoop with Jenny. I haven't chain-smoked American Spirits in years, but we stay up until dawn, talking about the uprising after the murder of George Floyd, the eons of violence our people have survived, the fear we feel because we chose to be artists. One of the inheritances of colonization is what I call *mysticynicism,* a persistent doubt of the Unknown, the Divine, the Sacred. When I toss quarters stamped with the face of an enslaver/first president to read divinations from the *I Ching,* the Chinese Book of Changes, it's not just some New Age shit, it's ancient shit. I use the book to illuminate situations that confuse me, like you, and I can't extricate how freely I read these words from what Jenny told me. How Chinese people and scholars were imprisoned and killed just for using the *I Ching,* for making art that calls truth to power. Sitting with her each night, I realize how relieved I am to be writing in a time that she is, finding the mystic and tender and traumatic in the past, as we imagine the future. I think about how she and I may have known each other in other lifetimes, too.

My entire space could fit inside your brownstone, I imagine, we've never been over to each other's houses, in the old world, when there used to be house parties. What's it like, having the space to hide?

This apartment is similar to all the ones I grew up living

in, close quarters, a single bathroom, very little sunlight. But my family owns this love hovel — this is ours. We've planted our roots in a city we've lived in for thirty years, most of my life, the truest home I've ever known. Mold-tinged tiles in the bathroom, mice and carpenter ants in the walls, whenever I feel repulsed by the cityness, I try to remember that these are signs that our home is inviting, a place where living creatures feel safe.

I write at the edge of a dining table that moonlights as a desk, I write late at night to dawn, as my man sleeps. I write by the light of three tall taper candles, fingerlings of light, their burning wicks I see as witches, *sati,* Hindu widows, witnessing flames, pain past. I feel shame writing about us, but that's part of why I write, writing is the form of art that can ruin, compelling judgment — even death — but to write in spite of this is to honor inner truth — greater than anything any man could ever give me.

The new LED streetlights give the nighttime the feel of a movie set or football stadium, emitting the same blue wavelength of light as our phones, making it hard for our brains to turn off and sleep. I miss the amber light of the old sodium halides. The world is so quiet at this hour, I only hear my own breathing and sighs, until the mockingbirds trill at dawn. I burn Tara Incense rolled by Tibetan refugees in India, banished from their homeland by Chinese occupation. There is a story behind every good, if we allow ourselves to consider the origins before we consume. My home is laden with traces of forgotten femmes, maximalist, mystic, sensuous shit, everywhere: vintage Navajo and Mexico ceramics, psychedelic Berber rugs, textiles, crystals, candles. My man built our floor-to-ceiling oak bookshelves, a grandeur the developers never dreamt possible for this old place. One wall is painted Oaxaca turquoise, fixed with an altar. A Buddha made of stone. A bronze statue of Shiva dancing next to a print of Kali stepping on him, blissed out.

A sphere of green opal, a nod to Islam among the idols; and a 1969 map of *India, Pakistan, Burma and Ceylon* — Bangladesh does not yet exist — all of the borders between the countries are bright red lines. When I trip on acid, they drip blood.

MUSK & OCEAN

> This beloved cheek, black as durva grass with its erect hairs, is victorious. Why here, Dravidian streaks sketched with musk?
>
> — Viryamitra, eleventh-century poet

The poet considers the black musk on his lover's face unnecessary, their facial hair — the lover's quivering hair standing on end — arouses longing itself. The lover may be masculine or feminine, in this precolonial time, there were freer, more fluid notions of gender, less delineation between cisgender women and transfemmes, or third nature, *tritiya prakriti*. Sanskrit, Persian, and Arabic literature are laden with ardent references to musk, for its pheromonal power, its faraway, mythic origins in the Himalayan forests of Tibet. Where you and I meet is a mystic crossroads, outside these contexts of power, where Hindus and Muslims were the same and not-the-same, at once, the realm of Sufi and Yogi mystics, poets, lovers, where the ghazal and the raga are unified sound, and the hypnotic fragrance of bodies smells like our musk.

Musk, a scented site of Hindu-Muslim confluence. Musk first appeared in Sanskrit literature by way of Muslim conquest, around the ninth century. *Navi-gandha,* navel perfume, after the dark scented grains in the male musk deer gland, found in the faraway forests of Tibet. In Islam, musk emanates from heaven, even said to be the prophet Muhammad's favorite scent. Al-Biruni, a Persian polymath of Islam's Golden Age, the great-granddaddy of Indology, wrote the *Kitāb al-Hind, Book of India*, and the *Kitāb al-Saydanah, Book of Pharmacy in Medicine.* In this latter work, Al-Biruni described the ancient city of Darīn, a merchants' port located on the island of Bahrayn in the Persian Gulf, where the musk trade thrived, as did the slave trade of Africans and low-caste Hindus from the subcontinent. From human bondage, empires of great opulence emerged. Arguably, religion, multiplied by toxic masculine hunger for power, ensured that Black and Dalit peoples suffered. Neither Islam, which preached egalitarian faith among all men, nor Hinduism, which believed in a strict hierarchy among them, is absolved of brutal violence or enslaving innocent people.

Muslim invasions heightened the fear among Indians, as the people came to be called by Muslims — so all Muslims became *mleccha,* foreigners, outsiders. As for the Arabs, they associated the ocean with the subcontinent, Hind. Bahri musk, musk that traveled by Indian Ocean to Arabia, was less desirable, though, than musk from the overland routes from Tibet; they believed that musk warmed the body, and exposure to the sea cooled its heat.

Perfumers became known as the *Darī,* for Muslim men smeared their faces with attars of musk, oud, amber, and to this day, *dari* is the same word my people use for the most iconic image of the Muslim man: his beard.

I'm a Muslim vegetarian. And no, despite common depictions in Indian literature, even Muslim meat-eaters aren't obsessed with animal sacrifice. Muslim vegans and vegetarians exist, hard as this is to believe for vigilante, vegetarian Hindu men who have lynched other humans — Dalit or Muslim — suspected of eating beef. Perfume wise, I'm not drawn to heavy animalic scents that reek of mammalian funk. But I have a small tincture of ambergris, the undigested squid beaks in sperm whale guts that they eject along with their feces. Before the eighth century, there is little mention in Indian ancient perfumery texts about this material. The word *ambara* meant sky, until the arrival of the Arabs, when it started to mean *ambergris,* after the Arabic word. By 1590, in the era of the Mughal Empire, the *Ain-i-Ak-bari,* a record of Emperor Akbar's administration, describes how fumes of *ambara* perfumed his chambers at all times.

Ambrette musk, extracted from dried hibiscus abelmoschus seeds, lends a softer, lighter note than synthetic musk, first created in a late nineteenth-century lab accident, when a white scientist named Bauer sought to make a more efficient explosive but got a fragrant surprise instead. Boom. From destruction, a rebirth, I suppose. We smell various derivations of that musk in all of our daily detergents, soaps, cleaners, a way to evoke so fresh, so clean. Near extinct because of the perfumers' demand for their sexual secretions, the Himalayan deer is no longer the source, even though you can still buy some online, on websites claiming no deer are harmed in the extraction process — but really, what stag wants anyone near its sac? As much as I seek to return to our precolonial fragrance culture, I don't want to limit myself to these ancient materials alone, since only the most privileged, royal, and wealthy had access to them. Synthetics have always been an equalizer, and even in ancient perfume culture, there are recipes for synthetic sandalwood, frankincense, and musk. No doubt my palette includes innovations from European laboratories, I am East-West. I write in English, after all.

When you fast, you become aware of how your body burns food as fuel, how thirst can drive you mad; after sunset I want to be inundated, forbidden, but I am doing this fast on my own terms. I smoke weed, I chat with you, I work myself into a fantasy. Inevitably, that paranoid moment after marijuana hits, I can hear Mojo's deep voice, *Drink some water, babe, you'll be fine.* His calm reassures me. My cunt aches, fasting makes me horny, hot and swirling with yearning for the forbidden — *you* — so I take a hot shower, lather my body in olive oil soap Mojo buys from a Palestinian co-op, hum fragments of Bangla or Bollywood tunes. I'm exhausted. I crave the raw scent of my own body, my own wetness. I crawl into bed next to my love, embracing his smooth backside, holding him, allowing his peaceful breath to lull me to sleep. But tonight, he is soaked in night sweat and I don't want to ruin my clean. I inch away from him and lay on my back, rubbing myself, less for pleasure, but to help usher me toward sleep. Our bodies together, a temple, you penetrate me, you release, I receive this death each night, our body smell oceanic, endless expansion in every direction, but I want us to go deeper. I think of a Bangla Baul mystic song, where Parvathy Baul sings about *bindu,* the dot that marks the beginning of the universe, the unattainable moon within, *adhir chand,* the moon beyond, the origin we can never trace to a single point, my clit to climax, the scent on my fingers the musk and brine of my own *bhumigandha,* ocean perfume, musk inside me, a cresting, crashing wave, released.

I'm wary, because this is not the first time that I've loved or been hurt by an Indian. We both feel hypervisible, and somehow invisible in America. Do you know how my people's stories are swallowed by yours? Do you see how this experience, of being Muslim in America, of being a non-Indian South Asian, turns us into a niche, obscured by India's long shadow? Do you understand some of us have inherited the ancestral pain of genocide? Something I share with Ilankai Tamils from Sri Lanka — but not you. This makes us feel our history is unknown, unspoken for. I fear that you will not know how to hold my pain.

Listen.

A few summers ago, I set out for Fort Tilden with two friends, a photographer and makeup artist. This beach is one of the dreamiest and quietest in our city, where the sun sets over dune grass and the waves are calmer and less deadly than the Rockaways. *Tirtha,* pilgrimage by bodies of water, is something I've always felt drawn to; this photo shoot felt like document-ing one of the places on Earth I consider sacred. The three of us, Black, Jewish, and Muslim femmes, painted ladies, one with purple hair, another with turquoise eyebrows, and me, wearing a vintage caftan, long and beige with hints of gold. I wanted to evoke free Muslim femme on the beach. Women alone by the ocean, sunbathing, undisturbed, is still rare in the Muslim world, even though in Bangladesh, whether by pond, river, or sea, you'll glimpse women bathing, swimming, fully dressed, as if no one can see.

We never made it onto that beach.

You can't take photos on the beach without a permit, said the weathered old white woman City Park ranger rolling up in a pickup truck as soon as we neared the sandy pathway toward the water. Beside her, a younger colleague, bored and not trying to get involved.

You didn't even ask us if we have a permit, shot back my friend Talysha, the makeup artist. *You're just assuming without asking us for one.*

We're not taking professional photos, I said. A white lie, the kind that people tell to get where they need to go without hurt-ing others, a lie meant to protect ourselves. We would use these photos for my small business, too small to warrant the bizarre rule of requiring business permits to use a public beach.

No photos without a permit, how many times do I have to tell you? You're going to have to leave, said the ranger.

We're going on the beach, you fucking hag, I spat. *We aren't doing anything wrong.*

She pulled out her phone. *I'm calling the police.*

My fury exploded. I lost control of my tongue: *Call the police, you fucking hag. We're gonna take these photos, we're gonna be fucking beautiful and you're still gonna to be a fucking hag. You're going to die an old hag.* I spat out these venomous words, the only attack I had against her was degrading her old age, her wrinkles, her ugly, scolding, scowling face; the one thing we folks with melanin can lord over a white person is how gorgeously we age on the outside. My poison enraged her, and she wielded her power, dialing in her complaint. She'd let the cops handle us, she didn't care if we were arrested or if we died, she wanted to teach us a lesson. Never mind the White Lie that we needed a permit to be by the sea, that land can be owned. We knew she'd never do this to a carefree white woman flowing in a caftan. Meanwhile, her colleague said not a word, still staring out the window. I almost felt sorry for the guy, stuck in this truck, but he hadn't stopped her from calling the police, so I hated him, too. She sped off, and I screamed once more: *Fuck you, hag.*

Within fifteen minutes, three armed policemen showed up in their own trucks, ready to take us down, we, the violators. *What the hell is going on? We were informed of a complaint.* The officers looked confused, and we went back and forth, little white lies: *We aren't taking photos of anything except me, it's my birthday, it's just for fun* — white cops do not care about Black and brown folks' fun. The most hotheaded cop of the three cocked his head, took an ominous step closer toward us, finally, fed up with dealing with us clowns. He shouted, *Well, why the hell are you still here, she told you to get off the beach, get off the goddamn beach!*

That is the moment, with the police, when you know speaking back will invite violence. And every muscle in my body wanted to scream at them like I'd screamed at the old white park ranger, but I knew we'd be arrested or that the tenor would shift to mortal danger if I came anywhere close to that rage. Without a word, seething, we stared down these three cops, they stared at us, the old hag had won, even though we all knew we'd done nothing wrong. They got back in their trucks, and we trudged with our heavy bags, down the gravel path, to the main road to catch an Uber. I flipped them off one last time, *motherfuckers,* as the police left us there, impotent with rage.

Let's go to Dead Horse Bay, suggested Sylvie, the photographer. Dead Horse Bay is named after the carcasses of horses strewn along the beach in the late nineteenth century, leftovers from a glue factory. I imagine the wretched stench of rotting horse flesh, the labor of those workers — immigrant or Black — who disposed of the dead bodies. Menhaden fish are found in these shores, the same fish that Tisquantum, who we learned was named Squanto, taught the colonizers to use to fertilize their crops. The minute we walked onto the land, the wildness and quietude enveloped us, calmed our racing hearts. I learned later from friends who'd grown up in Brooklyn that their families — Muslims — would be scared off the beach back in the 1980s by the racist white Rockaways residents. It is frightening to think how long white people have made beaches and oceans deadly, turning these sacred spaces into sites of violence and enslavement. Dead Horse Bay proffered immigrants and Black families a haven, a safe place to picnic with their families. Never mind that the entire beach is littered with washed-up horse bones, driftwood, and broken glass from antique bottles of cosmetics and perfumes and medicines from lifetimes ago. Swimming is hardly possible, but that doesn't matter, since so many of us never learn to swim. For Black and brown people, beaches are often toxic social space. Forbidden to us. As Sylvie took my photographs, and Talysha wiped the stress sweat off my face and painted me anew, the beauty around us was inescapable. Waves struck the glass, filling the air with the sound of chimes. Psychedelic blaze of a pink-orange sunset dipped below the sky-scrapers in the distance, and here, no partition kept us from the abundant dune grass. In the last few moments of our shoot at Dead Horse Bay, I discovered a piece of driftwood shaped like a three-foot serpent, a long, winding wood body I knew I had to keep.

That evening, I got home, exhausted. My rage morphed back into sorrow. I wept for hours. This beloved beach of mine ruined, by the cops, by a hateful white women's racism disguised as blame on us for breaking the rules, as if ocean could belong to the State. What shattered me is how the absolute mythology of white supremacy steals our joy. You know this pain, of being us, brown in America, we both lived in a post-9/11 New York City, but do you understand that it hits me differently as a believer in All — h? What hurt most happened afterward, though. I spoke to an Indian friend who called to check up on me. I considered her a muse, a femme to adorn with perfume made by my own hand, and even now, when I think of her, I think of the smell of my perfume on her warm brown skin, beach notes of gardenia, coconut, and jasmine, with sadness. She consoled me on the phone for about five minutes, expressed her rage at this old white woman for trying to ruin our day, before she launched into a great epiphany from a trip to Europe.

I realized that all of those artists who built the great cathedrals and painted the frescoes were poor Europeans, and they really weren't so different from us brown people.

What are you talking about? I snapped. *It's like you can't hold my pain without making it about you.* I got off the phone, even more upset. She saw us as one and the same, she knew what it felt like to be tormented by white folks growing up, in her neighborhood, her schools — we needed to band together. But right then, I needed her to hear how our differences were real. Everything felt so ugly. The experience triggered a lifelong ache of being born in a country that has waged wars in the name of fighting terrorism. Killing, torturing, and drone attacking hundreds of thousands of innocent Muslims. As a Christian in

America, she belonged to the dominant culture in a way I never had and never would. I'd been exiled from the very beach that she and I had swam at together. I wanted her to be able to sit with me in my pain around my Muslimness.

My anger broke our brown girl accord.

Besides the photographs, my only remnant of that day is this driftwood serpent, a premonition of my shedding. Of old ways, old friends, and falsehoods. All of this happened in the Before. Before you and I met, before the virus, before the city announced that Dead Horse Bay would close because of radioactive contamination, banishing us all from its eerie, musical shores.

PASSING

You know that I write this with a deep love for you, for our people, everything we share. In the name of healing, sometimes we need to break ourselves a little bit. As much as I have worked to untether myself from internalized Indocentrism, which I think is more pronounced as a child of the 1970s wave of immigrants, the child of people whose country, Bangladesh, was less than a decade old when they came to the United States. For me, Bangladesh felt legible only to other Bangladeshi second-generation people — we felt nothing like our parents — we all shared an intimately separate identity from the collective *desi* identity I shared with Indian friends. *Desi,* after *desh,* the synonym I used for the equally dissatisfying word *South Asian,* to denote a bond between us all, easiest to experience through the material culture of India: its clothing, food, Bollywood films, music. Both of us, South Indian and Bangladeshi, have felt the exclusion of our cultures in this patramyth of North India translated into the United States. Bedazzled *lehengas,* chicken tikka masala, *Kuch Kuch Hota Hai,* and the music of A. R. Rahman are simultaneously ours, but also not-ours. These signifiers let me connect to something fabulous, billions-deep and beautiful.

We have so many little things in common that sometimes our differences feel far away, but the fractures and cracks emerge when we occupy "South Asian" spaces — organizing collectives, conferences, campaigns, fancy galas — obscuring what is actually meant: India. They are most always run by upper-caste Indian Hindus. When it comes to economic security, money, recognition, institutional support, we, the peoples beyond India's borders — Bangladesh, Bhutan, Kashmir, Nepal, Pakistan, Sri Lanka, all the way to Trinidad and Tobago, Guyana and Fiji — are forgotten. We have less proximity to whiteness, our lands and histories outside the bounds of the Great Indian imaginary. We are absorbed into the Indian narrative, even though our ancestral traumas, our dissent, the way we live, work, dress, speak, listen to music, dance, all disrupt notions of a monolith. We know that to disagree, because of our differences in class, caste, skin color, and visibility, means inviting condescension or gaslighting by upper-caste Indians for breaking unity. I believe we need unity, too. But how can our ancestral separations be healed, how can we feel unity, if we aren't heard for how our differences are lived?

Being perceived as an Indian, knowing how to signify this identity in America, and even in India, when I've lived there, feels a bit like being a replica — a cyborg. When you're with a person who believes you to be just like them, you're having a great time, you are both *desi,* until you hit an uncomfortable topic — war, genocide, caste, color — and slip into a strange place of distrust. *Uncanny valley* denotes a dip in the human's affinity for the robot, at first the similarity, the likeness creates an affection, until the robot seems too human to be an actual human, so it falters. Disgust takes over, then a rejection of the cyborg. What makes us more human than our vulnerability, our difference? The cyborg, me, falters — something about me gives me away.

When a person learns the religion of my birth, that my people are Bangladeshi, not Indian, when I haven't known how to perform a Hindu *puja,* when I learn a person's uncle was in the Pakistan Army and may have killed my people in war. Broken bonds are hard to recover, it feels humiliating to move through pain that feels insurmountable. Eternal. But if our people's histories can teach us anything, it's that being known by outsiders gives us a greater depth of field to know ourselves, blurring the borders between us and them.

You're probably on a list somewhere, you joke once, when I complain to you about my phone's algorithm capitalizing the W in white — I don't believe that the inherent power of whiteness needs to be reiterated. I know that you've experienced an airport as a brown man in a post-9/11 America, but that's just it, you were a grown man during that catastrophe when you learned firsthand how fucked up it is to be a Muslim in an Islamophobic country. I don't tell you it hurts when you say that, not until much later, and you apologize, you felt awful for hurting me. I want you to imagine being a brown Muslim fifth-grader, a brown Muslim college student. How in the limited scope of the American imagination, my family's god, All — h, has always represented the brown peril, an enemy of the United States, just as Muslims in India, before and after Partition, have always been considered problematic. Do you understand how the pain of my brownness is not just that I am invisible to white people; it is that my people — Muslims — are considered to be difficult, dangerous, dissenting, by our own South Asian kin?

You and I first met in real life at a party; instantly, we felt a gravitational pull. I remember my dress, a vintage 1970s Don Luis de España maxi, the edge printed with psychedelic amphora — the green vessels used to transport honey, olive oil, wine across the Mediterranean, the smallest of them, *amphoriskos,* held perfume. I don't remember what you wore, probably something austere, professional in my boho opinion, wintry black, gray, or blue. Everyone felt a lot of stress about the situation in India. Massive protests had erupted all across the country, people enraged about the passage of the Citizenship Amendment Bill and National Register of Citizens. Citizenship became possible for persecuted religious minorities — Hindus, Buddhists, Christians — who sought to migrate to India from Muslim-majority

Pakistan and my motherland, Bangladesh. But any Pakistani or Bangladeshi Muslim would be excluded from this citizenship process. The implementation of this bill along with a National Register of Citizens — a register requiring birth documents proving Indian origins — threatened the citizenship status of Indian Muslims who came to India during Partition or the Liberation War of 1971. They could become stateless. This affected Bangladeshis, Muslim and Hindu families who'd moved to parts of India for property, opportunity. In the eastern states bordering Bangladesh, West Bengal, and Assam, Bangladeshi refugees, especially Muslims, are seen as people who don't belong in India — despite how porous these borders are, or how many generations back they migrated — India was home. Yet, according to the government, they'd never belong.

At the party, a jaunty Indian bro posed a question: *What's the endgame of all this? Like, what do we think is gonna happen?*

Genocide, I told him. *Genocide is the point.*

He flashed me a look — skeptical or confused — I couldn't tell. But I knew he didn't understand how that could be possible. Sure, the bill was draconian, but genocide felt a bit — much.

Less than two weeks later, a pogrom incited by a fascist political leader led to the death of fifty Muslims in Delhi, a city I love. Among the dead: a frail eighty-five-year-old woman, burned to death in her home in a fire set by mobs. The images set a chill in my heart, reviving the dread of Hindus beating and shooting innocent Muslims in Gujarat in a pogrom sanctioned by Modi, the deaths of forty thousand Tamils by the Sinhalese-led Sri Lankan Army; or even further back, to 1984, when three thousand Sikhs were murdered by Hindus after the assassination of Indira Gandhi.

After I said the word, *genocide,* I knew this dude would never understand how the specter of bloodshed lives on in me. He was just too basic. And a Brahmin. He'd never faced oppression for his caste. The racism he knew, I knew, too — being brown in America, being bullied for eating smelly food, being hairy, having a weird name.

But genocide is not a history you can tell from the outside.

The first time it occurred to me that I had no claim to India, that I was not of Indian origin, was when I applied for Indicorps, upon a friend's suggestion. I worked as an organizer in NYC and, heartbroken over a breakup, leaving the city for a while for a country I loved visiting as a youth felt like the right move.

I didn't get past the phone interview. The interviewer commented on how interesting my name was. I told her that my parents were from Bangladesh, that such secular names were common among us, and the interviewer went silent. And then, awkwardly, she told me that Indicorps was, well, *You, uh, need to be of Indian origin in order to be eligible. I'm so sorry, Tanvi. It's . . . it's stupid. Ugh. I'm sorry.* As if my grandmother and great-grandmother hadn't been Indians for some part of their lives. As if there weren't Indians who traced ancestors back to Bangladesh or Pakistan. India, for the non-Indian South Asian, is a part of our origin story, but we would never be imagined as a part of India.

When I was a seven-year-old in St. Louis, Missouri, we would visit the farmers' market on Saturdays. Amid the rows and rows of fresh summer fruit, peaches and blueberries and watermelon, I remember a smiling white farmer selling *Saddam Hussein Is Insane!!!!!!* T-shirts right beside them. That shirt, flames engulfing the dictator, shocked me to my core. They hated us, Muslims. They wanted us to burn and die. And then again, on the bus ride home, the principal's son taunting me along with all his friends, remarking on the ridiculousness of my name — *Islam, what in hell is that?* — and I remember staring at my friend, a bespectacled Black girl who mouthed to me, *They talking about you?* I remember sitting silently still, wishing I could transport myself home. This very same feeling is triggered again, when I see a mob of white supremacists storm the Capitol building, unhinged with racist rage. American terrorists in normcore who'd attack a Sikh or Muslim, totally ignorant of how the turban or hijab are symbols of devotion, marking a person as a believer, as equal under a higher power. Beauty that evades the white supremacist. Back then, my parents told me: *Don't tell anyone your last name is Islam.* Believing in All — h meant that I could be harmed. I would never belong to that mystical, benevolent rendition of brown, unless I lied about who I was.

Islam is my family's name, inextricable from us, but I reject modesty and submission. As a teenager, my body burst out of the clothes my mother chose for me, I was taller, browner, and more voluptuous than the women who came before me on my maternal side. I learned young that the brown-skinned feminine body is judged as unruly, lesser, hypersexual, by its shape, weight, color — and scent. I began to hide my body and the curried scent of home with perfumes that let me translate my sensuality to the world. A version of the feminine emerged in this liminal space between shame and sensuality — this is the place where I search when I write.

Passing as Indian, or rather, passing as Hindu, started after 9/11, subconsciously at first, I distanced myself from Islam, a name I'd never asked to be born with; I felt ashamed by the violence of men who wreaked havoc and horror in allegiance to All — h. I had internalized the self-hate fueled by the dominant culture's narrative — in the US and in India — of Islam's violence, without critiquing imperialism and Islamophobia. In my sorrow and shame, I lost sight of the parts of Islam that had some spiritual resonance, so I stopped fasting altogether.

At an old bodega that no longer exists, the Bhutanese brother behind the counter and I both assumed the other person was an Indian, until he noticed my given last name, Islam, on my credit card. Or a taxi driver might have been Bangladeshi and assumed that I was an Indian and Hindu, until he noticed my first name: *Where you from, miss?* If I felt up for a long conversation, I answered truthfully. But when I felt more antisocial, I would say I'm Indian, act a bit colder, more aloof, which never surprised him. Afterward, we rode in silence. Hurts me to think of it now.

When I lived in India four years after the attack, I never told anyone I was a Muslim unless they, too, were Muslims. Here in the States, Black people had always understood my family's faith, Islam, since the first Muslims in this country were Black, from the time of slavery to the Nation of Islam. We shared practices, calling a stranger *brother* or *sister,* or having Arabic names, Khadija, Fatimah. My own Sanskrit birth name — Tanwi — gave me an immediate kinship with Indians, but not necessarily a psychic one when we went deeper into where we came from. My reconnection to my ancestral Hindu — though the term *Hindu* is one that Muslim conquerors and traders gave Indians — came from Black people. Black yogis and astrologers and Ayurvedic herbalists and meditation circles. These were spaces where I felt comfortable to admit that as a Bangladeshi Muslim, I knew little about practices that felt like they should be mine. With Black practitioners I knew we'd all found our way to these traditions for healing ancestral trauma. I'd never learned that the roots of these rituals that I had been severed from could actually be traced back to my people.

I found solace in the ascetic-aesthetic that Americans crave to heal their own trauma, the benevolent forms of spirituality that felt a hell of a lot more fun than prayer, fasting, and modesty. I'm vegetarian. I celebrate Kali *puja.* I recite a Buddhist Tara mantra every morning. I probably know more mantras than I do *surah* in the Quran. Back then I knew nothing about how practices evolved, how the everyday femme divine goddesses worshipped for fertility, snakebite, malaria were Indigenous practices, stolen and absorbed into a pantheon of Great Goddesses, how the beloved festivals of Holi and Diwali were mythologized celebrations of the murder of Dalit Bahujan people, stories of dominant upper castes vanquishing lower-caste people, stories of *light persevering over darkness.* Even knowing this, I light a clay *diya,* holding the memory of Dalit pain, embedded in the candle's flame. Even when I visited Bangladesh, from my height and the way I spoke Bangla, people assumed I was visiting from Calcutta — my own people thought I was an Indian. During my last trip, I visited the Dhakeshwari Temple in Old Dhaka, I whispered mantras beside the incense pyre, not passing as a Hindu. These rituals are mine, too.

Fasting for Ramadan returned me to Islam for the first time since September 11, 2001. I returned to a young version of myself, an old teenaged memory emerged: Every day, after school, my Indian Christian boyfriend and I went back to my house, just a couple of hours before my mother returned from work. We hooked up while I fasted, dry-throated and titillated by our teenage, nubile first love, both of us thrilled by how effortlessly sinful I could be. Fasting was a mystery to him — *why do y'all do it?* — it was a mystery to me, too. I returned to this state, desirous and a bit delirious, falling apart, feeling ravenous between dusk until dawn's light, when I finish the night's writing.

This is the hour I eat *sehri,* so that I can make it through the day's fast, so I nibble on *medjool* dates and down as many glasses of water as I can. Dawn is the hour when Radha and Krishna must depart from fucking deep inside the *braj* forest, back home, back to their duties. In their union, Krishna makes love, not war, gender dissolves masculine and feminine. His beloved Radha and the other cow-herding Gopi girls bring out a softer side of him than we see in the *Bhagavad Gita* with the warrior Arjuna. Krishna revealed himself; I suppose that's the power of the feminine — it lets you closer to the softness of the Divine.

I'm drawn to you, but I'm scared to flash a rage that is safe to show my husband, because he understands where it comes from. But with upper-caste people like you, I've felt a derision, a condescension: *Oh my god, I would never be able to bring home a Muslim.* As a non-Indian South Asian, my orientation is different than yours — I care deeply about Bangladesh, about Muslims and Dalits. I care about little things, niches, countries swallowed by hegemonies. Couples who love and fuck across race, class, caste, genders, and sexualities feel an inexplicable Oneness. Despite the differences, when we become entwined with a person who we've been told we should never love, we want them more than anyone we've ever wanted.

Our American wet dream: naked brown skin, me, dripping in 24K gold, hot, fluid. Historically this gold might be a symbol of the shackled wife, but everything is hotter on a mistress. Are we Orientalizing ourselves, is our fetish *desh,* this ancient love we're trying to touch, smell, taste? We see each other as we want to be seen. How many hours in this parallel world do we lay on a floor, fucking, staring at each other, ecstatic, seen. Just as we've been taught to never ever discuss our trauma, we've been taught to deny ourselves what turns us on. Together we touch an innate part of us that was stolen by those who wanted us to believe ourselves ugly. Our ancestors' bodies, Othered by whiteness, judged not only by the color of their skin, but *the scent* of their skin. My ancestors' bodies, polluting to the Brahmin, but here, in this moment: none of that matters. We conjure this erotic vortex, where we are beyond the white gaze or caste, some part of us enamored by the hotness of this social violation, being Hindu-Muslim lovers. It's hard to imagine anything like differences in caste, religion, or the laws of a British colonial administration antagonizing any separation between us.

Maybe we're trying to get back to each other. Our masculine aspect one with our feminine, an innate, inviolable beauty we see in each other, a beauty that whiteness will never know, because they don't know us together, naked like this, in our utter truth, something they cannot steal, mimic, own, or possess. Isn't it sad, how in America, gorgeous brown-on-brown bodies feels rare? Your dick, perfect, chocolate brown, mouth-watering, circumcised — surprising for a Hindu, but not for an American. Your cut foreskin, the first permanent mark of your parents' assimilation.

ANCIENTS

Evidence of snake worship in South Asia can be traced back four thousand years ago, to the ancient Indus Valley Civilization — found in the remains of the settlements Mohenjo Daro, Mound of the Dead, and Harappa, on the land we call Pakistan today. Today, Hindu nationalist forces are determined to assert Aryan indigeneity, despite indications that a waning Harappan culture gave rise to a civilizational shift over a period of slow, steady migration and settlement. We don't know how the Indus Valley Civilization perished: Was it a great deluge, a flood, or did the rivers dry up in endless drought, parching the land and forcing the people into exile? Was it mass death by drought, famine, or fatal illness spread by the undead — a virus?

Throughout South Asia, there are traces of snake cults in Naga shrines. We cannot read the Indus script of the ancient Harappans, their language is a code that remains to be deciphered, but it is a language older than Sanskrit, older than the language of the Vedic Aryans. Archaeologists have unearthed an advanced, pre-Aryan, Harappan civilization, intricate urban planning, irrigation systems, water drainage and storage, metalwork of copper, bronze, gold, and silver, terra-cotta perfumery distillation pots, beads of carnelian and lapis lazuli, totems of feminine deities like tiger and snake goddesses, indicating worship: fertility, the Underworld, rebirth, and abundance. In these ruins, femmes appear as symbolic traces in history.

You are a goddess, you tell me, that the concept of a goddess was fashioned as a replica of a femme like me, Devi, the mother goddess. I know this feeling, I've felt it, too, in India, the motherland you haven't visited in twenty years. I do see myself in the gourd-hipped, almond-eyed, buxom babes carved into temples

— but worshipping a goddess is no guarantee that fleshy mortal women and femmes get respect. Kali, the Tantric goddess, still speaks to all the dark-skinned femmes I know, Black and brown women who understand rage and destruction as rebirth. Who among my ancestors first chose to leave their faith to worship All — h, a formless, genderless Divine? Yet Islam is tilted toward the masculine, even as its fundamental belief is the equality of all people under All — h. A world without caste, but has this ever been true for women, trans people, femmes? I learned to pray from a photocopied instruction manual — *Tarteeb of Salaat* — we didn't have enough money for Arabic school. I learned young that the sacred is there, waiting for us. As Muslims, my family rejected ideas of karma or reincarnation, but as Bangla Muslims, we still say the Sanskrit word *dharma* for faith, not *deen,* as you would in Arabic, the part of our Buddhist and Hindu ancestors' language we kept.

Great Goddess worship centers the feminine deity, allowing male devotees and priests to channel power, *shakta,* a masculine form of the feminine *shakti.* What does it mean to you when you call me a goddess? Do you draw power out of me for your own spiritual ascendance, to feel a fire in you that you've lost somewhere along the way? Do I reside as a love totem, worshipped on a pedestal, a constant reverb in your body, destroying everything you believed about yourself? I think of Donna Haraway's declaration: *I'd rather be a cyborg than a goddess.* As a woman of color — another term I dislike for its imprecision —

we are so often seen as part-machine, part-feminine — all labor. Goddess feels truer to my embodiment than cyborg, even as you and I merge into one by way of technology. Great Goddesses, the Devi, are an amalgamation of little traditions absorbed into a pantheon, emerging at the confluence of patramyth and the feminine divine.

When I was an NGO volunteer in New Delhi, I took a trip to Kolkata. One morning, I visited Kalighat, a Kali temple. My colleague Jaya and I took a few minutes in front of the goddess. Her long, gold tongue gleamed, her three saffron eyes reminded me of flower petals. I offered red hibiscus blooms, Kali's flower, and grabbed a *prasad,* a sugary *laddu* that I planned on scarfing down right after. I hadn't been able to keep food down for days, so a street sweet probably wasn't a great idea. *I certainly felt fucking destroyed and reborn,* I joked with Jaya, as we walked outside into the courtyard. This was true, I did feel emptied of whatever ego I'd had, felled by the *fuchka* and *jhal muri*. But I'd eat the street food all over again. We sat on benches to have our *prasad* and cups of chai. I struck up a conversation with a group of men who seemed to be temple regulars hanging out.

Where's your family home? he asked.

No soon as I uttered that my family mostly lived in Dhaka, the man got agitated. *Why is Maa Kali's prasad on the dirty bench? What kind of disgusting person are you, you have no respect* — he spat, pointing at the sweet that I'd set down to sip my chai. He seemed to be working himself up into a fury.

Maa Kali doesn't care where I put the prasad, what's it to you?

Aram se, yaar, said Jaya, *Relax, friend.* She stood up and raised her palms, signaling that he should calm down. She repeated the words, nodding gently. Her voice — in Hindi — broke his fixation on me. Their shared Indianness soothed him. The second I revealed my family lived in Dhaka, there it was, a gaping border, an uncanny valley between him and me, the cyborg disrupting a man's sense of my humanity. We were kin, until the detail of my origins gave me away. Suddenly, then, I became a person who didn't belong there. Here was a man, telling me, a woman taller, darker, and fiercer than he'd ever be, that I didn't belong at the Kali temple. I'd forgotten to pass as a West Bengali, upper-caste woman. I'd forgotten the animosity that some Ghotis, West Bengalis, had for Bangals. Mass migrations from East Bengal had contributed to these tensions. If the man realized I was a Muslim, Jaya knew it could've gotten very dangerous. He suspected I was either a lower caste or a Muslim, disrespectful of the *prasad,* so he took to yelling at me instead.

In a way, he was right. I didn't care about the *prasad.* A sweet treat could never be my gift to the goddess. I knew little about the details of a *puja* or *prasad* or high-caste worship rituals, and I didn't care. I felt a deep connection to divine feminine rage, darkness, and renewal. I am not a real Hindu, not by his estimation, not by the estimation of many, but who can deny me Kali?

○

Students of Indian history come across four names: *The Aryans, Dravidians, Dasas and Nagas.* Are the names *Dravidians, Dasas, Nagas* the names of different races, or are they merely different names for people of the same race?

— Dr. Bhimrao Ambedkar, *The Untouchables: Who Were They and Why They Became Untouchables*

Perfect Aryan nose, I tease you, the sound of this is ridiculous and makes us laugh. Aryan summons the Nazi, white supremacist and Hindutva buffoons, the light-skinned North Indian — we couldn't be further from any of those. I'm a few more hours in the sun darker than you. Your long, large nose, sharper in profile, most beautiful when you're sitting at your instrument, head back, eyes closed, you, tilted upward to the Universe. My nose is diminutive next to yours, the contrast between us straight outta the *Rig Veda,* the earliest of the Vedic texts, which I first read in college, in a course called Eastern Religious Traditions, taught by a white Orientalist scholar who knew more about Indian religions than anyone I'd ever met. I felt no connection to those hymns, they hadn't been spoken for my ears. In the text, Indigenous people are called the *Dasa,* a word that can mean enemy, slave, or devotee to god. The *Dasa* are described as alien and barbaric people, demonic, dark-skinned practitioners of black magic, blue-black as the later god, Krishna. They are speakers of a strange language, distinguished by their small, snub noses. Horses, the light spoke-wheeled chariot, and iron technology marked the arrival of the Aryans, the authors of the *Rig Veda.*

Arya means noble, a person of status, speaker of the Aryan language and ritual sacrifice — nothing to do with a white Aryan race or blond hair or blue eyes, not until thousands of years later, when European Orientalists insisted on a shared ancestral kinship between Europe and India, a connection to erase traces of their Semitic or Islamic past. In the *Rig Veda,* Ahi Vritra is the snake god and enemy of Indra, the Aryan god of heaven, thunder, rains. Snakes are the creatures that horses most fear, their venom possibly fatal if the bite is on the nose.

We are Dravidians, my father said to me once, about our origins, this lineage that you and I share. Most likely farmers, given where our family home is located. *Dravidian* is a Sanskritized form of the word *Tamil,* your people's ancient language, from the word *Dhamila.* Like so many of these names — *Hindu, Tamil, Bangla, Dasa* — they are not what people called themselves, but names given to them by outsiders, the travelers, traders, and settlers who made their fortunes on the land we now call India.

When I tell you how to pronounce your name in Bangla, you joke that it sounds funny, a warbling of the elegant Sanskrit sound of your name into a mouthy Bangla version: *Oshoboshoshosho* to your ears. I wonder if you know that this is an ancient Aryan reaction to Dravidian languages, like Tamil. That this inelegance you hear in my tongue as I say your name is how the Aryan speaker distinguished himself from the men he considered uncivilized, *mleccha,* the barbarians, the ones who didn't know how to speak Sanskrit or were too impure for sacred rituals. My ancestors, the low-caste farmers, snake-worshippers before they knew Islam, fishermen, forest dwellers in the far reaches of East Bengal — *mleccha*. This word, *mleccha*, likely evolved from the language of the Indigenous people in North India who encountered the Aryan speakers, but would be hurled at Indigenous people as if they were the ones who didn't belong.

Folks like us — horsemen and snake femmes — have been lusting after and fucking each other for thousands of years. I imagine these Vedic Aryan horsemen like the white cowboys of the American West thieving Native land, cattle, and women, then forming a country as if no one had ever been there before. As the Aryan speakers migrated across the Eurasian steppe, expanding and settling east toward the Ganges, women and femmes became another commodity, either as wives, a status symbol chained to preserving honor and home — or as whores. Woven into this narrative of conquest, there must have been people who broke the rules, fell in love, deep true love.

o

> *Nāga* (n.) snake, women of *nāga* type; — A woman who has a pointed nose and sharp teeth, slender body, complexion of a blue lotus, is fond of sleep, takes pleasure in the company of many persons ... loves sweet scent, garlands and similar other objects, is said to possess the nature of a *nāga*.
>
> — *Natya Shastra*, a Sanskrit treatise on performing arts

I learned to read Devanagari script, but my tongue is still timid in Hindi, childlike, sometimes flirtatious when I flow in it, learned by way of Bollywood and a course in college. Devanagari translates to *script of the city of gods,* rooted in the eighth-century script Nagari. Abode or city, *nagara* is a word of Dravidian, Indigenous origin, its root word *naga,* after the First People. *Deva,* the Divine, god, is masculine, an implication that men are keepers of sacred written knowledge.

False friends are words that sound similar in different languages, but with significantly different meanings. False friends might be false cognates, words that emerged together but diverged, like the word *burro,* meaning donkey in Spanish, butter in Italian. False friends might share the same roots, stemming from the same tongue, but as they were spoken and spread and people used them to mean separate things, the words forked paths, broke in meaning. Can we ever truly know how words emerge, if they can ever be traced to a pure origin? Words mimicked, stolen, forced, and, finally, adopted into language, as friends and enemies speak them, over and over, until they're so much a part of us we can't imagine they came from outside.

The Indo-Iranian tongues, Old Avestan and Vedic Sanskrit, diverged more than three thousand years ago, as these peoples split apart during migrations of the nomadic horsemen from Iran to India. The Aryan speakers who moved eastward kept the sounds of their old tongue as they absorbed the language and sounds of the Indigenous people — the Naga — whom they encountered, intermingled with, raided, or conquered. Perhaps, over time, the sounds and meanings of the words changed. Citizenship, being a *nagaraka,* has never been guaranteed to Indigenous people.

I still have my paperback of Vatsyayana's *Kama Sutra,* which I bought in a bookstore in Dhaka. Ol' Vatsyayana wrote on a plethora of seductions, from how men can effectively fuck other men's wives, to instructing courtesans on the art of seducing the *nagaraka* — her scent must intoxicate him, he needed her outside the confines of his sexless marriage, the way you need me. You are the *nagaraka,* the man-about-town, the ideal citizen, yearning for someone to seduce.

To seduce you.

I name myself the *nayika,* since this is my story. *Nayika,* the courtesan, a heroine of the story or film, but there are hundreds of Sanskrit words for the prostitute: *varangana,* the outside woman; *veshya, patita,* fallen woman; *paricharika,* a domestic worker; *devdasi,* a servant of god, temple dancers of the Isai Vellalar caste, whose moves have been absorbed into modern *Bharatanatyam* dance, I always wanted to learn, but never did, because of money. *Rati,* a beloved woman of the night. *Jatini* — the female lover of a married man — but this is my story, not yours.

There are countless names for so-called bad women, but in these texts, Brahmins like you, you're never the bad men. Romantic, spiritual, worldly, otherworldly, but never the liars, the cheaters, the frauds. Bad men are demonic and subhuman, the men of the lowest castes. They are the men forced to live on the outskirts of town, even as they maintain every part of the community with their labor, their actual blood, sweat, and tears.

Versed in the sixty-four *kala* arts, ancient sex workers held immense troves of artistic and worldly knowledge; they were dancers, writers, drummers, actresses, singers, polyglots and poets, perfumers and spies. *Kala,* the word for arts, cosmic time, the color black, deep, dark-skinned beauty, and grace for men to possess. For their impressive repertoire of skills, *gūna,* the *nayikas* were owned by the State, passed around for pleasure by Brahmin priests, paid for by kings, elite men-about-town. Yet in so many ways, these women and femmes were free: they lived in their own communities, at the outskirts, rejected by the social order but free of the chains of marital bondage. Who were they? We know little about these women and femmes; they are figments in these texts, objects to chase, flirt with, and fuck. We don't know why they left their husbands — probably because girls as young as ten married twenty-five-year-old men, like so many of our grandparents. Banished outside of organized society, they were widows, queers, transfeminine and transmasculine, the adulterer, the infertile, the sexually free, the impoverished, the daughters of sex workers.

I used to be versed in lying as a youth, my first loves were all rooted in lies I told my parents. Your lies feel as though you and I are lying to our parents — your wife — protecting her from harm. I've always found that as much as I tried to hide myself — they always knew. I suspect this is true for you, too, whether or not your illusions allow you to see that. Your face, a decrescendo, imprinted with a decade of sadness, half bottles of wine at night, that, I imagine, numb the distance between you and your wife. Mojo and I don't have a television, we hardly drink booze, we are present, fully. We live in a small apartment, always up in each other's space. There is no space for hiding. There is no room for lies between us. Despite your meticulously manufactured illusions, the versions of yourself you want the world to see, somehow, I believe that I know some of the most beautiful parts of you.

Sex workers knew freedom at great personal and emotional cost. Their lovers were their private audience, one who paid them for their time. In turn, they listened to these men's sorrows and heartaches, the stresses on the job, the fantasies they played out as they fucked, feeling each other's sweat, cumming, scratching, meeting each other on intellectual levels. These femmes renounced tradition for freedom, beauty, and pleasure, far away and safe from the dead-end chains of heterosexual, reproduction-rooted, upper-caste marriage. But they could be discarded, just as wives could or should expect to be cheated on. Erotic texts want us to believe they only lived to fuck the *nagaraka*. Sex workers like Amrapali, one of the first of Buddha's disciples, endowed public works, the building of temples, canals, roads, schools, and gardens with her own hard-earned money.

They held an ocean of knowledge in their minds and bodies, they held their lovers, they built the worlds. They faced the constant threat of violence. Once the *nayika* could no longer perform, once men perceived them to have lost their youth and

looks or if they became infected with disease, they had to rein-
vent themselves. They would become spinsters, spinning textiles for the State until their deaths.

The specter of the prostitute in South Asia is vaster than the
labor of sex — they are my ancestral foremothers — to which
all societies owe the evolution of aesthetics, art, beauty, and
culture.

Wives among the upper castes: virtual wards of married men,
who needed them to run their households while their husbands
were free. In the *Kama Sutra*, wives are expected to know every fucking thing, from what seasons to plant and sow seeds to
how to cook, manage money, accept their man no matter what
his mood, all while putting family, home, tradition, husband
first. Does your wife — who cooks your every meal, keeps your
household in order, birthed your child — have no idea about
the depths of your sexuality? I feel the pain of this dissonance
between your life and your longing. *Nagaraka* and *nayika*, lovers who never stand besides each other, hand in hand, open and
out to the world, perpetually secret to protect us from judgment and to protect wives from humiliation. I am the femme
who will never get named in your story, just as I won't name
you in mine.

Mustapha and I have an open love, one that I feel humbled to
experience in this life. When I tell him — *I have some new erotic
feelings* — I begin weeping. Open relationships in theory are
much scarier in practice. As soon as you admit your feelings, you

need to find the boundaries of this wilderness. Borders. I don't want to lose everything that we've worked for years to have, after the years I felt loveless and unlovable and ruined. Damaged. But we're committed to this lifelong work of queering romantic love, so he doesn't judge me, he doesn't discard me. He doesn't see us — or me — as ruined. *If you want to sleep with someone else, I want to sleep with someone else.* He says the words and the thought pulls my heart into a knot. I stare at him, bewildered by the idea of his body fucking another person. My man has an ancient face — a halo of brown curls, a long, aquiline nose, lush lips, and ocean eyes — I can stare at him endlessly. His stellar kindness still feels rare among heterosexual men I meet. I know the women he's drawn to will be drawn to him, femmes of color, mixed race, sexy, loving, nurturing. Their lissome yoga bodies like his own, bodies that trigger a discomfiting awareness of my own flesh and flab, years of growing up in a society that worships his blue-eyed beauty. He would find polyamorous, open, wondrous women. I'd probably want to be friends with them. Leaving me — with what? You.

CHOYA NAKH

I want to scratch my nails down your back, you write, and I want that, too, because I love all manner of scratching and massaging, but hilariously, I'm reminded of Vatsyayana's numerous finger-nail-scratching techniques in the *Kama Sutra.* I can trace your scratch all the way back to these ancient texts. Of course we're familiar with the *Kama Sutra,* suspicious of this exoticization, this Eastern erotic narrative that erases the fact that these texts were written for privileged men, and divided women, femmes, wives, into hierarchies. Somehow, though, reading the *Kama Sutra* again feels a bit like seeing ourselves in medieval pornography, hot, sexed bodies eons older than us, but so familiar, not alien like a kid growing up in the 1970s and 1980s, in America, this land of our birth.

In the erotic text *Nagarasarvasva, The Complete Man-About-Town*, the Nepali Buddhist priest Padmaśri sought to make the *nagaraka* feel his sexual prowess, his virility, his *kama*. He drew the feminine body as a riverine map of pleasure, so that they, *nagaraka,* could chart her channels of desire, the *nadis,* or rivers that carried her *kama* from her toes, to her clitoris — love's umbrella — to her belly, neck, lips, and cheeks, up through her head. *Nadi* theory pervaded all of science, yoga, medicine, and philosophy in the ninth century, and lovemaking was no different. Whisper a few mantras on pleasure points all over his Beloved's body, visualize them in the shape of the diacritic mark, the moon-dot, *chandrabindu* — so that these symbols and syllables would flood her, make her fluid, ready to fuck you. The meeting point of all *nadis:* the mouth. The part of your body I will know best.

There's an incense in the *Nagarasarvasva* called Ratinatikantha, Beloved of the God of Love, undoubtedly referencing a *rati,* a lover, a woman of the night, the sex worker the *nagaraka* knew as his true Beloved, not the dutiful wife unable to captivate him.

Choya nakh is one of the base notes. *Nakh* means fingernail, after the crescent moon-shaped shell operculum of sacred conch
and other mollusks. Choya nakh never makes an appearance
in Sanskrit literature, no trace of it outside of perfumers' innu-
endos, in formulas composed of riddles that need to be solved
to figure out the ingredients. Scent of a loose woman is one
such riddle — and the answer: choya nakh. Like the fingernail
scratches from a lover. Whereas musk or oud from East Bengal and Assam were exotic extractions, choya nakh, found on
beaches all along the Indian Ocean, sold plentifully in the market, common, taken for granted as a prostitute, and so unnamed
in great works of art. These books offer men's perspectives on
their lovers as sex objects, aphrodisiacs, escapes — and perfume
sets the mood.

I have a small bottle of choya nakh from India, as well as an
onycha tincture from the natural perfumer Mandy Aftel, whose
iconic book *Essence & Alchemy* was an early part of my perfumer journey. Choya nakh is smoky, a bit like burnt hair, with
a mineral marine quality. It's made by roasting and distilling
seashell operculum in large *choya* vessels. By contrast, onycha
tincture smells like ocean droplets on skin, sweet leather, the
body after a day on the beach. From Mandy, I learned that the
ancient Jewish *Ketoret* incense had this animal component, onycha. These details remind me how across race, gender, religion,
we share olfactory histories across space-time, rivers leading us
to the same ocean. Our references and what moves us as perfumers is as different as it is the same, especially when we don't

speak from a place of mastery or dominance. We all come from peoples who knew incense smoke as an evocation of the Divine, just as they knew that liquid perfumes let us bathe ourselves when we can't touch the water.

We live in a time where everyone wants clean, nontoxic beauty and fragrance, as if thousands of jasmine petals extracted by solvents is somehow cleaner or less toxic for our bodies and environment than lab-created jasmone cis, which, ironically, makes a jasmine note smell more real, like a living bloom. I return to Auranone, a creamy musk with hints of sandalwood and jasmine petal, adding a few drops, along with the oils of ambrette, onycha, and choya nakh, diluted in unscented coconut oil — it's like I smell your skin on my skin. Each of these materials is a fixative, giving the perfume a bodied, lasting impression, a resounding base note. Perfume, as cyborg, a synthetic-natural hybrid, a simulation of past, present, and future, at once. A way to chart the uncanny valley between what I fantasize about and my day-to-day life. With and without you. As much as I want to summon the ancients, there's no returning to our past, we can only ever be constantly present, and perhaps this is where I feel myself slipping with you, the surreal present, where I become undone, dissolved.

When we finally meet again, *in real life,* it is New York City summer, we are teenagers together, dream boy, dream girl, lip-locked, tequila soda and gin and tonic at this SoHo hotel feels like the parties we'd throw at a Ramada Inn back in high school. With this liquid courage, I hold you, pull you in for our first kiss, I can smell last night's dinner, the faint curried scent of your wife's cooking off your chest, thick with black hair peppered with gray. Our noses touch, we stare at each other, eyes wide and dark, aroused as we kiss, our mouths locked, as though reunited after a long separation. After eons. We kissed, and kissed, more wildly than each of us had kissed in years. Your body smell is what made me feel as though I've known you for lifetimes. We aren't supposed to be here, but we've already been here. *We have to stop,* I whisper, at some point, and you pull away immediately, spell broken by that moment, we'd read everything on each other's faces. Later, you name our emotions: tenderness, warmth, desire, melancholy — and a little fear. I had missed that part of new love, when each precise, new realization about yourselves, together, makes you weep.

BURNING

If the only way you know how to live is by burning, then
at the end all you will have left is ash.

— Kazim Ali, Day Thirteen, *Fasting for Ramadan*

Sisters! Come, let us pledge to give up saris made from foreign cloth; scorn British bodices, chemises and socks; start using rosewater and attar instead of lavender, and free ourselves from wearing shoes meant for foreign ladies that make us stumble. Only then will we be able to benefit our country. A huge variety of dhotis, silk saris and fine cloth are manufactured in Bombay, Dhaka, Pabna, Nadia and Murshidabad. These clothes are both glamorous and durable. If we use these materials, our money would stay within the country, artistic activity would get a boost, and the poor weavers and labourers would be able to earn themselves a frugal meal through work.

— Khairunessa Khatun, "For the Love of the
Motherland," 1905, as translated by Anusuya Ghosh
in *Women in Concert: An Anthology of*
Bengali Muslim Women's Writings, 1904–1938

Most of my Bengali Muslim literary foremothers from the early twentieth century remain virtually unknown. The educationist Khairunessa Khatun led a village night school for Muslim women who observed *purdah,* the veil, and could not travel during the day for school. So, she traveled from home to home, asking families for permission to let their daughters learn. She called for a boycott of British goods, not only textiles, but the canned milk, cigarettes, white sugar — British customs she felt were killing her motherland, India. Even the way people smelled had changed, the Mughal-influenced perfumes of rosewater and attar, flowers steeped in sandalwood oil, had given way to English lavender, the scent of my own grandmother's favorite soap.

Bengali Muslim middle-class women wrote prolifically in the early part of the twentieth century, as India fought for

Independence from the British. They wrote alongside up-per-caste Hindu women and men, as well as their own Mus-lim middle-class male counterparts — all of these peers held conservative ideas that never imagined Muslim women as free, intelligent, literate, or capable of choosing their own futures. These writers addressed Muslim women, calling on them to become conscious and liberate themselves from the limitations of religious conservatism. They had less mobility and education than Hindu and Christian women, but the disdain for Mus-lim customs like wearing a burqa meant they had to make their own worlds. Despite how radical these women feel to me, it's incredible that my foremothers' voices have been severed from Indian history, as their voices went unheard in the nationalist dialogues, written out of the patramyth.

I am the first of my kind. I hear this phrase often, I've said it myself, among people who've never encountered a version of themselves in history or literature. But I've found more solace in the realization that in the thousands of years of human his-tory, someone, at some point in time, shared the same tendrils of thought as me. This notion of being first dishonors the intu-ition that all knowledge is collective, a continuation. This idea of being the first of our kind is a construction of dominance, a patramyth. Each time we utter *I am the first,* we are forgetting. We forget how Muslim women have long been cast as being both behind the times and, in hindsight, ahead of their time, vi-sionary, but born in a society that never knew how to read them.

o

The Orient needed first to be known, then invaded and possessed, then re-created by scholars, soldiers, and judges who disinterred forgotten languages, histories, races and cultures in order to posit them — beyond the modern Oriental's ken — as the true classical Orient that could be used to judge and rule the modern Orient.

— Edward Said, "Orientalism"

Scientia sexualis versus *ars erotica,* no doubt.

— Michel Foucault, *The History of Sexuality*

Before the British Raj, before Empire, the first wave of colonizers were zealous capitalists, the British East India Company, a private corporation led by an unstable sociopath. After winning the Battle of Palashi in 1757 against a minor Mughal Nawab in Bengal, Siraj-ud-Daulah, with forged documents and bribes rather than brilliant war tactics, these colonizers transferred the wealth of Bengal to the East India Company. By 1765, the East India Company intimidated their way into *diwani* rights, total stewardship of their new conquest, and the subsequent years led to their amassing obscene wealth — estimated at around $45 trillion in today's money — as they ravaged the people of India, who suffered famine, torture, heavy taxation, and death. They were ousted from power by the Crown after the 1857 Sepoy Mutiny, the first struggle for Independence from British rule, one hundred years after they stole their way inside. Vying for power through violence led to seismic shifts in material culture, the draining of wealth and disappearance of Indigenous knowledges, which undoubtedly led to revolutionary struggles for freedom. In order to make sense of a land where they were strangers, the British had to remake not only a map of the territory, but a new imagination of India that named them as master.

Since the time of the ancients, everyone has been obsessed with the deviant femme, the bad woman — the prostitute. As a person to desire, possess, scorn, and punish. Sex workers integrated the first wave of the British East India Company men, who were encouraged to *go native.* These lovers provided pleasure and comfort, nursed them back to health when their fragile British asses exploded with diarrhea, gave them local intelligence that would ultimately allow them to better understand the people they wanted to rule. These women were the first point of contact, but little is known about them, erased in the making of modern South Asia.

British Orientalists were oriented toward the Brahmin; they translated texts written by upper-caste medieval men because these white people felt a kinship with the highest castes among their subjects. Both Orientalist and Indian upper-caste men imagined the past, present, and future of Indian civilization through ancient texts. Ancient and medieval texts, like the *Kama Sutra* or the *Manusmriti,* became absolute assessments of a Great India's erotic, exotic, golden past, the time before the

Muslim conquests. As with all conquests, there are simultaneous violences and emergences: as Muslim conquerors pillaged temples, killed innocent people, raped Hindu and Buddhist women, they built magnificent wonders, changing the architectural, literary, social, political textures of culture forever. The Indologist Max Müller's work — which unfortunately and forever conflated the Aryan language with an Aryan race — drove home the point: that though the white colonizer and the colonized Brahmin were kindred, they possessed different bodies and drives. The European Aryan was visionary, courageous, an aggressive adventurer; the Hindu Aryan was spiritual, intellectual, a serene philosopher. Long-lost brothers.

The *Manusmriti,* the Book of Manu, the most well-known of the Dharmashastras, reified the absolute power of Brahmin men in their ideal society, just as the *Kama Sutra* or *Nagarasarvasva* imagined the men-about-town as the ultimate lovers. In medieval India these texts were largely irrelevant to the masses of everyday people, for good reason, since Manu doomed the lowest castes: *their dress the garments of the dead* — vintage — *their food from broken dishes, black iron their ornaments, they must always wander from place to place.* Upper-caste women were objects to be controlled in the *trivarga,* the three aims of a Brahmin householder's life: his *dharma,* religion and duty; *artha,* politics and worldly aspirations, *kama,* his sensual, sexual desires. *Shastras* were codified patramyth, centered on men's worldly power, spiritual transcendence, and sex. Women and femmes — of all castes — were polluted bodies worth only as much as their beauty and youth, their purity as wives and protectors of patrilineage.

Manusmriti became the blueprint for British Raj. Laws divided the population, tried to save native women from native men, who were ridiculed as unmanly, weak, savage for their practices, including the gruesome spectacle of *sati,* burning widows on pyres. Brahmin Indian Hindu men and the British colonizers constructed women's bodies as sites of domination and control. Spinning the *Manusmriti* as sacred code let them criminalize Dalit and Muslims, whose labor and exploitation and impoverishment made the colonizers rich beyond imagination. They evoked caste as an essential narrative, natural, inevitable, a desirable progression in Indian society, culminating with Brahmin men as the rightful inheritors of a liberated India.

Colonial officers of the British Raj brought along their wives and children. White women's presence, coupled with repressive Victorian sexuality, ensured that there would be no shacking up with once-tantalizing Indian lovers. But for the Irish and working-class British sailors and soldiers who kept the Empire running, the administration allowed them sex to release their animal urges. Registers were created. Women and femmes were forced to reside in the Lal Bazaars, red-light districts organized around fucking British men. Damned by an extensive patramyth: literature, surveys, calls for social reform, colonial registers, and codified laws that policed Dalit and Muslim bodies. The 1868 Contagious Diseases Act gave authorities permission to go after women suspected as prostitutes — they could be gynecologically examined without consent, arrested, detained, sent away to be worked to death in a penal colony. An 1881 Census in Bengal declared all unmarried women *fifteen and older* prostitutes. All Dalit and Muslim women and femmes were considered prostitutes. They were seen as illiterate, uneducated sexual deviants at the mercy of their sexist, violent men, and so their writings, debates, books, and articles are virtually unknown from this period. By this logic, my people, feminine people from East Bengal: prostitutes. No wonder our grandmothers were married as children.

Women left India forever, crossing the *kalapani,* black water, to work as indentured laborers, known by various names: *girmit,* as in the *agreement* of indenture; *jahaji,* as in those who traveled on ships; or *coolie,* like *kuli,* the Tamil word for wages or hire — to places like Guyana, Trinidad, Fiji, Mauritius, and South Africa. On the Andaman Islands, British officers banished Independence activists and freedom fighters to a brutal prison, the Cellular Jail, where they were often tortured or worked to death. Across caste, women sought to escape Brahminical patriarchy, leaving abusive families and marriages and widowhood. After enslaved Black people were freed, white overseers flooded colonies with indentured Indians. Outnumbered by men, women found a new sexual freedom. They held the cards, they could choose their partners, swap, or have several lovers. Loving across caste no longer carried the same stigma. Caste bondage broke in these new homes.

I wear these copper bangles I bought in a market in Kanyakumari, the southernmost tip of India in Tamil Nadu, at the confluence of the Arabian Sea, Indian Ocean, and Bay of Bengal. The ends of the bangles are lingam-shaped, little metallic dicks. I heard that copper helps with blood circulation, from another musician I loved. My hands cramp when I type or write by hand, so I've always wanted this to be true. In the States, *chode* is slang for a dick chubbier than it is long, unlike these slim copper cocks. *Chod* means *fuck,* or *fucker,* slang still used among South Asians — *matachod,* motherfucker — its root the Sanskrit word *chodna,* to excite, animate. In Tibetan, *chöd* means cutting through the ego, involving a Tantric Buddhist ritual where meditators visualize the body as a symbolic feast to be devoured by all beings. *Chöd* releases ego. Maybe it's a *desi* thing, but I love an acronym. *Cisgender heterosexual oppression and dominance: CHOD. CHOD* upholds oppressive patramyths, applicable to any dominant cultural group — cisgender, feminine women are not immune — power is upheld by patramyths asserting their superiority. *CHOD* is palpable in the *Manusmriti,* or the *Kama Sutra* — which even offers a miscellaneous section with intense, seemingly painful instructions on penile enlargement — there's an underlying Brahminical panic about caste impurity, having a small dick, or lower-caste men and Muslims stealing their women. The presence of British colonizers drove their emasculation home, so revisions of these old texts became imperative to wrest back not only land, but their manhood.

Young Brahmin girls married off to older men ensured her family's caste status. And yet, their old husbands weren't expected to maintain relationships, only money and familial alliances. Practiced among the highest caste, the Kulin Brahmins, men could marry multiple wives — their scathing critique against Muslim polygamy did not seem to apply to them. Is it surprising that a teenager might fall in love or sleep with someone closer to her age? If she was caught, social suicide. Losing her caste status. Kicked out of her home. Or worse yet, mortal danger, if her husband died. Widows, young and old, needed to be desexualized, stripped of their sexuality, hair shorn, white-clothed, starved of spice, onion, garlic, anything that might elicit their inner fire. And for strict families, only by burning herself alive as a *sati* could a widow immortalize herself as proper and pure. Otherwise, they saw her fate worse than immolation: prostitute. These rigid bounds of femme identity and womanhood saw all feminine people as potential sources of ruin. Sex workers, ruined women, and, yes, wives, could be taken by force, embedded with all the pain and pleasure of men who've always needed them. Kept them secret because of their own fears of being ruined, a laughingstock, losing their devoted wife, their family, their rightful place in the imperial culture.

○

The real remedy for breaking caste is intermarriage.
Nothing else will serve as the solvent of caste.

— Dr. Bhimrao Ambedkar, "Annihilation of Caste,"
1936, an undelivered speech

Is there not a part of us that wants to experience this love as an intermarriage, a world where an Islam and an Iyer are together, without a second thought, the hot and healthy Hindu-Muslim romance we never get to see in films or television?

Growing up, my parents never told me much about caste, as Muslims they referred to Hindus as a monolith. I owe what I know to the writings of Ambedkar, the iconic Dalit jurist, scholar, and architect of India's democratic constitution, namely a speech he never delivered, "Annihilation of Caste," which called for the eradication of the caste system, and more controversially, Hinduism itself. India's digital archives include volumes of his writing and speeches, strangely housed on a website for the Ministry of External Affairs, although no thinker is more prolific about India's Internal Affairs. Ambedkar wrote extensive theories on the origins and development of Untouchability, the ostracism and violence his people faced for being outsiders in the Hindu *varna* system. *Varna:* caste and color. Dividing human beings into four castes — the most revered, the Brahmin, the priests; Kshatriya, the warriors; Vaishya, the merchants; and Shudra, the peasants — meant that anyone held in the lowest status, once called the Untouchables, could, and should, be destroyed.

On March 20, 1927, the day before the vernal equinox that year, Dr. Ambedkar and his followers performed a *satyagraha* — a nonviolent resistance in the style of Gandhi — at Mahad, another city in Maharashtra. They drank water from Chavadar Lake, forbidden to Untouchables, whose lips would pollute the lake, according to the Book of Manu. Just as he wore his tailored three-piece suits, he encouraged Dalit women to wear their saris as upper-caste women did, rejecting forced exposure of their breasts and legs. They were beaten by angry caste Hindus with sticks and clubs for this social violation. Some found refuge in Muslim homes. Afterward, the caste Hindus cleaned the waters with prayers and cow shit and piss. As if human lips were somehow more polluted than animal excrement. Later that year, on December 25, 1927, Ambedkar planned a second *satyagraha,* with a brilliant, irreverent act: burning the *Manusmriti.* This dangerous text had justified the humiliation and death of Dalit people for far too long.

In the patramyth of India's Independence, Gandhi is the beloved hero, but he renounced the Mahad *satyagraha.* Ambedkar never forgave, nor forgot, the Mahatma's abandonment.

Ambedkar believed intermarriage, as well as conversion to a new religion, could offer his people the protective power of belonging to a community. He knew that if Muslims were at-

tacked, other Muslims would ardently come to their defense
— all over India, if not the world. After he contemplated Islam
seriously for years, Ambedkar decided to convert to Buddhism.
On October 14, 1956, along with 365,000 Dalits, Ambedkar
and his followers liberated themselves from a society that demanded their endless suffering in every lifetime. That day, they
were reborn.

Whenever you and I have a fight, it's a rude awakening. Reality
check. When I learn that you don't own a physical copy of my
novel, my hurt is electrified by rage: *You're hiding me, you've got
a million books, but you don't have room for mine.* My sensitivity
to erasure as a Muslim femme heightened in your Brahmin man
presence. You don't think of yourself this way, but I do. Modern
readers love electronic books, they're the ones you keep closest, you tell me, but for me, a person who makes fragrant and
text artifacts with my hands, who cherishes the scent of a book's
pages, who is the first person in their family to publish a book
in English, with the same publisher of the first English books
my parents knew as children in Bangladesh — owning the physical copy means you care enough about me, your Beloved, to
make me a part of your archive. While I am still alive.

*When you make people who already feel small in the world feel
smaller, it's nasty. It hurts.* You apologize, over and over again,
distressed and shocked by my outburst. You wonder: How
could I ever feel erased by you? Perhaps you have no idea what
it feels like to give a decade to writing a single work of art, be

paid an entry-level nonprofit year's salary for it, a Bangladeshi wage, $1.35 per hour? What would you, a wealthy Indian man, know about that?

I crawl into bed with my man, crying about this fracture that feels final. *He doesn't even own my book,* I say, and as soon as I say it, my man chuckles at your rookie mistake. He holds me tight and kisses the back of my neck, sleepily murmuring, *You always see the profound beauty in things that no one thinks are important. And that is important.* He falls right back asleep after this sage declaration. I cry for a while longer, releasing, exhausted from writing, from you. Foolish me for believing love could thrive under lies, or be limited by smallness, thrift, deceit. I lay beside my lover for lifetimes. He is the person I remember to return to the water with, a return to our baby selves, when we swim at the beach, shower, drink a cool glass of New York City tap. He knows how I am drawn to niches, obscure places, how small things matter. He is the first man who held my hand in public, who never sought to hide me, never felt ashamed of me or how much he wanted to fuck me, never lied about me, never fettered me with toxic ideas of femininity, who accepted me for my incandescent rage and secret softness, as a queer, a wife, a whore, a goddess, a nobody, a star — everything, hand in hand, under the sun. Infinite.

INDIA TRIPPING

I always return to the East River to reset myself, watch the sunset and moonrise. Instant pilgrimage a stone's throw from my house. Ancestral land of the Munsee, one of the Lenape tribes, stolen by Dutch and British colonists, who ravaged the people with smallpox, influenza, yellow fever. Wild, how European tourists spread the virus here, 1600s redux. Settlers misheard and named the New York State towns I grew up near: Monsey, Haverstraw, Tappan, Ramapo. We can never be sure these are proper names that the Indigenous people called themselves, but even after their descendants left for places like Ohio, Ontario, Oklahoma, they were absorbed into iconic tribes, like the Delaware and Mohican. Invisible Indians are a myth, though. Their living descendants, the *vasanas* they leave behind, evidence of existence by way of deeds, records, birth certificates, pottery, and violet and white wampum — beautiful money made from sea snail shells — circulated until the pale-skinned conquerors minted coins in their own image.

I meet up with my friend Ajay by the river, greeted by the scent of weed, Black and Mild, aquamarine from the water, praline from the nearby ice cream shop. Depending on the block, in June you can catch a perfumed whiff of linden blossoms, the sperm scent of pear trees. Where questionable toxic superfund sites and the old Domino factory once stood, developers built high-rises and offices and manicured parks on the waterfront. My neighbor remembers when there were only factories everywhere — a candy factory even — when cabdrivers wouldn't want to cross the bridge over to the Southside in 1980s Williamsburg, when drugs, violence, and incarceration tore families apart, and mothers fought for their kids to live.

Ajay and I met in India, two Americans in Delhi. Ajay would be the *nagaraka,* my courtesan to his pimp, procuress to procurer. Just as I am a Hindu Muslim, he is a Muslim Hindu, his myriad knowledges of the Muslim world, from the Roman ruins of Damascus to Uzbek textiles to the Silk Road routes in Afghanistan, teach me about the lands Islam connects me to, just as I connect him to a feminine divine that feels to him ancestrally Hindu. To know someone in such a prismatic way is to experience different iterations of them: dance partner, romantic lover, toxic lover, roommate, squabbling spouse, estranged sibling, best friend, kindred. Ajay has known the full terrain of my emotions: rage, longing, softness, and sorrow.

Maybe this can help you heal the wounds you have with Indian men, he tells me, his brown eyes wet at the edges. *But not if he creates more trauma.*

I want to recount the only dream I've ever had about you, at least the only one I remember. I have an aversion to remembering dreams, often I want to leave them as soon as I awaken. Disorientation without a clear memory of what happened scares me. This time, though, I text you to tell you. You are my audience, after all. Dream, fantasy, memory, experience: with you, these bleed into a whirlpool of the same sensation that we've given different names.

We lay beside each other in a four-poster canopy bed draped in diaphanous mosquito net, like the beds our grandmothers slept in. Our view is the ocean, right there, in front of us, black waters haloed by moon.

Look at the stars, you say.

I can't see them. I remember feeling anxious, as I do in life — without my glasses, stars disappear. More ominously, the light pollution of the city makes it impossible to see them anymore. I look, but I can only see blackness and a faint glimmer of light. You take my hand and we step off the bed. There is no wall, no partition between us and the night sea. We walk onto the beach. *See.* We tilt our heads upward. Millions of stars. Staring at the same night sky our ancestors would have seen.

○

The sacrificial fire was lit; air all around was filled with the smoke and fragrance of incense and burnt-offering. The reverberations of the Vedic chants threatened to burst through the cloth walls of the pandal. I was lost in watching the head-movements that accompanied the chant of *"Svaha!"* each time a libation was poured. All this was extremely new, unknown, never seen before. I was totally engrossed, at one with the chants and the incense.

— Kumud Pawde, "The Story of My Sanskrit"

Kumud Pawde, the renowned Dalit Sanskrit scholar, learned to read and speak Sanskrit despite the thousand years forbidding women like her from ever learning or hearing such things — the *Manusmriti* warned that even listening to the Vedas could mean a punishment of pouring molten lead or lac in a Shudra's ears. Despite all the people along the way who bullied and belittled her quest, Kumud Pawde had a few upper-caste mentors who despised these prohibitions, taught her this forbidden language. It was her husband's name, which indicated a higher caste than her own, that let her finally through the door to becoming a professor. Hearing the chanting of the word *svaha* made the Sanskrit come alive to her. Kumud Pawde felt these words belonged to her; she became more incensed when an upper-caste woman noticed her watching and yelled at her to leave. I felt something similar when I heard Ravi Shankar's *Chants of India*, which became an iconic record for me, released the year I survived what I'm not yet ready to talk to you about. When I listen to the record now, I hear these beautiful chants, but now I hold space for Ravi the survivor, who experienced sexual abuse as a child. When I hear his music, I can hear how creating sounds from this primordial place healed him.

Svaha, the last utterance of a mantra, the last word in my Buddhist one, *Om Tare Tuttare Ture Svaha,* which I chant every day. In Tibetan, *svaha* means *so be it,* in Sanskrit, *well said.* Named after a nymph who wanted to love the great Vedic god Agni, a minor goddess, as they're called, but I see her as necessary, like the kindling that clings to the fire, letting us see the beauty of the flames, as we feel the warmth. I'm drawn to fire, I describe my energy this way; the part of Hindu traditions that drew me in were the sacred fires of a *havan,* where offerings are burned to the gods. I had always imagined I'd marry beside such a fire, but I didn't, I married by the ocean. I grew up in a faith that forbade idols, forbade goddesses, we should know

no divine besides All — h. But what is ancestral never dies, perhaps, and so, this utterance *svaha* reverberates, returns me to a
pre-Islamic abode within. I think of what's left of us, a message
here or there, nothing too unsettling, but even these are like
little embers of wildfire, enough of a spark to blaze. *Svaha,* the
femme inside the flame, the last breath of a mantra meant to be
chanted by men — the end.

You haven't been to India in twenty years. We've read lifetimes'
worth of stories about the spiritual sojourns to your motherland, but it's still rare to read the perspective of a Muslim, Dalit,
non-Indian South Asian, who experiences this motherland
as an outsider. Even getting my ten-year visa to go is a trip. I
need documentation of my *parents' origins* — photocopies of
their decades-defunct Bangladeshi passports from *before* they
became US citizens. I made sure that I looked as "Indian" as
possible, so I wore a bindi, a kurta top, making sure nothing
screamed too Muslim. I rode the train far out to Richmond
Hill, Queens, to a mom-and-pop Punjabi-owned spot.

Go for five-year, said the husband, smiling. *It will be easier
than ten-year visa.*

Bangladesh is not so much a problem, the wife said, both of
them were sweet, but real as hell. *Pakistani passport has more
trouble.*

I want to go for the ten-year, I told them. *I love India.*

We all smiled.

I paid them $650 for applications for me and my partner,
crossing my fingers that the Indians at the embassy would let

me into their country. Waiting for the visa depressed me, a reminder again of how silly this is, this blatant xenophobia, this notion of Bangladeshi *origins,* as though our origins started with our nation's formation in 1971. What about the thousands of years before that? What about the Indians from West Bengal who have the exact same Bangladeshi origins as I do?

I got the visa.

I remember my solo journeys across India, wondering if I'd be as brave now. One of my favorite places had been Rishikesh, a town by the Ganges named after Vishnu, which translates to *Lord of the Senses.* Each morning, I practiced yoga and sat in meditation by the sacred water, trying to heal from a heartbreak back in New York. I stayed at a small hotel near Lakshman Jhula, a suspension bridge on the river. Within a few days, after late-night conversations that went until dawn, the hotel manager and I become lovers, enamored with each other, stealing moments after he'd finished work. Hidden in the basement that he'd decorated with block-printed blankets and pillows and *diya* lights. Certainly I was not his first guest, nor the last. We were the same shade of brown; he felt familiar, dimpled cheeks, strong black eyebrows, lithe. What struck me then is how I experienced an Indian man I'd not yet come across in Delhi. He'd left his small town to find honest work in this dreamy yogi weed-smoke-swept place; he wanted to meet foreigners, but when he saw me, a *desi* foreigner, he'd stopped chatting with the Israeli couple he'd been talking to and came over to my table, where I ate dinner alone. Would this man feel comfortable had I come with my upper-caste friends? I suspect not. Without the judgment of friends, family, we could be our total selves, strangers, kind and loving for a short week, knowing we'd never see each other again. We crossed that uncanny valley, between feminine and masculine, American and Indian, Muslim and Hindu. I saw myself in his gaze, soft and amorous, wanting to feel all of me, brown-skinned, Bangla, free.

○

> From my childhood, my sense-organs had been sharp and vigorous. My sense of smell, in particular, had sharpened beyond limit . . . . I couldn't bear the smell of *shikakai* mixed with the smell of their hair. Their bad breath, too, was unbearable. And, in spite of all this, they found me disgusting? So, even at that young age, this emotion of disgust taught me to think. It inspired me to be introspective. At an age which was meant for playing and skipping around, these thoughts would rouse me to fury.
>
> — "The Story of My Sanskrit," Kumud Pawde,
> Dalit Sanskrit scholar,
> on ostracism as a youth by upper-caste girls

Eleven years later, I returned to India with Mustapha, but this time I had long, rather luscious hair and, more importantly, I was married, not a single twenty-four-year-old living with two American women. So I felt treated with a certain respect

I hadn't known. There were a few encounters — at the airport, the hotel — when an Indian man couldn't believe that my white-passing husband was married to me. I wondered if they were thinking: A. *Why would you marry her if you could be with a white woman?* B. *Why are you with him, you should be with an Indian guy.* Unclear. There were moments when people couldn't believe our names were our names. When we dropped credit cards, they were confounded by how we two turned out to be a Mr. Mustapha and Ms. Islam. Later, I wondered if I'd imagined the discomfort, but for the first time, I had a partner tell me what I felt as a Muslim in India was true.

We stayed in a flat beside the ruins of Hauz Khas Village, the same neighborhood I had lived in with Ajay. Each detail in the house felt like sacred geometry, from the rugs and hardwood floors, stonework mosaics and Islamic window grilles on the verandas. The grounds near the reservoir's lake were as lovely as I remembered, but this time I could hardly breathe, the air blackened by smoke and pollution. Wafts of smoke lay thick on New Delhi, from the burning of farmlands that surrounded the city, from the diesel of millions of trucks and autos and cars, from the outdoor fires lit to keep guards warm in the January cold. I took Mustapha to visit my most beloved of Delhi's Mughal ruins, Humayun's Tomb, but the palm trees leading up to the tomb had been decapitated by pollution, they bore no leaves or fruit. Veils of smoke gave the ruins the feel of a mirage.

One night, my coughing and breathing became so belabored, we decided to escape to the Hyatt Hotel. We inhaled that pristine air, just as we inhaled the mediocre Chinese food that cost nearly a hundred dollars, a berry tart, and cups of chai. We lingered in the lounge for a few hours, debating whether or not to blow a ridiculous amount of money on a room. We inhaled deep breaths as inconspicuously as possible, loath to return to our smoke-swathed Airbnb. Finally, we left. What a macabre vision of the future: Air Hotels.

That January, from the scale of Narendra Modi propaganda, the sheer size of his smiling, avuncular image on billboards — we felt his reelection was sealed. Street dogs wheezed, as children skipped in alleys of Hauz Khas with their bare feet, their eyes watery from the smoke and cold. We passed them hundred-rupee notes whenever we had them on us, knowing that more than anything, it assuaged our guilt. A year later, after the virus struck, millions of migrant workers, Dalit and Muslim, among them Bangladeshis, lost their labor for lockdown, traveling by foot back home. Humiliated by the police along the way, sprayed down with pesticide, forced to hop like frogs. The cessation of labor cleared the pollution, and the air in India's cities was cleaner than it had been in years. Fresh air would be short-lived. After the virus surged, mass pyres cloaked the city in smoke.

We booked a trip to Goa, where my old roommate Julia had lived off and on over the last decade. Her people hail from Brazil and Peru; she grew up in the States, but Goa is home. As a

Portuguese colony until 1961, its relaxed vibe is different from any other part of India. There's a lot to love as a traveler, the people are super chill, never too pressed by the presence of a foreigner; and the lushness of those verdant hills, Agonda's quiet, white-sand beaches, along with the flow of alcohol, drugs, reggae or electronic music, made Goa the perfect escape from Delhi's noxious air.

On the plane ride, I watched the film *Padmaavat,* which drew the ire of both Hindu and Muslim fundamentalists for their depictions of the titular Rajput queen and the Sultan Alauddin Khalji, who, incidentally, built the reservoir at Hauz Khas. It's undeniable that the movie is tilted in favor of the Rajputs protecting their kingdom from Muslim invasion. It is rife with caricature of Muslim hypermasculine bloodthirst. The final scene of the film ends with the glorious beauty of Deepika Padukone aglow in frightening firelight, ready to burn to death with all of her courtesans, her last stand against Khalji's battling army. What do you call a group of *satis?* A *jauhar.* The lesson: choose mass-immolation over being dishonored by rape by Muslim men. I couldn't help but wonder, what would I have done in that moment? *Hai, All — h,* I exhaled. Whew. That final image of her beautiful face just before committing suicide haunted me into silence for the rest of the ride. I felt sickened that, somehow, we were supposed to believe her act as the ultimate expression of a woman's purity.

As soon as we arrived in Goa, the salted air of the Arabian Sea opened up my breathing. We stayed right on Agonda Beach, in dreamy and simple bungalows owned by a Nepali woman. The staff came from all over India and Nepal, there for the busy season, and they immediately started to make us feel at home, though they'd left their wives and children to be there — to make enough money to last the rest of the year.

It felt good to breathe.

There's something about being a bodied brown thick femme in a bathing suit in India — something I would never do in Bangladesh, as it would certainly evoke judgment and ire from conservative Muslims that feels too close to home. And honestly, it's only possible in Goa because of the Euro vibration running through it. I took full advantage of the protective aura, and my white-passing husband, knowing that no matter what, I'd be treated as a guest, a foreigner exempted from the rules of modesty. But a brown booty hanging out of bikini bottoms is still a rare sight.

When I strolled onto the beach in my bathing suit, I felt the gaze of these brown men who worked these bungalows. They did not bother to hide their appreciation of my curvaceous body. I loved every second of it.

One morning, Mustapha and I laid out blankets on the beach, ready for an early afternoon swim. Within minutes, a young woman came up to us, her child wrapped in fabric against her body. *Didi, sister, please, na, give me something so my child and I can eat,* she asked, in Hindi.

We were in our bathing suits and had no money on us. I apologized and started to tell her to come back later, but just then, a pack of dogs started running toward us, barking viciously at the girl. They circled, snapping and growling at the young woman, who started screaming and crying in fear. I leapt up and started shouting, *Jao, kutta, jao, go, bitch, go!* Did these dogs respond to Hindi? Konkani? I had no clue. I didn't feel afraid of them, not for myself — they clearly were out to get the young woman and her baby. We knew they wouldn't hurt us.

Mustapha and I stood between the woman and her wailing baby and the frenzied dogs. I enveloped her in my arms, shouting at the dogs to leave her alone, until one of the waiters shooed the dogs away with a stick. Finally, they retreated.

Sorry, didi, sorry, I said, *sorry, sister, sorry,* over and over, in English-Hindi, embracing her as she wept. *Come back, didi, okay? We will have money later.*

We were outsiders, but the beach dogs never bothered us. The dogs only barked at Dalit people who passed by. Had they been trained by other humans, upper-caste people, to terrorize? Were they identifying them by the scent of their labor, where they lived? There are toxic aroma chemicals present in environmental and human waste, which the world's poorest people are exposed to because of their proximity — cadaverine, putrescine, formaldehyde. These chemicals imprint themselves in the body and the brain, affecting mental and physical health. Even after the day's work is done, sweeping and cleaning, the nightmare, the sensorium of labor, is inescapable.

We stood there as mother and baby wept. Her baby was too young to remember this moment, but trauma would become indelible memory. I looked into her face, this young woman and her child, both of them beautiful, brown, the undeniable loveliness of her lips, lashes, the ovals of her face — how could anyone deny her anything but love? She and I looked at each other, our eyes wet with heartbreak. We did not see the girl and her baby again.

RUINS

> I guess I'll see you next lifetime...
> — Erykah Badu, "Next Lifetime," *Baduizm*

My fury and your fragility at odds, whenever we reckon with our differences, how our interaction is suffused with pain. We cycled over and over the same terrain, working through something insurmountable I imagine we felt in past lives. I couldn't explain the feeling. Neither with reason, nor religion — and I didn't want to. I didn't need to. I just wanted to feel this mystery of loving a brown-skinned man whose body felt cleaved off my own, bound together we formed a cosmic whole. High-caste, low-caste; Hindu-Muslim; masculine-feminine — dissolved. After our last fight, it was clear that it had become too difficult to speak. We took space. I don't want to re-create the loops and cycles of trauma we've known before this.

No one talks to me the way you do, you told me once. I don't think you mind, I think you need me to tell you the truth. Your power keeps people from speaking the truth to you, but I don't know any other way to be. When I'm mad at you for not under-standing the chasms between us — class, gender, sexuality, caste — you react by retreating into a mood. Silence or sadness. My first response is to tend to your pain, as I push my own sadness at my smallness aside. You are as intoxicating as you are toxic, like a perfume, aroma chemical ruins of the natural world. Poison in small doses lets us ride that edge of death, reminding us what it feels like to live. During our affair, I've dipped back into familiar poisons, cigarettes and candy, even my late-night joints hit different, weed is less of a medicine, more of a smoke screen.

Holding your patramyths makes me sick. Sick to my stomach, unable to be nourished, loose shits, breathing shallow, chest tight, heart racing — trauma that I didn't know I still carried like this. Are you a bad man? I see the sweet part of you, the teenaged part of you; in my depressed state, I let myself open to you, a portal into that part of me that holds this longing old as time, for an Indian boy to love me, make me feel like I am worth something, make me feel pretty when I felt completely invisible. Shitting whatever I ate, day after day after day, for months and months and months. Mourning what my body remembered, which I'd stopped naming as active trauma, but there it was. I shed my body's weight for a lighter one, before I knew violation. I cut my hair, in the fashion of widows and survivors of rape and war, foremothers who were burned, dismembered, discarded for the fear their sexual power and vulnerability elicited in powerful men. My new hair looks more like yours. This is my shorn self, a shed, shredded self, a return to my adolescent body before I knew violation. I molted like a snake. *Naga.*

The last time you and I see each other, the night begins with both of us on edge. Hurt has a way of collecting in the throat, lumping into awkward silence. Touch softens us. Soon, we are laughing, petting, giggling, staring over a plate of overpriced pasta in Manhattan. We hail a cab to the East River. It is the coldest night since winter, wind blows off the water, we are shivering, clinging to each other for warmth. In the distance, the glow of the Manhattan skyline. Two slim beams of light, twin ghosts of the towers we will never forget — is that the day we became one or separated? — the ruins of them clear as this moment. Above us the white moon, full and waxing, kissing, mouths are where the rivers within meet, whispering the only good mantra in English, *I love you,* I let go of you, *I love you,* I cannot be absorbed in you, *I love you,* goodbye. A month later, you send me a photograph, your eyes are as melancholy and brown-black, beautiful. I can't read the longing in them any-more. Your intensity makes me shudder. I'm not sure I can stare at you this way, here, at the crossroads of this uncanny valley, I feel revulsion at this virtual you. Without touch, without scent, you are a simulation. I need to protect my language. This love filled me with new language, but to learn it, I need to let go. I write to imagine freedom, even though I write in the language of power. The language of the colonizer. Can I ever be in pos-session of my power if I am with you? Not only is this ancient love — it is ancient pain.

In the ruins of the Indus Valley Civilization, scientists extracted DNA from I6113, a female-assigned skeleton, more than four thousand years old. From the cochlea, a part of our inner ear, shaped like a sea snail's spiral, they determined that she had a genetic mixture of ancestral Southeast Asian hunter-gatherer and Iranian-related ancestry. What I6113 did not have: the steppe ancestry associated with ancestral North Indians. This study flowed back into Hindu nationalist discourse: So, was the Indus Valley Civilization an indigenous Vedic Aryan culture or a Dravidian Tamil culture? Were these ancient people related to descendants in North India or South India?

Let me offer a reorientation — East.

My ancestors — our ancestors — were among the people who settled, migrated, labored, loved and fucked and lived and died in the Indus Valley. People destined to be written out of this ancient civilization, because future patramyths would deny them a place in history. Their origins lay too far in the wrong direction. Forever outsiders. I consider the possibility — the inevitability — that some of our ancestors from the now-mysterious Indus Valley hailed from the far eastern reaches of the subcontinent. Places like Bangladesh, Tripura, Assam. We will never know if I6113 is definitively from the eastern reaches of India. There is no place for her in Indian history if we imagine her from East Bengal. Why not? Who will ever offer me evidence proving it true or false? Don't we all want to see ourselves in history? I want to. Your people are mine; my people are yours.

We can't read these ancestors' language, we can't hear their music or smell their scents, but we, their descendants, know them. We are them.

You and I haven't spoken. We are separated, for now. Lost in our work: you, on your artifacts of sound, me, writing this text, making perfumes. Each composition is its own universe, with its own accords. Art to be experienced on other bodies, in ears, eyes, noses; bodies that will die, and so, the memory of our work will die with them. Melody, musk, a scattering of shells, an ocean of *vasanas* that we leave for each other, for the world. They are how we remember, how we disappear. How we love. *Svaha.*

Romantic Scientist

Perfume as Frontier

NOTES

Sandalwood & Oud

CLASSICS

Baj found me, his first child, to be the exact image of his mother, Lutfunnessa, who died when he was twelve. *Janani Manutu abar esheche,* he would say to me as a child, which translated to *Ma's come back again.* I suppose when children are born, we want to give them Earth free of discord, where there are no bloody assertions of identity, where they know nothing about violence for as long as possible.

Just before my birth, Baj completed his PhD in chemistry, a subject that he chose because of the beauty of Dhaka University's Curzon Hall, named after Lord Curzon, the man responsible for the 1905 Partition of Bengal. Had the medical college building not been such an eyesore, his fate would've been different. Baj never wanted sons. He saw it as luck that he'd been given daughters. I've thought of my father's discomfort with having sons as a fear of having to teach or embody masculinity in America, which would pressure him to keep his affectionate nature at bay. He preferred science to sports, pacifism to war. He worked as a scientist, but nurtured a clandestine imagination: he painted, sculpted, studied Bengali music, gifted with a sonorous voice that spans two octaves; he loved long drives, of which there had been many, when we moved from one university town to another; he loved excursions in nature; he was a daydreamer, a bit lost in the clouds, but with a mean streak, a lightning strike, flashed when he felt provoked. After his brother's death from a heart attack, Baj had to step into a new role as father and provider for his nieces and nephews, who lost their parent as children, just as he had. Baj fit the trope of a Romantic Bengali man, a *bhadralok,* an upper-caste gentlemen — like the ones we encountered in Bengali films and literature — only Baj is Muslim. He had the gentleness, but not the caste.

During the war, my father visited Ma's house in Tongi. She was a teenager, my father in college, her older brother's best friend. He would sing songs, often at night, astonishing my mother and her siblings. They were mesmerized by his size (he stood a foot taller than everyone in their family) and his knowledge about nature, literature, music. When he sang, he escaped into his own realm. Music still escapes my father's body effortlessly, lips whistling old Bangla tunes or playing the *bashi,* a bamboo flute, his fingers at home on the expanse of a harmonium, those soft, diffused notes that sound underwater, thick, hirsute fingers searching the pearlescent keys for his song. When he sings, he looks lost in a dream, eyes slightly open, his voice clear as water smoothing river stone. *He sings to me all day,* said Ma once, her voice broke, remembering why she fell in love with him.

Their generation was part of the 1970s wave of scientists and doctors and pharmacists who were admitted by the 1965 Hart-

Celler Immigration Act. There have been earlier waves of Bengali Muslim men, seamen escaping the harrowing, inhumane conditions of British steamships to live in Harlem, in the late 1800s until 1947. They fell in love and made families with Black and Latina women, absorbed into the bloodlines of their descendants. The gilded, 1920s, Orientalist aesthetics of the flapper, swanky in silk, would not exist without the textiles and wares of those early immigrants who peddled Indian goods. By the time my parents arrived, their people had recently become Bangladeshi. Students and professionals from all over the postcolonial world left their new countries, in a global draining, a de-braining, of young people who could've (would've, should've) built their own countries' futures. Instead, they helped build modern America. Ma never thought they'd stay here. She thought my father would get his degree, work a few years, and they'd go back home, to live out their lives, die, and be buried in their *desh*.

I think about how our human quest for fragrance has been a slow violence against the Earth, but a necessity for dealing with our own filth. Remains of prehistoric plants and animals trapped in the primordial mud of our oceans, swamps, lakes, and rivers, with time and high temperatures and great pressure, transformed into petroleum-laden rock. From this petroleum, about a third of volatile chemical products, pesticides, paint, ink, glue, cleaner, and perfume are derived. Human exposure to volatile compounds of fossil origin comes from automobiles and everyday chemical products. Not all of these are derived from petroleum; natural essential oils emit volatile compounds into the air, too, and require millions of flowers and trees and intensive human labor. There is a deep cost to fragrance, but long ago, humans burned fires, fragrant woods, their perfume offered an escape from the stench of the world. *Perfumers are creative chemists,* says Baj, glad to see me sharpen my scientific mind through scent formulas. He taught me about global warming early, devising a science project on our coffee table. We filled three test tubes: one with dry ice from his lab, one with regular ice, and an empty tube of air. We positioned a lamp in front of tubes, and I recorded the temperature in each tube with a thermometer. The carbon-filled dry ice test tube got hotter and hotter, of course. A vial of glass, like a perfume, a microcosm of our planet.

GIFTS

When I was three, we drove from Texas to Alabama in a Toyota Celica, a rust-scarred hatchback, blasting '80s music, Baj's favorites: Donna Summer, Queen, Boy George, George Michael. He sang with the flamboyance of Freddie Mercury but without the moves. Wanderlust by way of economic necessity, we moved from town to town for elusive science jobs. His brainy detachment from his body, from hours locked in the lab, threw his back out. I remember seeing my father laid out on the floor of our Houston apartment, debilitated by pain, the largest presence in my life hobbled down to where I stood. From a young age, I identified more with my father. He and I were both a bit bow-legged, brown-skinned, messy, with the countenance of big cats — he a lion, me a tigress. Our voices have the same texture, soft and deep, although mine is more femme and smoked from cigarettes. I used to sneak cigs outside my bedroom window, masking the scent with body sprays and incense, but the thought of me smoking hurt him deeply — my grandmother had died of throat cancer, perhaps caused by chewing *paan*. Every betel leaf stuffed with sweet and bitter carcinogenic plant and mineral bits offered a little escape from life, just like my window tokes.

Somewhere in my parents' house, there's a Vanity Fair Music Time! record player that Baj gifted me in 1986. I owe that record player my Americanization. What's more tragic for a non-Christian kid than being left out of Christmas? We memorized Christmas carols from a Disney album Baj bought us. I begged him for a tree, so he obliged me. Year after year, we lit up a three-foot plastic tree on my dresser. I played Blondie and Tina Turner on repeat, dancing in a bathing suit, the closest thing I had to a leotard, memorizing the lyrics to "Heart of Glass" and "Private Dancer," as if I knew how a broken heart felt. My icons were irreverent Black and white women, an approximation of the femme I wanted to be. Dance as a future never was on the table. Besides not being able to spare extra money on lessons, dance was reserved for private pleasure, not public performance. Did the aversion come from Islam, which stressed modesty, or the British, who vilified *nautch* girls — dancers and courtesans and sex workers? What moves a body to music is beyond *dharma* or *deen,* beyond the scope of any imagination that holds men as the ultimate expression of who is free.

SCIONS

A month before I turned five, I started kindergarten at the Learning Tree Elementary School, in Auburn, Alabama, which seemed to me a land of football fanatics and a small community of Bangladeshis. I was the youngest in my class. From the first day, I became a target of a young Persian girl bully. Our skin, the color of almonds; mine the color of its roasted sheath, hers the meat. She stated the obvious fact: I was dark, and she wanted me to know she thought I was ugly. Both Black and white kids would ask me: *You Black or you white?* I didn't know. So I answered, *Tan,* like the crayon, the first part of my name.

One day, the Persian girl refused to let me hold the doll she'd brought in for show-and-tell. I'm uncertain whether or not I started crying, or if my teacher, a young, freckled white woman, noticed what was happening. Miss Michelle had each and every student raise their hands. *See how we're all different colors? Some of us are white, some of us are Black, some of us are in-between. Nothing wrong with that.* My bully and I, in-betweens, avoided each another after that, too small to know that one day, we'd be seen as the same enemy.

In 1969, a community of Black Muslims in the Nation of Islam bought one thousand acres of farmland enveloped by a dense pine forest, in Ashville, Alabama, a town two hours from where we lived. Sold by a white car salesman who appreciated their moral uprightness and segregation — no drinking, no white women. As soon as the deed was signed, the white people who lived nearby—thought to be Ku Klux Klan members—unleashed a series of intimidating attacks: they shot dead and poisoned cattle with cyanide, destroyed the salesman's lot of cars with acid, and burned his office down, right before Christmas. Shaken by the toll of violence, the farmers moved their surviving cows to another ranch owned by the community, in Greene County, which was predominantly Black. *No use staying where the people ain't civilized,* said the manager of the property, John Davis. *We don't want any profit, we'll sell to anybody, including the Klan.*

These Black Muslim farmers aroused an old fear among the white people who did not want them living nearby. Among enslaved people, 20 percent of them were Muslims, who held on to their traditions, even if outwardly they proclaimed to be Christians, a practice known as *taqiyah.* They prayed on mats and *tasbih* beads, they fasted, and they wrote secret letters and books in Arabic, a rare literacy among enslaved people. The long notes of the *adhan,* their call to prayer, were submerged in the sounds of the early blues.

I could hardly inhale the scent of southern flora, abundant with magnolia, longleaf pine, wisteria, and moss, buildings quilted by mold in the damp wetness of summer. My small lungs were saturated with pollen and moisture, leading to bouts of bronchitis or pneumonia. Southern *vasanas* live in dormant corners of my mind, revived whenever I've returned to Alabama, Georgia, Louisiana. After school, Baj tried to lift my spirits away from the daily bullying with visits to a local pecan grove. We gathered as many pecans as we could; cracking them open at home, I savored those first tastes of southern food: black-eyed peas, fried chicken, mashed potatoes and gravy, sweet pecan pie. A rich break from our staples of *daal,* rice, fried mashed *bhortas* of vegetable and potato. We celebrated my fifth birthday with a rich chocolate cake. I snuck sweet bites from the fridge after my parents had gone to sleep, the first memory I have of being ashamed to eat food. In the afternoons, sometimes a peacock would appear outside the window of the bedroom that I shared with my baby sister. I crumbled a handful of Ritz crackers in my hand and tossed them to the peacock, who fanned open irides-cent teal-eyed feathers while eating my gifts, flashing me beauty in return.

In 1986, as we gathered pecans in Alabama, my father had not yet become a citizen of the US. Did he know about those pecan trees, who'd planted them, who died on them? At that time, I hadn't heard the phrase *the bloody birth of Bangladesh.* My bully and I were too young to know how we, the children of new Muslim immigrants from Iran and Bangladesh, had inherited this country's history, or how Islam connected us not only to each other, but to the first Black Muslims, who held on to their faith and traditions even as white people enslaved them on this land. Did Baj realize then, that here, in his new country, trees were mausoleums hiding in plain sight?

Near our old apartment in Auburn, there is a trail of trees called the George Bengtson Historic Tree Trail, named after a white research forester and plant physiologist at the University of Auburn, Alabama. A great man, I'm sure. These trees are grafted from scions of heritage trees. Among the trees planted: *Lewis & Clark Osage Orange. Trail of Tears Water Oak. General Jackson Black Walnut. General Robert E. Lee Sweetgum. Southern Baldcypress. Johnny Appleseed Apple Tree. Mark Twain Bur Oak. Lewis & Clark Cottonwood. Helen Keller Southern Magnolia. Amelia Earhart Sugar Maple. Chief Logan American Elm. Lincoln's Tomb White Oak. John F. Kennedy Crabapple. John James Audubon Japanese Magnolia.*

No trees are named for Muskogee, the First People who died in the millions during epidemics, displacement, and land raids. Under the buildings and homes and replanted forests are remnants of Muskogee earthwork mounds, temples, and trenches, a complex network of pre-American cities. There is a single scion named for a northern Indian Iroquois, Chief Logan, another for the Trail of Tears, the only nod to the suffering of Indigenous people. There is no mention of Sacajawea, never mind that Lewis and Clark would've been lost in the American wilderness without her. George Washington Carver Green Ash is the only scion named after the Black inventor and scientist. No Black or Native women or femmes are named. No mention of a single civil rights leader, which Alabama birthed aplenty: Coretta Scott King, Rosa Parks, Angela Y. Davis. Imagine a Zora Neale Hurston Sweetgum or a Margaret Walker Poplar.

Fifty miles away in Montgomery, the four men wrongfully accused of murder in Lee County — Mr. George Hart, Mr. John

Moss, Mr. Charles Humphries, and Mr. Samuel Harris — are tattooed on one of the eight hundred rusted steel beams that represent the victims of lynchings across Alabama's counties, a necropolis honoring massacred fathers, sons, mothers, and daughters. Just down the road, at the Legacy Museum, there is a wall of named mason jars, filled with soil collected from lynching sites, dirt, and tree matter. Hues of rust, black, and Gulf Coast sand are time capsules of earth and blood. In this trail of patramyths, Robert E. Lee and General Andrew Jackson are remembered as Great Americans. We know their savagery is what once made them Great. As they turned fellow human beings into aliens and animals, by enslavement and genocide — in Africa, in Asia, in the Americas, and in all of Europe's colonies — white people mythologized their savagery into a patramyth of supremacy.

RELICS

In photographs of Baj when he first moved to the town of my birth, Carbondale, Illinois, he possessed a laid-back, scientist cool — fitted in bell-bottoms, muttonchops, a slim-fit batik or velour shirt under a lab coat. All chosen by my mother, his young bride. In those photos, he was clean-shaven, but Ma preferred Baj with facial hair, she felt it made him appear kinder. When Ma joined him in the Midwest a couple of years later, he grew a mustache, looking a bit like one of those Greek-Buddhist Gandharan sculptures of the Buddha. Gandhara, as in *gandha,* perfume, for the spices and fragrance the people used to anoint themselves. Sculptors chiseled the Buddha's features to Helle-

nistic perfection, but with the aura of an Indian, a light smile
on his lips, a skinny mustache. They captured a true syncretic
union of Greek and Indian cultures. The Buddha never wanted
idol worship made in his image, but it's hard to deny the beauty
of those Gandharan *bodhisattvas* and their handsome swagger.
As remote as our people were from the Gandharan civilization,
in the far western reaches of the Peshawar Valley of present-day
Pakistan and Afghanistan, the vast expanse of Buddhism connected us, as Islam would, too.

Baj taught me to collect facts, fragments of history, the remnants of nation: coins and postage stamps. I preferred earth
shards, rocks, and seashells. Each time I read one of my library
books, my father hassled me to write a synopsis of everything
I'd just read on an index card. Boxes of index cards held details
I might possibly need one day in the future for a book. My father had dreamt of being a novelist, he had the imagination, but
could he ever let loose, be provocative — a freak? If not in this
lifetime, he left the task of writing to his daughters. Baj's tendency to hoard possessions that could one day come in handy
— a nine-volt battery, a magnifying glass, a motherboard — is
a psychic remnant of living through war, where anything could
be stolen. Visitations to the library held our connection to our
father's inviolable self — gentle, brilliant, wise, never angry.
One did not have to be a rich or an ambitious man in a library.
Everything was free.

We never went camping or anything like that, but we did see beautiful places in the middle of America, in long drives across the country to the Rocky Mountains, the Meramec Caverns in Missouri, the Ozarks in Arkansas. Once, at a lakeside picnic in the Ozarks with other Bengali families, Ma tried to teach me to swim the way she'd learned: by throwing me into the lake. As soon as I got into the murky water, a giant log stabbed my knee, I started screaming. *What, what? Just float!* she yelled, trying to keep me in the water, as the wood splintered deeper into the wound. When they pulled me out, my knee had been split open, a gash that should've probably been stitched, but we just used Band-Aids, leaving me with a crescent moon scar. I wouldn't learn to swim for another twenty years.

SANDALWOOD

I meet the son of the legendary perfumer Carlos Benaïm at a mutual friend's dinner party. Benaïm is the nose behind some of the most iconic Western fragrances worn by my father and me, like Ralph Lauren's Polo Green, released the year of my father's arrival to the States, 1978, the gold-capped emerald bottle a fixture in our bathroom. Baj has never bought himself a cologne; he admits that perfumes are perfunctory, gifted by Ma. The most resonant notes of Polo Green are its sunlit pine forest with bursts of mountainous herbs like thyme and lavender, as it dries down into musk and woods, reminiscent of old book pages, the dry scent of cedar, like pencil shavings and grassy patchouli. For

Baj, wearing it is a sort of scent drag, a masculine imaginary of the American frontiersman.

Benaïm composed the perfume gifted to me by my first boyfriend in high school, a fifteen-going-on-thirty-five fragrance, Elizabeth Taylor's White Diamonds. The rhinestone-encrusted bottle made me feel like a rich bitch, strong enough to overpower the scent of curry that nestled in our clothes.

As we sat around a fire pit, Benaïm's son asked me, *What's your favorite perfume note?*

Sandalwood, I answer, wondering if the truth was too obvious an answer, aware that being a self-taught perfumer brought about the feeling of impostor syndrome. In the Western, white male-dominated perfume world, becoming a master means scenting the masses with the backing of a multinational laboratory. None of the reasons that called me to perfume.

He smiled and said, *That's my father's favorite, too.*

Buddhist tradition rooted itself in our land before Islam, rising to prominence under the Pala kings, who ruled from the years 750 to 1161, until the Sena warriors who hailed from Karnataka in South India overruled them, establishing their new Sena dynasty. They instated a rigid Brahminical social order in Bengal, and, slowly, Buddhism started to wane. After being burned and pillaged and abandoned, Buddhist *stupas* survived as ruins, but long lost their odors. They were once fragrant abodes, for in the heart of the monastery lay the perfumed chamber of the Buddha, a *gandhakuti,* where ritual offerings of incense, handprints of sandalwood paste, and flower garlands summoned the presence of the Buddha in his absence. Whenever the Buddha happened to be in a town, he stayed in the *gandhakuti.* In the *Lalitavistara,* a second-century CE biography of the Buddha, his mother's womb is described as an embryonic palace, its innermost chamber made of *uragasaracandana,* or sandalwood imbibed with the essence of snakes. Sandalwood cooled the body, evidenced by nesting serpents that crawled on trunks in the summer heat.

Throughout Buddhist texts, references to snake deities, the Naga protectors of the Buddha, are mentioned. Mucalinda, the one who raised his cobra hood, offered the Buddha shelter from a rainstorm, right after his Enlightenment, in Bodh Gaya under a sacred fig tree. I imagine these stories immortalize everyday people as Divine, turning the humble man who'd held up a tarp to protect Buddha from the rains into a myth. Throughout Hindu scriptures, sweet fragrances — lotus or sandalwood — are associated with the cosmic and caste purity. Likewise, the malodorous smells of garlic, onion, fish, blood, or shit are judged ritually polluted, the sensorial landscape of lower-caste people. Buddhism radically broke from Brahminism, destroying any notion of purity and pollution, for all beings were both pure and polluted. All beings could attain Enlightenment, and all beings could end their suffering of rebirths, the cycle of *samsara.* Laypeople participated in all devotional rituals, laying down *malas,* flower garlands, lighting incense, or smearing the body of a *vihara* with their sandalwood-pasted palms. They built the Buddha's funeral pyre of sacred woods, like sandalwood and oud, woods known as *anaryajam* or from non-Aryan lands where his teachings flourished. After his death, incensed relics of his ashes, called *sharir,* or body, were housed in perfumed jars. Excavations in the mid-nineteenth century uncovered these lost reliquaries in the ruins of a Gandharan monastery.

Sandalwood oil is extracted from its heartwood, which takes ten to thirty years to become viable for distillation. The strength and scent of the wood led to its prolific use for architecture, Ayurvedic and Chinese medicine, incense, and, by the nineteenth century, Western perfumery. Sandalwood has been discovered in the South Indian charcoal record around 1400–1000 years BCE, and the word *candana* is thought to have the same root as the Tamil word *cantu,* for fragrant powders wetted into a scented paste. Warm, creamy, and affordable sandalwood synthetics offer nature a respite from human extraction. Its importance in Indian perfumery is evident from the formulations in the *Gandhasara, The Essence of Perfume,* or *Sandalwood,* a medieval Sanskrit compendium. By 1792, the Sultan of Mysore declared sandalwood a holy tree and forbade its sale to prevent overharvesting. When Indian sandalwood no longer became available to the Chinese Buddhist merchants because of this decree, they began trading with King Kamehameha, who conquered and unified the Hawaiian Islands. And so, Hawai'i entered a harrowing era of sandalwood trade. In 1819, after the death of Kamehameha, his son Liholiho ascended to power. Liholiho struck foreign trade agreements on sandalwood credit, forcing forest laborers to pay impossible taxes to cover his debts. His appetite for luxury led to overharvesting the trees — and decimating native *'iliahi*.

Today, I use precious drops of Royal Hawaiian sandalwood from a family farm reviving native forests of sandalwood that once flourished on the islands. It's curious how sandalwood trees are parasites. They need host trees like whistling pines and acacias to draw nutrients and water from their roots. Just as royalty inflicted their rule upon the people, without their hosts, sandalwood would never survive.

PABNA

My ancestral home is in Pabna, a city on the northern banks of the Padma River, a distributary of the Ganga. This house has an eternal quality to it, built in a timeless way of imagining communal space. Traces of my father's artistry live on in that house, a sculpture he made of my cousin Deepa, pen-and-ink drawings, books of ragas with his notes. The unassuming white stone structure felt most alive at the back of the house. Every bedroom opened up to a veranda that faced a courtyard rimmed by mango and guava trees. Free hens pecked at insects in the dirt. The ambience invited visitors to laze and stare at the sky. Separate from the living quarters are the outhouse and kitchen, the place that always felt most in need of reimagination, where the women who married into the family, like my father's stepmother, were relegated to prep and cook meals all day, every day, for their lives. In my father's family, there is no deeper bond than blood. Wives, like my own mother, remained at the edge, outsiders, never held at the center.

That first summer I spent in my father's childhood home, I was ten years old. My cousin Tutul, my late uncle's son, gave me family birth records. I drew a family tree of our ancestors going back seven generations, to a patriarch named Keramat — *miracle* in Arabic — revealing that we'd been Muslim at least two hundred years. Our family's original name, Sardar, means *chief,* a term often used to address a turbaned Sikh man, probably because the men in my father's family are tall. In the tradition of most Bengali families, last names changed from generation to generation. We were Islam because we followed the Western convention of taking our father's last name. I think about how this choice reveals a lot about my grandfather, who gave his sons the last name Islam, a simple declaration of faith. Unlike the folks who adopted names like Sheikh or Sayyid to assert a bloodline past the Khyber, claiming themselves the descendants of Persians, Afghans, or Turks rather than descendants of lower-caste people who converted to Islam. That we are all a mixture of the travelers and settlers and Indigenous people of Bengal is the truth.

But I am no descendant of Mughals — I am the descendant of farmers.

SUFIS

Our Sufi masjid of the Turkish Jerrahi Order gave me a magic sense of solace inside a house of worship for the first time.

Whenever I'd go during middle and high school, I felt at peace. The small brick cottage invited worshippers from Turkey, Albania, Senegal, Pakistan, and Bangladesh. During Ramadan, we prayed on the lush Turkish rugs laid on the floor of the light-filled prayer room, and afterward we feasted on everyone's home-cooked dishes in a communal iftar. The leaders of the mosque led us in a Sufi chant, swaying their bodies to a song in a language I could not understand, but felt in my veins. In the Jerrahi masjid, the whirling and swaying and singing embodied the Sufi concept of one's total dissolution into the Divine. We listened and wept, sated our hunger with delicious food, ascended to All—h as the mystic chanting grew louder and louder. I had never sung prayer aloud before.

Still, during *namaaz,* I resented how I had to stand behind Baj and the other men, who recited their prayers aloud — allowed — for them. Whereas we women and femmes whispered. I didn't mind the whispering — to be honest, I preferred whispered prayers, I didn't want others to listen, or to hear my mistakes on Arabic words I didn't understand. But I wanted to stand beside the men, to break this idea that we needed to be separated. They say this is to protect women from the male gaze, to avoid distraction or desire. My feminine body detached me from this freedom that Islam afforded Baj, and the brotherhood he felt during Friday *jummah.*

After I left for college, my parents transitioned to a larger masjid, led by a Pakistani imam, where more South Asians worshipped. When I visited, my mother, sister, and I entered the women's prayer room from the basement, a dark, cramped space, with a television that showed us the men's prayer room. We heard the sound of their *namaaz,* all of them surrendered in that gorgeous, golden light, but we were relegated to the downstairs darkness. These microcosmic divides felt like we mattered less than the men. I've debated whether or not this is true, but to be relegated to the back, the bottom, has never felt good. Perhaps hidden women's prayer rooms have an older history, an evolution out of necessity, in light of violent attacks against mosques, I don't know. I never went back.

Sufis brought Islam to Bengal. No one was forced to convert, we did so to break free of that horrible caste system, said Baj. Perhaps by the time our family converted to Islam, no one held a sword to their necks, but that Islam eradicated caste prejudices or spared Hindu, Christian, and Buddhist people who kept their own faiths and practices is untrue. When we mention India, I hear an undercurrent of contempt in Baj's voice, more embittered after he missed me at the Jaipur Literature Festival. One of his thirty visa application pages had a mistake — an incorrect address of a family friend's home in Kolkata instead of his hotel. His error cost him the visa, which the consulate denied Baj twice, even after he corrected the mistake. It's not so easy for men named Muhammed with Bangladeshi origins to get into India.

I remember the day that Baj awoke wide-eyed and as scared as a child after his back surgery, his American desk life eventually catching up to him. Seeing him like that jolted me with the realization that one day he, too, would die; one day, I would lose the privilege of being parented, of being loved, I would lose him. He never prayed much when we were children. After that surgery, Baj started to pray. He had lost a few inches in his spine; now closer to my height, we were finally eye to eye. He prayed in a chair, for the prostrations had become too hard on his back. I'd never seen him pray much before that; he kept a scientist's distance from religion. After his surgery, he found a way to bridge the unknowable with the practice of *namaaz,* a private place where faith and science live inside him, in quantum equilibrium.

Years later, when Baj and Ma traveled to Mecca for the Hajj, the journey bound them together as spiritual pilgrims, ensuring their afterlife entry to heaven. He returned home with quiet awe, humbled by the Oneness, circling the sacred black cube of the Kaaba, along with millions of his brothers. In the eastern corner of the Kaaba, there is a black stone mounted on the wall, a remnant of pre-Islamic goddess worship, when the Quraysh tribes of Arabia worshipped Al-Lat, a mother goddess who rode a lion, like Durga, a feminine form of the word All — h. Some believe this stone is a piece of a fallen meteorite. There are traces of primordial cosmic odor in meteorites, trace notes of sulfur, honey, puke, and tar.

Sometimes I think of Baj akin to that sacred black box — all that I'll never know about him, because of how he set himself aside to be present for us. Where did men like him fit into the masculine imaginary of nation? He chose science over sports, art rather than war — where did he see himself in the fight for the birth of their country?

EXALTED BIRDS

Have ye seen
Al-Lat and Uzza

And another,
The Third goddess, Manat?

These are the exalted birds,
Their intercession is to be hoped for.
— from Surah Al-Najm, The Star

In the Surah Al-Najm, these lines appear in the Quran, the *qissat al-gharānīq,* or Story of the Birds, later known as the Satanic Verses, acknowledging the three goddesses of pre-Islamic Arabia: Al-Lat, Uzza, and Manat, represented by a feminine body, a sacred tree, and a white stone, respectively. In Islamic accounts of this *gharānīq* story, Muhammad is said to have recited these revelations at the Kaaba while in assembly with leaders of the Quraysh, the mercantile tribe persecuting him and his followers. Though the Quraysh worshipped feminine deities, this did not preclude the practice of infanticide of female-assigned babies or the abuse and enslavement of women. Uttering the names of these goddesses — and calling for their divine mediation with All—h to bring them into Islam—Muhammad compelled the Quraysh to halt their violence. Later, however, the archangel of Revelation, Jibrīl, visited Muhammad, informing him that these words had been implanted by Satan. There was only one true All—h, and no pagan deity could ever be acknowledged, the Divine could never take on a human or idol form. The Prophet recanted, and the persecution by the Quraysh continued.

Over the centuries, Hadith scholars, who recorded Muhammad's practices and sayings, debated the truth of this incident, which called into question the issue of a prophet's infallibility —how could the messenger of All—h be tricked into uttering words about bringing pagan goddesses into the fold? Other scholars accepted the incident, praising Muhammad's ability to admit error in his quest to transmit the Divine, a sign of his innate truthfulness.

Salman Rushdie's *The Satanic Verses* reignited this arcane controversy. Incensed Muslims the world over burned and banned and fatwa'd the book condemned as blasphemous for its portrayal of the Prophet and his wives. This didn't keep Baj from buying the book for our home library. Books transported us to other worlds, offered freedom from our bodies, revealed the absolute and inviolable freedom of an author's imagination. Books were transcendent, so inviolable we were taught to never accidentally touch one with our feet, to never let a book touch the ground. Reading a book, no matter what its contents, no matter how profane—raised consciousness, which made them sacred. I felt afraid to even touch *The Satanic Verses,* intimidated by its red-and-black spine, by the title itself, unaware of how these lines traced back to a feminine divine. I feared sin as early as four, when I first heard the story of Iblīs, the archangel closest to All — h, whose hubris and fall from grace turned him into Shaitan, the Satan. When I heard older kids say phrases like *fuck you, shut up, you're stupid,* these words felt like an unspeakable undertow in a new ocean of sounds. I had not yet learned the concept of sin, or *gunah,* as we called it, from Persian. *There are no bad fingers,* Baj whispered back, gently pressing my middle finger down into a small fist.

NIGHT BOAT

Where did you live during the war?
Pabna and Dhaka.
Did you want to fight in the war?
I did want to. But my father was old and alone. So I stayed with him.
Did you feel safe?
Of course I did not feel safe. No one feels safe in an occupied home-land.

Back then, there were hardly bridges, we had to take boats and ferries everywhere, Baj tells me on the phone. In late summer 1971, near the end of the Liberation War, my father caught the last ferry back to Pabna from Dhaka University. As soon as he sat on the ferry, his heartbeat quickened — he was the sole civilian on the boat — all the rest were Pakistani Army men. He kept still, his eyes avoiding contact, but a young Punjabi solder struck up a conversation with him.

My village is very green, much like your country, the young man said. They reminisced in English, a language that unified them despite all attempts to divide and conquer. Baj was terrified but aware that he needed to stay calm and pleasant to assure his safety to make it out of that ferry alive.

Suddenly, the young soldier's superiors beckoned him over. Though Baj couldn't understand their language — likely Punjabi — he could tell that the officers were pissed at the kid for talking to one of the locals so openly. They avoided eye contact after the admonition.

When the ferry docked around nine o'clock in the evening, my father caught the last bus back to Pabna. Another Bengali who'd been on the ferry rode with him. They struck up a conversation. Still shaken by the encounter on the ferry, my father invited the Bengali man to stay the night at his father's house. Traveling late at night could be dangerous; one could be caught in the crossfire between guerillas and the army. He wanted to offer a haven for his countryman.

He turned out to be a nasty, terrible fellow, my father told me. No soon as the man arrived at the house, he began bragging about his plan when he returned to Kushtia. He planned to steal land from his neighbors — Hindus — whom he despised. It dawned on my father then, the gravity of his mistake. So relieved had he been to be with a fellow Bengali after that night boat ride with the Pakistan Army men, despite the nice exchange with the Punjabi soldier, he'd unwittingly brought a dangerous man — the worst kind of traitor, a Bengali aligned with the occupiers — into his home.

I wonder — who did that frightening stranger have to kill to get that land?

CONQUESTS

My father recounted the story of Bengal's conquest in ten minutes, something that had taken me months to research. In the year 1204, when the old king Lakshman Sen sat down to eat his dinner, a short, squat and scary Turk-Afghan general, Muhammad Bakhtiyar Khalji, rode into town with a cavalry of horsemen. Horsemen, as always, brought the chaos. Disguised as horse traders, they made their way to the king, and threatened to kill the old man unless he ceded the throne. Sen surrendered and departed quietly for Sylhet, the easterly hinterland of Bengal. Khalji and his men had ransacked the famed center of Buddhist study, the Nalanda monastery in Bihar, but the glory of his violent conquests was short-lived. Drunk with power, Bakhtiyar Khalji planned to conquer the Land of Snow, Tibet, traveling the northern tea route from Bengal through Nepal. Unversed in treacherous mountain warfare, tens of thousands of his men were killed by Tibetan warriors. Two years after he penetrated Bengal, as a humiliated and defeated Khalji lay ill in bed, he was stabbed to death by one of his own men.

That fateful night shifted the destiny of the Delta. Over the next five hundred years, vast swathes of the rural people became

Muslim. In the beginning, the Delhi Sultanate minted gold coins to honor the conquering of Bengal, stamped with the image of horses, a primordial symbol of men's power over the Bengali population. Situated so far east from Delhi, Bengal's rulers sought to break free from North India's grasp. By 1342, they went rogue, an independence that lasted for two and a half centuries, until the final reintegration of Bengal Subah into the Mughal Empire under the Emperor Akbar.

HAREM

On our first family trip to North India, we visited Akbar's red sandstone city, Fatehpur Sikri. Our tour guide, whose accent sounded almost southern from the way he drawled his words, reminded us about Akbar's syncretic approach to rule, how he engaged Hindu and Muslim scholars in public debates, and only drank water from the Ganga for its sacred powers. We walked through the three palaces of his wives — each one's abode reflected their religious milieu: Christian frescoes, intricate Hindu and Jain temple motifs, and the one that struck me most, the smallest of the three, for Akbar's Muslim wife. In the Hujra-i-Anup Talao, the walls were carved delicately as if the sandstone were wood, into a honeycomb pattern once inlaid with mirrors and diamonds, which were all stolen in the years after Akbar abandoned Fatehpur Sikri to conquer Punjab.

If you were to light a candle in this chamber, said our guide, *these thousand mirrors would reflect its light.*

I loved the smallness and intimacy of this nest, a perfect escape for lovemaking, writing poems, a private world apart from the squalor of the imperial harem, which housed five thousand women. *Harem,* in Arabic, holds a dual meaning, a sacred space, a sanctuary, but also that which is forbidden, *haram.* For the Mughals, military conquests included the collection of women as tribute, reifying the significance of the harem. In North India, Rajput princesses became a part of Akbar's harem of thousands, pawns and pledges of allegiance by the defeated. Members of the harem included young, lithe, and beautiful virgins, wet nurses, survivors of war captured as booty, as well as all the women in the emperor's family. Guards protected them. No men allowed, but castrated boys "gifted" as revenue payments to the emperor, many who hailed from Sylhet, in far eastern Bengal.

SYLHETI OUD

When I was researching my first novel, my sister and I visited Sylhet, near the Jaflong border between Bangladesh and the hills of Meghalaya. The lushness moved me, our people were from more southerly, flatter parts of Bangladesh, I reveled in the green. We took a walk through a tea garden, passing a grove of slim trees, their bark stripped in the pattern of camouflage, almost like birch, but deeper in color — they were agarwood — from which oud oil is extracted. Agar, like the word *agarbatti,* or incense. When the trees are infected with fungi, they respond by producing a thick, resinous heartwood. Its scent is woodsy, animalic, with a touch of kalamata olive and stone fruit. I have some shards of Sylheti oud from a fifty-year-old *kala kat,* black-wood tree. I held these tiny bits of trees in my fingers, as if I were holding a roach, and burn them, inhaling that creamy, charred chocolate smoke.

Today, half a pound of pure oil runs for nearly thirty thousand dollars, distilled from Sylhet, one of the original birthplaces of this oil. As Buddhism spread from India across Asia, incense of oud became laced into ritual offerings in Chinese temples. Oud became an encounter between East and West Asia, a meeting in the markets of South Asia. Just as musk connected Tibet, India, and Arabia, so, too, did oud. Beloved by Arab merchants and royals, oud was one of the *al-usul,* the central five aromatics, including musk, ambergris, camphor, and saffron — all of these associated with exotic locales far from Arabia — from the Himalayan mountains to the Indian Ocean. Luxury is never about proximity, just as in love, we yearn for some distance to know how much we want someone.

One evening, my sister and I decided to venture downhill from our lodge to watch the sunset at the edge of the forest. We caught the late-afternoon humdrum of the village, children playing in their yards, chicken and goats nibbling around, a woman making dinner, squatting to slice her veggies on a *boti,* a scythe she held down with her feet. We found a spot to watch the sunset, and snapped a few photos to document the glow of golden-hour on our skin. Everything grew still. Quiet.

Hardly ten minutes had passed before we heard an old man

shouting, *Ja! Ja! Go!* He held a giant walking stick and waved it around. We raised our hands, *OK, OK, we'll get out of here, calm the fuck down,* I muttered under my breath. We knew he wanted us out of there, but we didn't understand Sylheti.

We started hiking back to our lodge, but the man stayed close behind us, still agitated by our presence. We quickened our pace. Darkness had come fast after the sunset we hadn't even gotten to enjoy. It seemed that all the cute kids playing in their yards, with their mothers watching close by — they'd all disappeared. The only people out were men. Men playing football, men walking in pairs. We kept our eyes straight ahead. I did not fear I would be harmed that evening, but I still felt afraid. My body and breath constricted by the possibility of harm. No matter where it moves, whether in the forest or in the city, the femme body is tracked. This stranger had gotten so agitated by the sight of two girls unaccompanied by men, so close to dusk. Later, I realized that we knew nothing about what he may have witnessed during the war. Seeing the two of us sitting alone in those woods triggered that old man, patriarchy, no doubt. But —

What unspeakable things had he seen?

Nature is not guaranteed to femmes. Perfume lets me concoct a simulation of these sacred woods I can't walk alone without fear, a ritual of the future using ancient materials. In the patramyth of modernity, we've come to see ourselves as separate from nature, separate from each other, as if we can disassociate

our humanness from the insides of a forest. The processes unfolding among trees is not separate from the arc of a human
life. Sandalwood, a parasite, would be nothing without coex-
istence; and the spirit of oud, its depth and richness, blooms
as it becomes sick, as it decays. Laying down these base notes,
I remember that a perfume is a journey, one that the perfumer
begins backwards. These sacred woods are the beginning of my
process, of my people's olfactory story, they are the dry-down,
the way the scent will fade on the wearer. How my intention
— the story I wanted to tell — will end on their skin.

CAGED BIRDS

> I was like a caged bird. And I would have to remain in
> this cage for life. I would never be freed.
>
> — Rassundari Devi, *Amar Jiban, My Life*, 1868, the first
> autobiography written by a Bengali woman in Pabna

We learned our first Bengali songs in the shower. Baj, in his
swimming shorts, transitioning my sister and me out of baths.
I remember that the scent of our father's preferred soap, Irish
Spring, felt too masculine for me — I preferred the softer musk
of Caress — but we used whatever soap we bought on sale,
like the bread, cereal, and cold cuts that were also on sale. He
wanted my sister and me to be versed in music as well as science,
for our economic and emotional security. *Music is for your mind
and soul,* he would say when I complained about practicing my
violin. The songs we sang were sweet, simple tunes, their lyrics

— as far as we know — penned by the Great Poet and India's first Nobel Laureate, Rabindranath Tagore. *Phule, phule, dhole, dhole, flowers sway in the breeze.*

Back then, I didn't know how Tagore represented the epitome of high Bengali culture, belonged to the Bengali *bhadralok* class that renounced caste but lived all of its privileges, or how his family had owned ancestral *zamindari* lands in East Bengal for generations. Tagore often lived on a houseboat on the Padma River, and many of the motifs in his poems show his love for the Bengali countryside. He opposed a divided Bengal so deeply that he pronounced the day of Partition, October 16, 1905, a national day of mourning. In a way of processing this loss, he took to the streets, tying a *rakhi,* a sacred thread, on the wrists of Hindus and Muslims, a symbolic effort to remind everyone of their Bengali bond. I wonder if he considered how this iconic Hindu tradition might have alienated the Muslims?

When we sang, I felt as though I were in my own world, reveling in the crystalline acoustics of falling water and our music bouncing off the walls. We were young enough to bathe with our father without shame of our bodies, and old enough to know that we should never ask him about his scar.

On one of my visits to my father's hometown, we visited the grounds of the Pabna Mental Hospital, the first in Bangladesh. The area felt peaceful, a wash of blue, brown, and green like much of the riverine countryside. *Pabnar pagol,* the crazies of

Pabna, I've heard in passing, a lewd reference to people struggling with mental illness. Unspoken is another history of the
institution, which became a site of rehabilitation for women
raped during the war. Whenever I got loud or aggressive or
flaunted wildness, Baj would call me *pagli*, crazy woman. Being
shrill and unstable were undesirable qualities, the sort that belonged to a woman who, throughout history, ended up locked
inside.

Your dad has the hands of a brute, a boyfriend told me once,
pissed that he couldn't drink a glass of wine to break the ice
with my Muslim parents over dinner. That would've had the
opposite effect, I tried to explain. That I'd grown up attend-
ing dry parties with my parents, without the social lubricant
of booze, seemed unthinkable to him. We broke up soon after. That observation struck me. I'd never thought of my father
as a brute. I remember Baj's gentle voice and loving bear hugs
wrapped around me, and when I think of his hands, I remember him combing and braiding my hair, comforting me during
illness, painting my face green on Halloween. I dressed up as
a witch for years. I relished those hours free from being a girl,
a night when demonic evil became acceptable. With my long
black-and-white-streaked wig and black wax in my mouth that
made me look toothless. I cackled witchily, flashed my blackened teeth, sealing a win in the mall Halloween costume con-
test. I won a thirty-dollar gift certificate to spend in any store.
I offered the prize to Baj, who never bought himself anything
luxurious. He'd gotten a job interview and he needed a new

pair of shoes. Opportunities for steady work evaded my father in those nascent years of his career. We shopped together for a pair within his budget. I loved giving him something, for once. With my own money.

I have a faint memory of a fight, the outline of my parents. I am five, watching. Baj and Ma shouting, she is hunched over a sink, weeping, dishes breaking, his arm raised, face angry, me running, hands covering my ears, hiding in the closet until the shouting stops. A strand of my parents' memory, I am not a full witness. But I remember the pressure of our lives, would there ever be enough money or space, the feeling we would never get there, wherever there was — *I want to go home* — even though that's where we were supposed to be. Home.

My own rebellion started after my first period, as my new breasts and hips delineated the forbidden, a boundary that no one could cross. I rejected modesty. I didn't want to cover my arms or keep out of the sun, I hated any commentary on my body, like whenever Baj called me a little fat girl, somehow saying the words as if giving me a compliment. He seemed genuinely shocked when I screamed him out. He didn't get that the words didn't translate to English the way he thought they did. By fifteen, he discovered that I'd been sneaking out of a downstairs window to meet my boyfriend, and Ma found a box of photographs of me posing provocatively with said boyfriend and empty cigarette packets under my bed. They grounded me indefinitely. I was trapped inside. I wasn't allowed to leave the house except for school, my mall job, and after-school clubs, like the literary magazine, where I let out my troubles in poems.

One afternoon, I'd had enough. *I fucking hate you,* I screamed. I locked my door and cursed my parents for this sentence of antisocial confinement. I threw a hole puncher and successfully punched a hole — in the drywall of the first house he'd ever owned. I threw my violin and broke its neck, stunned at the splinters along the scroll. As much as Baj wanted me to play, to be a virtuoso, settling for virtuous, I refused to give him the satisfaction.

Baj banged at the door, livid at my outburst, and I opened it, wanting him to see how much I hated them for caging me. *Janwar, animal,* he said, flashing rage right back at me. It was the harshest word he spat when provoked. He raised his hand, and I wondered if he would hit me, I glared at him, waiting, but as soon as our eyes met, he lowered his arm, his body deflated, he softly whispered, *Why, Ma,* unable to slap the likeness of his own mother.

When I came out to my father: *What do you mean, queer?* Baj furrowed his brow in concern at the only word he didn't approve. He saw the words from my bio in a play program, an unmemorable performance: *Tanwi Nandini Islam is a Bangladeshi Marxist Feminist Queer Femme Artist living in Brooklyn.*

You mean psychologically, not physiologically, right? He repeated the words, unable to ask what he meant — *do you sleep with women?* I thought about the Trinidadian femme I met on a dance floor, at some New Haven bar near Yale. Her slim waist adorned with a belly chain that kept getting caught on my short-lived belly button ring. Mouthful of long hair, salted kisses, the full fleshiness of breasts in my mouth, finding her clit with my fingers, as if I were touching my own.

I wouldn't let Baj push me into the corner of his mind that could accept what I was telling him. *That's not how sexuality works,* I told him. I started to explain that I was femme, I was attracted to masculinity, trans men and butch women. I still loved dick. What did he need to hear?

Baj started to write down the words on a napkin — *butch, femme, queer, transgender, bisexual* — like those new worlds of knowledge I wrote on my index cards, a synopsis of my sexuality, but on a scrap that he'd throw away.

UNKNOWN BIRD

Will you always write about subcontinental characters, Baj pondered once, *with alternative lifestyles?* Would I always write about desi queers? *Yes,* I told him. *I want to write people I never grew up reading, people like me.*

Writing outside of the dominant culture feels this way, a constant pull toward trying to name and locate ourselves in a milieu that never imagined us. We reach for our futures, at the same time we reach to the past, trying to figure out how we got here.

Baj's nickname for me, *Pakhi,* or bird, imagined the freedom he wanted for me, for my mind, to be unfettered, unrestricted, when I danced or wrote, he knew I existed outside of boundaries he understood. Sometimes he said the name came from a romance adventure novel that he'd read as a young man, *Green Mansions* by the Anglo-Argentinian author William Henry Hudson, after a feral young woman, Rima, who lived in the Amazon. She spoke in tongues that let her communicate with birds. I never liked the reference, for the Bird-Girl is killed, burned to death as she hides from native tribes in a giant tree. Did he see the ultimate freedom as death? Other times, he joked that when I wasn't old enough to eat solid foods, he'd chew up the pieces and feed me the mash, akin to how birds feed their young. Perhaps transmitting a Western idea of pioneers charting the wilderness helped him make sense of how I would always be my own person, a part of him, apart from him. I see how we've grown up together my whole life, Baj and I, how he translated me through what he understood of the West.

When I first heard the album *Bauls of Bengal,* recorded in 1966, the songs of these mystic musicians felt rooted in the body, the soil and spirit of my fatherland. These songs have been passed down generations by the mystic musicians of Bengal, known as the Fakir or Baul, all committed to their memory. Written words were never as trustworthy as what we hold in our *mon,* the mind-heart. Listening to their music, the resounding message is that our body is a microcosm of the universe. *Moner manush,* person of my heart, referred to the Divine inside us and everyone else. I heard a new reason for Baj's nickname for me, the phrase *achin pakhi,* the unknown bird within, the Divine stuck in the flesh cage of the body, like a bird ready to be boundless.

INFINITE BLUE

If you would know All — h
Go to the infinite blue.
Who is this you call All — h?
Almost formless embodied in light
In his embryonic avatar
He meets his Beloved.

— Lalon Shah,
a Baul-Fakir mystic poet and philosopher

Baj recalled a trip to Bangladesh, when he and my mother visited Shilaidaha, the ancestral *zamindari* lands of Rabindranath Tagore. They encountered a blind singer, sitting under the starry flowers of a bakul tree, playing tunes on his harmonium. They gave him some money for his performance, delighted at this happy surprise. An ice cream seller sold Ma chocolate-and-vanilla-dipped bars, which she bought for the people who stood with them as they listened to the man play.

On those lands, there once lived a Baul named Lalon Shah, also known as Lalon Fakir, who lived more than a hundred years and died on the same date of his Libran birth, October 17. Whether he was born Muslim or Hindu is unknown. Lalon composed thousands of songs, but he never wrote them down.

The songs of Lalon Shah were finally collected into a thirteen-volume oeuvre called *Haramoni, Lost Jewels,* by the folklorist Muhammad Mansuruddin, who invited Rabindranath Tagore to write the foreword to the first edition.

Tagore admitted the extent to which he drew conceptually from Bauls, even though he didn't mention Lalon Shah by name: *I have adopted the Baul tunes for many of my songs. From this it can be seen that at some period of time, Bauls' tune and voice got assimilated in my mind in a natural way.*

The performances of Lalon, living on Tagore's land, playing his one-string *ektara,* a lute made of dried gourd and bamboo, undoubtedly affected his rapt audiences. Surely the *zamindars,* the landowners, bore witness, too. Lalon's songs are invisibly imprinted in Tagore's body of tunes. How many were drawn from Baul melodies? How much of his philosophy drew from Baul conceptions like *moner manush* — person of my heart — a gender-neutral Oneness with another, with oneself?

For an artist, there's a fine line between assimilation and extraction, borrowing and theft. But for Lalon, would this matter, if his truth found its way into another's heart? If men who yearned for worldly power spread these messages of love — did it matter if the origin became absorbed in the patramyth of a Great Man? Would Lalon even give a damn?

Femme people are rarely cast in the light of Greatness, our bodies predestined us for erasure. We learned and loved the songs and surahs of Great Men, like Rabindranath Tagore, like Muhammad, shapeshifters of consciousness, who implored their fellow men to be more humane, men like my grandfathers, men who married girl children. Facts a feminist must square with faith.

Six months after my sister and I took that trip to Sylhet, the four of us visited my birthplace, Carbondale, Illinois, to revisit our parents' old haunts from their first years in the States. We would visit the apartment complex I'd grown up in, now dilapidated and abandoned. Hard to imagine it bustling with international students. Baj drove us on the highway, past endless fields of blond corn and green soy, just like we used to as children, the scent of the McDonald's we'd scarfed down minutes earlier clung to our clothes. My mother had provoked my sister into answering a question she'd kept secret for years.

No soon as my sister cried out the words, she collapsed into my lap, sobbing.

Baj responded, slowly, *What?*

He looked at us in the rearview mirror, confused, but trying to keep his eyes on the road.

My sister sobbed, I stroked her hair, pleading with Ma — *love is love* — until at some point she conceded, *I can understand why two women would love each other.* Baj said nothing. I stared upward at the great expanse of that midwestern sky I'd forgotten, a sky that seemed to envelop us all, as my father drove, stunned, silent, staring into the infinite blue.

~~Orientals~~

Perfume as the Other

NOTES

Incense & Spices

OCEANS

A mother snake always protects her baby snakes by swallowing them if danger comes around.

> — interview with Mildred Heard,
> a formerly enslaved woman from Georgia, 1937,
> *Federal Writers' Project: Slave Narrative Project, Vol. 4,*
> *Georgia Narratives, Part 2, Garey–Jones*

Capital comes dripping from head to toe, from every pore, with blood and dirt.

> — Karl Marx, *Capital*

Horsemen rode through villages, capturing strong, beautiful and young people whose lives they'd ruin for their own gain. In preparation for market, medicine men concocted ceremonial baths of brewed plant roots laced with the powers of forgetting, to cleanse people of their old lives. Hausa traders made their captives eat a legume they called *màntà uwa*, forget mother, its toxins intended to steal the memories of everyone they loved. In the markets, mountains of cowrie shells, harvested by South Asian laborers in the Indian Ocean, were used to purchase and enslave West Africans on the Gold Coast. Their jagged little teeth an omen of how they sucked the blood of innocent people.

Twelve million Africans were stolen by European slave traders and more powerful groups in their homelands. Forced across the Atlantic Ocean on massive, heaving ships to a brutal New World, chained on a harrowing voyage, in a sensorium of torture: collective excrement, illness, blood, and putrefaction of wounds. Pungent smells wafted off the coasts, revealing the cargo — whether they carried spices or enslaved people. Islam, which preached equality, still sanctioned slavery, if a person was a *kafir,* a nonbeliever; or captured during *jihad,* a holy war. Like the Hausa traders, Arab traders justified slavery in the preceding centuries to force East Africans to labor in the salt marshes of their harsh desert. Riding the monsoon winds across the Indian Ocean to the eastern coast, Arabs brought goods from India and China — silk, spices, porcelain — and returned back to Asia and their own land with rhino horn, elephant ivory, gold, and enslaved people, *Zanj,* an epithet meaning Blacks. These people crossed the Indian Ocean to work in mines, as household concubines, and as military.

In the name of Christian salvation, the Portuguese, Dutch, English, and French defended their right to own slaves. From the "Enlightenment" onward, Europeans fashioned themselves as modern, rational, the future of humanity. Far, far away from the brutality unfolding in their colonies. The patramyth of a free market erased slavery as the genesis of capitalism and Empire. By the nineteenth century, pseudoscientific racism emerged as a strategy of dominance, from eugenics to miasmatic theory, a belief that foul odors held poisons. Europeans feared inhaling night air, since they believed the vapors of noxious smells could make them sick. The fear of contaminated water kept white people from washing their bodies with frequency, an irony not lost upon the colonized. Africans originated the trade of scented resins, like frankincense and myrrh, so often associated with church, but as whiteness claimed property, purity, intellect, and the sweet-smelling as its predestined virtues, Blackness became a void — landless, immoral, superstitious, and stank, destined for hard labor and damnation.

Conjuring ancestral knowledge and their own deep botanical connection to the lands they labored on, enslaved Black people birthed a new sensorium of resistance. They healed their bodies in illness with plants: pine needle tea, sassafras to cleanse the blood, comfrey to heal wounds, and snakeroot for serpent bites, a fatal hazard they encountered in the fields. Honeysuckle and rose petals steeped in benne oil, sesame seeds brought on the ships from Africa, perfumed their skin. Poison proffered an escape, a vengeance on white enslavers: with the milky sap of little *mancenillier* apples in Martinique. Speckled green leaves of dumbcane swelled the tongue and throat, forcing master to shut the fuck up, or white oleander, so toxic that water from a vase of the blooms killed. Mixed with crushed glass, verdigris, and snake venom — dinner assured death.

White enslavers' fear of poisonings and escapes sharpened their cruelty. By 1704, slave patrols started in Barbados, spread to South Carolina and eventually all of the colonies. The first police were horsemen armed with whips, and bloodhounds, trained to smell the scent of a runaway's clothes, ravaging any Black person caught while trying to get free. If they happened upon a stream or a river, wading in the waters to throw off the dog's nose could save their life.

By 1833, after intense pressure from abolitionists, the British abolished slavery. It would take another thirty-two years to abolish slavery in the United States. Laws never deter men's greed. Smuggling increased the slave trade in Africa, where more people were enslaved than in the Americas. Twelve million Africans crossed the Middle Passage to the Americas, and another six million traveled an older route, in the other direction — across the Indian Ocean — to work the clove, nutmeg cinnamon, ginger, coffee, and sugarcane plantations on the Maluku, or the Spice Islands of Indonesia.

Colonizers manipulated the people and the land in battles they fought to gain power over each other. They'd rather destroy all the nutmeg trees to create scarcity and demand. After the abolition of slavery, plantation owners grew desperate to save their crops from ruin in the colonies, in the Caribbean, and in the Indian Ocean. They recruited people to leave India, a homeland that never felt like home, as they were punished for caste, gender, widowhood, sex work. More than a million left for colonies, half of them in the Caribbean, as indentured labor, crossing the same dark waters as so many before them.

ORIENTALISM

Master Perfumer: Oriental is a reveur, a dream, a fantasy, nothing offensive. There is no other term as nice and general and dreamy. Oriental means exactly the style and beauty and luxury before the colonies! Oriental is untouched and genuine. "Colonial" style is not Oriental at all! The Orient comes before the colonies! From when it was feared by the Occident, when the Orient was invading the Occident—and cutting a few of our throats!

Me: I think white and European perfumers can learn from perfumers who are Black, Indigenous, Arab, Asian, Latinx—we exist—we who create not only transcendent fantasy, but objects of immanence, this world we live, connecting us to the ancients, to our ancestors, to a time before colonizers named us and erased us, our smells, our scents, and bottled them into fantasy.

Master Perfumer: Go have a smoke, calm down, and chill out.

I got into a public online debate with an iconoclastic French *Master Perfumer* — I call people what they call themselves. We argued back and forth for a while, with me and other perfumers of color trying to educate him on how for peoples who'd been colonized by Europe, the term *Oriental* is racist and made so many of us feel Othered. How could the word *Oriental* — derogatory to East Asians in modern parlance — ever be expansive enough to contain the vast histories of Africa, Asia, the Middle East?

Another perfumer in the discussion sent the Master Perfumer a copy of Edward Said's "Orientalism," to re-Orient why discontinuing his use of the word *Oriental* mattered. "Orientalism," a revolutionary text, became a revelation to me as a young feminist, mind-blowing as a perfumer. As Orientalist scholars embarked on their translations of *ancient texts, languages, civilizations,* they helped colonial rulers make sense of Empire. Knowing their subjects made it easier to categorize, divide, and conquer them. Perfumers summoned these faraway lands into temporal sensory experiences. Perfume as little museums of the colonies, a fragrant addition to the social and scientific discourse, yet another *generalization, an immutable law about the Oriental nature, temperament, mentality, custom, or type.*

Coined by the French fragrance house Guerlain, the Oriental fragrance family emerged alongside Empire. Notes of sandalwood, spice, vanilla, and incense expanded the nineteenth-century European perfumer's palette, as did the aroma chemicals in their laboratories. While the colonial project was underway — and the prices of raw materials were driven down by the endless capacity to exploit human labor and the creation of new synthetic materials — Parisian perfume houses became the locus of Western olfactory culture. Perfume became a mode of sensory imaging of the Other and the fragrant material of the Orient. Most Western writing on perfume focuses on its capacity for transcendence or escape. Allures of luxury and the exotic nature of the materials described in purple, perfumed prose. This is what first drew me in, language that is lyrical, historic, romantic, and scientific, at once. There is inventive signature in the way independent perfumers describe their creations. Yet I often find the opulent, canonized, big-brand Western perfumes powdery as the dusts of conquest.

The Master Perfumer meant to tell me that I couldn't understand what he meant, but I knew very well what he meant, I'd encountered this among many white and upper-caste people before him. There's this Western desire to connect to something beautiful, abundant, and mythic — like the rose-scented sails of Cleopatra's ship, all things ancient Egypt, Ayurvedic healing and yoga, traditional Chinese medicine. They yearn to belong to a sensuous past that existed before the colonizer arrived, before the violence and the genocide. But did that past ever exist? Oriental is an erasure of the actual living, breathing descendants of the Orient, the native people, the laborers, the low caste, the massacred, or the enslaved — the very people colonizers believed too inferior to comprehend their own ancient greatness. They are disturbing to acknowledge because the colonizer must acknowledge the crimes of history. *That's not even what we meant! We mean the beauty! The dream!*

The modern obsession with clean beauty and perfume codi-
fies colonial language — what does it mean to be clean? Does it
acknowledge that someone, somewhere is getting dirty harvest-
ing the roses, the sugarcane, the turmeric?

I knew the Master Perfumer would never hear me. He wanted
to hold on to the fantasy, the dream, the Great Past. Who was
I? Unimportant, hypersensitive, too woke. Not a Master. The
rêve de l'Orient mattered more than the descendants of colonial dreams that more resembled nightmares. The next day, the
Master Perfumer admitted that the French fragrance archive
Osmothèque, a bastion of European fragrance culture, used
the term *Ambrée,* not *Oriental,* for the thick, sweet viscous resins and spices often used in these perfumes. My words held no
sway with him. The declaration of an institution he respected
changed his mind. Master's tools include condescension and
gaslighting others' reality, so I never expected an apology or acknowledgment.

In homage to their tradition, I won't bother to name him.

European perfumers transformed the spiced bounties of the
colonies into their own classics. Oriental perfumes, a fetish object, a way to *formulate the Orient,* while not *even trying to be
accurate,* as we are reminded by Said. In their attempt to insert
themselves in these histories, they construct ahistorical, inaccu-
rate mythologies, rather than a continuation of a practice.

Jacques Guerlain's most iconic perfume, Shalimar, released
in 1925, tells the love story of the Mughal Emperor Shah Jahan
and Mumtaz Mahal, a king courting his Beloved in a royal gar-

den. The brand still proclaims this fragrance as the *first Oriental perfume in history.* As if the ancient practice of attar-making simply didn't exist. In 1989, Guerlain released Samsara, *an elixir of seduction for a woman who has found harmony and balance.* Strange, since *samsara* refers to the life of the householder and the endless cycle of rebirths. Being released from this state to experience *nirvana* is a fundamental aspect of Indic thought. *Samsara* has little to do with harmony and balance.

Names are important. Western knowledges, including perfumery, have been rooted in an obsession with scientific classification and categorization of every facet of the biological world — and at its worst this has enacted great horrors on the planet. There have been initiatives to undo the damage to the environment and the laborers by the largest European multinational fragrance and flavor companies, like Symrise working with vanilla farmers in Madagascar to eradicate child labor and abuse, or Firmenich replanting oud trees in Bangladesh. Some of us are using those materials, sourcing from farms we know will give back to the earth and the local people, recalling real places, ancestral lands, and pain. How we use perfume to ascend social class or trauma fascinates me more than glamour. When I compose a perfume, I want to transcend families and classifications. Perhaps that makes my scent memories illegible to some. *This smells more like a place, than a perfume,* I read in a review of one of my fragrances, Mala, inspired by fragrant flower garlands and trails of incense, a dirty rose inspired by New Delhi. *Precisely, bitch,* I want to tell her, I made that perfume as a brown-skinned woman in a brown-skinned land, and I wanted to hold the city close to me. For some of us, language, trauma, labor, and land cannot be extricated from why we perfume.

BLOOD BROTHERS

> You can't hate the roots of a tree and not hate the tree.
> You can't hate your origin and not end up hating yourself.
> You can't hate Africa and not hate yourself.
>
> — From a speech delivered the night after Malcolm X's home in New York was firebombed. He was assassinated a week later on February 21, 1965.

Once, during Ramadan, when I participated in an educational exchange program between college students and inmates at Greenhaven Prison, I uttered *as-salaam-alaikum* as I walked past brothers donning beards and kufis waiting in line to go outside into the yard. The masculine reverberation of *wa-alaikum salaam* down the hallway made me shiver. Islam made us kin, instantly.

Muslims make up 9 percent of the US prison population, even though we are 1 percent of the US population. Many found Islam while incarcerated, just as Malcolm X discovered the teachings of Elijah Muhammad while incarcerated. *The Autobiography of Malcolm X* is banned across prisons in the United States. After he broke from the Nation of Islam, he went on Hajj to Mecca, renaming himself El-Hajj Malik El-Shabazz. There he felt kinship with Muslims from all over the world, even blond-haired and blue-eyed ones, which began to shift his consciousness about race. He visited leaders of Muslim and African nations. In Algeria, he met the first president, Ben Bella, a revolutionary who fought for the Liberation Front, the FLN. During his time in Africa, El-Shabazz built a Pan-Africanist, Islamic brotherhood. These bonds threatened Western imperialism, and the US government surveillance of him became intense. The tyrannical Muslim man and the criminal Black man were incendiary figures to annihilate.

On February 21, 1965, El-Shabazz was assassinated by men in the Nation of Islam. Despite evidence of the FBI's and NYPD's surveillance and infiltration into Malcolm X's inner circle, the FBI maintains the patramyth that he was killed by fellow Black Muslims. In the photographs of his lifeless body in the Audubon Ballroom, the Japanese American activist Yuri Kochiyama cradled his head in her arms. Nearly forty years later, I met Kochiyama in her studio at a senior home in Oakland. We sat in her room, where books and papers covered every corner. When I hugged her, her body felt both frail and strong at the same time, but as we spoke, I felt how the fire of revolution still moved her to the core, unnerved by how the two of us, Asian American women, traced the genesis of our political awakenings to the same man.

o

I visited the Casbah ... in Algiers, with some of the brothers — blood brothers. They took me all down into it and showed me the suffering, showed me the conditions they had to live under while they were being occupied by the French .... And they also showed me what they had to do to get these people off their back. The first thing they had to realize was that all of them were brothers; oppression made them brothers; exploitation made them brothers; degradation made them brothers; discrimination made them brothers; segregation made them brothers; humiliation made them brothers ....

— Malcolm X, in a speech
at the Militant Labor Forum, May 1964

In 1956, on an evening in Béjaïa, a port city on the Mediterranean Sea, Mustapha was on his way home after picking up some grapes from the market. Caught on the street just past the 7 p.m. curfew, he was arrested by French officers, who accused him of being in the Algerian National Liberation Front (FLN). He was an electrician, and owned a business with his brother. They wired homes in the region with electricity, and owned a fleet of trucks. All things the French considered dangerous, a gateway to handling weapons or making bombs. The echoes of his screams in the alley as they dragged him away live on in his eldest son, my father-in-law, and these stories live on in his namesake. They never found Mustapha's body.

His namesake is my partner, Mojo, a portmanteau of his grandfathers' names, Mustapha Joseph. Postcolonial inheritances sealed our bond when we met. As the son of an Algerian man who met and fell in love with an Irish American woman, Mustapha is a descendant of two legacies of struggle, Algerian and

Irish liberation. He is Berber Kabyle and Irish, I am Bangla. Berber, *barbar,* the sound of language the Greeks and Romans found unintelligible, just as the people of the eastern subcontinent were *mleccha,* ritually impure to Brahmins. We, the barbarians. Not that you can tell such things by how we look. If we held our tongues, kept silent in conversations about Israeli occupation rather than make it known we believe in a Free Palestine, sure, we could pass as non-Muslims, him as a white man, me as his Indian Hindu wife. But such a thing is unthinkable. Our people didn't die for us to be colonized, ashamed of who we are, who we come from.

We watched *The Battle of Algiers,* a film we've both seen before, but for the first time together. Now, I belong to an Algerian family. *The Battle of Algiers* explodes the French patramyth that the Orient had *come for their necks,* and thus was theirs to rule. Europe's world wars could not have happened without their armed forces from South Asia and Africa — forced to bear arms is more accurate — to fight for their respective European colonizers. Fighting for nations that did not recognize them as true citizens left a bitter taste. When the Viet Minh defeated the French in 1954, another world became possible. Vietnam's victory inspired the Algerian Liberation Front toward an insurrection.

For far too long, the French had denuded and occupied the best land for themselves, turned those gorgeous Mediterranean beaches into a North African getaway, a place to sunbathe and drink wine from Algerian grapes and snack on Algerian olives. They displaced Muslims who did not drink wine to grow vast vineyards, wine they shipped across the Mediterranean and rebranded as their own. They turned the people into misfits on their own soil. When Frantz Fanon lived as a psychiatrist in Algeria, he witnessed the grim effects of colonization on the people of Algeria, he wrote about how even breathing became *an occupied breathing. It is a combat breathing.*

o

> We must watch the parallel progress of this man and this
> woman, of this couple that brings death to the enemy, life
> to the Revolution. . . . The one radically transformed into
> a European woman, poised and unconstrained, whom no
> one would suspect, completely at home in the environ-
> ment, and the other, a stranger, tense, moving toward his
> destiny.
>
> — Frantz Fanon, *A Dying Colonialism*

Brotherhood became the face of Revolution the world over. Yet, the most riveting sequence in *The Battle of Algiers* shows the struggle through the eyes of Algerian women. Each of them undergoes a makeover, and they turn themselves into French women: hair dyed blond, clad in Chanel, in preparation for their grave task. They flash demure, unassuming smiles at of-ficers, who let them pass, they plant makeshift bombs in clubs and cafés, places where the *pieds-noirs,* Algerian-born French people, leisured. By turning into French women, the revolutionaries escape the colonizer's suspicious gaze. When the bombs detonate, this violence in the name of liberation exposes the fragility of French occupation on a land that was never theirs to claim.

Imagine, a postcolonial film released in 1966, a mere four years after independence, that cast revolutionaries as actors. They offered testimony with their own bodies — evidence of the white violence collectively survived by colonized and enslaved peoples the world over. *The Battle of Algiers* immortalized the freedom Algerians won with fresh blood, becoming a blueprint for all peoples overthrowing imperialists. The Black Panthers screened the film to initiate new members into their vision. As a revived pan-African consciousness grew, Algeria became a haven for exiled Black Panthers, providing refuge for revolutionaries absconding the country of their birth. My father-in-law remembers them around town, at parties, in the Casbah, wearing their black leather jackets and their berets, reminiscent of the French military, but on them, they symbolized the oppressed taking back their power.

Today, waves of migrating laborers from Algeria, West Africa, and Syria have crossed the Mediterranean Sea on precarious makeshift boats. Drowning in those waters before they reach their destination is the true migrant crisis — not their arrival as refugees in Europe. They bear the inheritance of enslavement

and war. What does Europe expect now? That they could forever dissociate from the white terror unleashed in the colonies?
As if the past would bear no influence on the future, as if the
reckoning would not someday arrive.

Once my father-in-law, Loucif, smelled a perfume I made,
Night Blossom, a bouquet of North African flowers, Egyptian
jasmine, and Tunisian neroli, blooming open on a bed of sandalwood. It reminded him of an attar his mother once wore.
This simple joy of smelling took him to a place back home, to
his youth.

Seven years later, on the night Mustapha and I celebrate
our love ceremony, the cool green of that Hawaiian night air
swirled with the scent of lit joints, the sweet-sour booze breath
on everyone's lips. Our friend and DJ, the artist Azikiwe Mo-
hammed, turned up a Bollywood tune. Our fathers, two Muslim men, a Bengali and a Berber, both had lived through wars,
deaths of a parent and brother. They moved from the edges
of the tent to the center, they stomped their feet and pumped
their fists, in that moment, everything lost in the past and the
fears of the future disappeared, we were all here, we were happy,
and for the first time in my life, I saw my father dance.

Beloved — Perfume Interlude

HEART

Blue Chamomile

Rose Petals

Saltwater Accord

BASE

Blood Cedar

Auranone

When I started making candles on my stove top, it never occurred to me to start a business. But selling at a local market, I made five hundred dollars in one weekend — a bit more than a week's worth of the unemployment I'd been collecting after losing my job. I received a random message on Instagram from a photographer named Kali about photographing some of my perfumes and candles. We met up for the first time in her apartment in Brooklyn, where she photographed altars of candles for a few hours. Seeing my work this way affirmed that I was embarking on a new path toward economic independence. Never to be a subordinate to a man, or a white person, ever again.

At the end of the evening, we smoked slim menthol cigarettes, the mint crush so familiar to me from high school, even though I never smoke them now. Truth is, I've met the people I love most over a cigarette, sealing a friendship with the accord of smoke. Kali and I sat on a sofa, puffing and chatting. I admired the fabric, an elegant taupe brocade, smoke-tinged and decades old, but its grandeur undeniable.

Where'd you get this incredible sofa?

It belonged to my Grand.

She's got great taste.

She's a writer in the Hudson Valley.

That's where I grew up, there's only one — oh my god.

She smiled, I died. *Toni Morrison.* We smoked more skinny cigs on that gorgeous couch, and then I left Kali different fragrances as a trade for the photographs. One of them, Nāmaka, named after the Hawaiian goddess of the ocean, is a composition of salted wind, grapefruit skin, waxy gardenia petals, sampaguita jasmine, coconut milk — *Paradise* — a sweet fragrance that dries into musk, like a day spent on the beach. Later, Kali told me that her grandmother inhaled that perfume and needed her own bottle. I sent this offering to the ocean goddess to the Greatest.

A few months before her passing, I created a Beloved perfume, to evoke the vast sensorium of Blackness that Morrison embedded into her characters, their landscapes and bodies, their scent memories, their sensuality and homes, their *vasanas* of life, before and after liberation. Beloved is rife with olfactory memory, the traces of the past that linger, akin to the haunting of Sethe by her baby daughter, whom she killed to save her from enslavement. Inspired by Morrison's notes, the composition opens with a meadow accord, of African blue grass and American sweetgrass, a duet of lost motherland and homeland, *chamomile sap,* a thick oil the color of sapphires, like the sticky flowers growing on fields, the *shameless beauty of the farms* of Sweet Home plantation. Blood cedar and rose — which mark the arrival of the carnival, *the closer the roses got to death, the louder their scent* — give the perfume a dark, wound-red color.

Saltwater and musk, for Sethe's sweat and her tears, as the perfume dries down, I want the wearer to feel the heart of how I read Morrison's work as a Bangladeshi Muslim femme, that the emergence of beauty is an act of survival, necessary for a people to heal shattering sorrow, as they honored the pain and joy of their ancestors perished by genocide. Perfume, a metaphor for a flooding of memory, as Morrison wrote: *All water has a perfect memory and is forever trying to get back to where it was, where we were, what valley we ran through, what the banks were like, the light that was there and the route back to our original place.*

II

HEART NOTES

Lovers Rock

Mother Tongue

Mati

Other Tongue

Mala

Mala

Ngozi

How You Love

Lovers Rock — Perfume Interlude

HEAD

Sri Lankan Black Pepper

Peruvian Rosewood

HEART

Sri Lankan Clove

Sri Lankan Cinnamon Leaf

BASE

Atlas Cedar

Brazilian Tonka Bean

French Tobacco Absolute

Himalayan Fossilized Amber

Somali Frankincense

Indonesian Sandalwood

Madagascar Vanilla

Cosmic, we'd say afterward, about the night we met. We were in front of a now-shuttered nightclub in the Lower East Side. I'd been on another date with a Vietnamese copywriter who dreamt of being a rock star. He had a decent voice, his face pink from whiskey and the attention from a small crowd of Asian women that formed around him. *I guess I'm with the band,* I said, sarcastically, trying to plan my escape — when I noticed a handsome man watching me awkwardly hanging around my date. I read him as Arab. When I made eye contact with him, he shyly averted his gaze. I walked up to him and asked, *Were you staring at me? Yes,* he told me — and after a few minutes of small talk — he told me he played keyboard in an Afrobeat band that I'd seen play in college, I told him I'd just moved to the city and wanted to be a performance artist. He was ten years older than me, Japanese and Jewish, not Arab, and at thirty-two, he was the oldest person I'd ever considered fucking. I broke free from my date. Made up an excuse that I'd just run into an old friend. The words did not feel completely untrue.

He bummed me a cigarette and we left to get a drink at another bar. *You're lovely,* he said. Soon, we started making out. He still lived with his ex, and I had just moved into my new apartment in Bed Stuy. Nothing but a futon mattress on the floor — not even a bedsheet — so we grabbed a sheet and a candle from his place and then went to mine and fucked on the floor. The August night buzzed with that humid, indolent New York City heat made for nights like that. I remember him inhaling my scent, marveling at the naturalness of my odor. *You smell earthy, just like . . . body.* As natural as coming together felt, he had trouble falling asleep next to me — a sign we were doomed, perhaps, but at that age, you ignore signs that say you can't have what you want.

That night marked the beginning of a longing I had never felt for another person before. Longing that I'd never fulfill. We found ourselves in a lovers' arrangement common in cities, when you see each other after midnight, once a week or so, sometimes dinner if he felt up for a date. I wanted more, but he had just gotten free of a long relationship, and I'd never been in one. We dated other people. I gravitated to people who reminded me of him, quiet, reserved, people who moved with diligence and discipline in their art. Masculine, but soft. When I couldn't bear our arrangement, I cut myself off. But I wanted to smell him. I traced his scent back to the source, the Brooklyn Bangladeshi-owned oil shop Madina on Atlantic Avenue, an institution. Named for one of the two holy cities in Islam, the word *al-Madina* simply means the city, and the shop's visitors include Black and Muslim entrepreneurs, fragrance aficionados, folks who want to smell good for cheap, imams who sell the oils to the prison commissary, making perfumes available to inmates. I would purchase five-dollar roll-on bottles of oil to smell him in those periods we were off-again.

Lovers Rock, my rendition of V, now one of my best friends, failed to capture the essence of that Madina oil. Nevertheless, the perfume became a signature scent for many, who return again and again to replenish this bottle of intoxicants. I wanted to make something addictive, eschewing ideas of masculine and feminine. I wanted to rouse the way I once craved the spiced incense of his body, the frankincense and myrrh oil hustled on sidewalks from Harlem to Bed Stuy. The perfume evokes sex — a heart of Sri Lankan spices, an after-hours dry-down, the sweet smell of sex juice, as you lay next to a person you want to devour, edible gourmand notes of vanilla, an oil that is deep, dark, viscous, and black, with none of the associations with white childhood innocence, for the laborers who hand-pollinate the world's vanilla are youths in Madagascar. Amber woods hold the narcotic note of tobacco flower like a cigarette pulled fresh out of the pack. Ironically, all of the notes are restricted or banned by European fragrance regulations; the tobacco, clove, black pepper, tonka bean are all allergens. Lovers Rock is a composition that tells the story of conquest. Its notes are remnants of the past, forgotten jars in the pantry, a reminder of how the spice and slave trade stole the lives and labor of Black and brown people across the Atlantic and Indian Oceans.

Mother Tongue

Perfume as Mother Language

NOTES

Jasmine

Speak the language of beauty, scent, erotics, and love—
dangerous things to erect because they're an affront to
empire and exploitation.

— Jenny Zhang, voice note, 2020

Bangla: language I speak now to your grieving daughter,
this language the bodies of women were once broken
open for.

— Tarfia Faizullah, *Seam*

FORKED TONGUES

Serpents smell with their tongues, I learned, when I touched
one for the first time. I was five. The school principal, the
largest red-necked white man I'd ever laid eyes on, jaunted into
our kindergarten class at Robert E. Lee Elementary School. He
wore aviator glasses and a boa constrictor draped around his
shoulders, as if he were a drag queen. He grinned, delighted by
our fear. *Who's gonna touch her?* I held my best friend's hand,
gingerly, as we stepped toward the giant snake to stroke the
brown saddles of its throbbing, curved body, careful to avoid its
tongue, the part that seemed the wildest.

We were brown-skinned, we wore our hair in braids, hers

coconut-oiled and neat, mine baby-shampooed and messy. We spoke little — we still felt quiet in English. Somehow, we knew we were neither Black nor white like the other kids in our class, but since we couldn't communicate with each other in our different South Asian languages, somehow, we realized we weren't the same, either. Her name rhymed with my sister's nickname — this is how I remembered her when I departed from the world of school and she disappeared from my mind. Though I didn't speak it aloud much, Ma had already taught me to read in English, I was among the few who could read simple books. So I imagined spelling my Indian best friend's name *Brommy,* but it must've been that her name was *Brahmi,* like the Ayurvedic water hyssop that strengthens memory. Maybe she was named after the ancient script of India, or the feminine energy of Brahma, the great divine Hindu masculine. I can't be sure.

We never had playdates like American-Americans, so we never had a chance to yell each other's names. When I finally went to Brahmi's house and met her parents, my parents were hitting up their yard sale. We'd left Alabama in that rusty hatchback to move to Columbia, Missouri, another university town, and were still collecting furniture. My parents were there to buy her parents' bed. A couple hundred bucks for them meant an upgrade for us. On the drive back home, it dawned on me that we'd said our last goodbye. Like most of the broke immigrant transients, students, and postdocs in Columbia, Missouri, her family was moving onto the next university town, the next dream. I remember feeling depressed.

You did what? Ma recoiled when I told her about the boa, given her lifelong fear of snakes. Touching the snake was the first of many times that something that I'd done would shock her. My first-grade teacher, Miss Patty, believed I didn't speak English or had a learning disability. She hadn't bothered to find out that I'd been reading for a couple of years. She agitated me, insisted on calling me Toni, dusted crumbs from those orange peanut butter crackers she ate all day onto our desks. Her commentary and concerns on my report card made Baj livid, so he arranged with her to do a presentation about Bangladeshi culture for my class, essentially explaining our existence. He shared everyday artifacts: a *tabla,* a plaid fabric *ghamsa,* photos of boats strolling the river. We were from a faraway country, but instead of feeling inexplicable or invisible, or even embarrassed, I felt proud that Baj captivated my classmates. Maybe his care persuaded Miss Patty of my worth, because she began to treat me with more respect. For the psychological warfare of American public school in Missouri, my prize: a damned red, white, and blue ribbon embroidered with an image of the Confederate general Robert E. Lee. I was Patriot of the Month.

Language, like memory, between a mother and her foreign-born child, is a forked tongue, a constant state of translation, uncertainty, a flicking between each other's strange words and experiences, like a snake sensing its way in the dark. Before language, we inhale each other, as mother and newborn, as old as our reptilian selves, as our bacterial ancestors navigating their chemical environments with a primitive sense of smell. A couple of years later, my left eye started to wander, my young vision deteriorated — I believe this is when my scent sense grew keen.

I like to move in the darkness. I still prefer to spend the early hours of the morning — when I've stayed up late enough to meet the sun, or when I first awake after a good night's sleep — seeing the world as a blur, with my true sightlessness. More often than not, I tend toward insomnia, waiting for the world to quiet so that I can write when the veil between this life and the underworld of consciousness thins. My full sight — the one that my body knows — is a haze of amorphous shapes. Orbs of light. Contact lenses offer a "correction," making my disability invisible, but I love that I cannot see. I need my disability to access that deep brain, the words I can't find with sight. I love being fucked when I can't see my lover, but I can taste, touch, and smell them in the blue glow of dawn. I need to know that I can navigate the world without my sight one day. In case there's a war, an attack, glaucoma, macular degeneration — any future where I need to accept that I cannot see.

In July 2005, I participated in a prisoner-of-war simulation with the artist Coco Fusco and a group of women artists for her film *Operation Atropos*. I experienced what a day without being able to see as a prisoner of war would look like, and I made it through but not without freaking out. This is what it means to grow up knowing that your people survived a war, I suppose, you foretell futures where your body may be stolen from you. Without being able to see clearly, I'll feel my way through a drawer for clothing I want to wear, guided by color and touch; I map the layout of a table, a bookshelf, finding a book by the color of its spine, reading it two inches from my face. When I make a perfume, I make sure to smell it on my skin, eyes closed.

Sometimes I write with my eyes closed, like lying awake in the darkness, each thought already written in my body, deep in the ocean of mind, at the confluence of memory and fantasy. I learned to type without looking when I wrote orders of protection as an intake counselor for the Family Court in Poughkeepsie, New York. Tasked with typing up the details of an assault, my fingers wrote the survivor's words, no soon as they uttered them, my eyes never left their face. Even when they couldn't look at me, I wanted them to know that I was listening. Most of my clients were women experiencing dire abuse by their husbands, who would show up once in a while, in a macabre turn, to retaliate against her word. I had only been fooled by one man. He wept for his wife who'd cheated on him. With his large brown eyes and matching leather jacket and seven-year-old son beside him — he moved me so much that I told him everything would be okay. No soon as I filed his order of protection, a couple of days later, a woman with the same distinctive last name arrived, head wrapped in a scarf. *Look what he did to me,* she whispered, removing the scarf, revealing large bald patches and thinned brown hair. He'd mixed in Nair hair remover, to make her ugly, make her pay for cuckolding him, which she only did to escape the beatings, the constant berating. He'd rather poison her than be seen as a fool. It scared me how easily I believed him.

I was a formula baby, I never latched on to my mother's breast, forming an immediate separation between her body smell and my own. Did powdered water drink make Ma incomprehensible to me, did it affect my ability to sense her, to sense danger, at least as a child? Even now, when I hug her, her body smell indistinguishable from mine, my sister tells us neither of us has a malodor, and when Ma showers off the cooking, she still smells like soap and air to me.

I got into trouble early as a baby for snaking across their apartment floor in Carbondale, Illinois. After sleeping most of the day, I came alive late at night until dawn, the same hours I keep now to write. They'd often host other Bangladeshi students, all of them playing Scrabble, my dad and his fellow PhDs, men trying to make complicated words, while Ma, who expanded her English by way of MTV and board games, often won with big-value short words: *love, money, zoo, yes.* The men smoked cigarettes and drank. They sipped late-night cups of *cha,* moving on to a long round of Trivial Pursuit, oblivious to me, baby scumbag gnawing on their butts, beer, and tea bags.

My grandmother lived with us off and on throughout my childhood, from about age three to seventeen. We lived in a modest two-bedroom apartment, and, to my embarrassment at the time, I shared a room with my little sister and grandmother. Three twin beds in a row, the same spatial arrangement of an orphanage or hospital at wartime. I barricaded myself with a pillow, creating a psychic wall between my family and me. My grandmother's fears of sin, and suffering, were born of every parent's worst fear: the death of her twenty-four-year-old son, my Uncle Masud, who died in his sleep. No autopsy, and so, the mystery around his death remained unsolved. Her tragic loss haunted Nanu in every waking moment, and even at night. For years, she couldn't eat his favorite foods, lychee, mango, and *pi-yaju,* the lentil fritters we loved to eat during Ramadan. Nanu seemed to be in permanent mourning at night; her constant remembering of how she'd only had him for twenty-four years ruined each and every night's sleep.

I have no memory of my first trip to Bangladesh, after Ma's father died in 1984. I know only photographs of me as a toddler, several shades lighter than I am now, before I found my true caramel tone closer to Baj's skin. There are photographs of me eating rice and *daal* balled into little spheres, screaming while being bathed in a tube well, cradled by different relatives, each of them, I imagine, spoke to me in Bengali, so that little by little, by the end of that trip, I learned our mother tongue.

Writing is the form of art that can ruin, even as it protects us by moving us toward consciousness and truth. It never escapes me, knowing that my people — artists and writers — were killed because they lived a life of thought. Throughout Indian history, the thoughts of Muslim women have been ignored, overlooked, regarded with a sense of being ahead of this time, or out of place. This is the conundrum of being invisible, and very much seen. I italicize non-English words because they look

more beautiful that way. Since we can't honor the beauty of
their own script and still be legible to most readers of English,
I want to give the words their own space. Some think of italics
as othering, but I *am* Other when I speak my mother language.
Words in Bangla or Arabic or Urdu have their own weight separate from English. America took my first language, mother language, gave me my life language. I don't recall the feeling of my
first language fading as I learned the language I write, love, and
fight in best.

What little I knew about my mother's childhood in Bangladesh
had a mythic feel: a snake had fallen from the ceiling onto her
head as she slept in her crib; she survived smallpox as a young
girl healed by a village *kabiraj,* the medicine man; during the
war, a Pakistani soldier snatched a magazine out of her hands
to see what she might be reading on the train — it pleased him
that a Pakistani actress was on the cover, so he left her alone.
Riding death's edge, in each instance, she survived, through a
lockdown living in a stick house overlooking a giant pond, enamored by a visitor, her brother's best friend, the tall whistling
scientist who'd become her husband.

My tongue is thick in Bangla, the words rough like shards of
sweet jaggery my grandmother mixed into boiled milk and rice.
Dudh-bhat, or milk-rice, offered by a milkmaid named Sujata,
revived the Buddha after he spent six years as an ascetic, emaci-
ated, living on the extreme frontiers of renunciation. Her gift
is believed to be *kheer,* a sweet rice pudding, cooked for hours
over a stovetop. But I imagine upon seeing a shriveled tree

god in need of some nourishment, she whipped up something quicker than *kheer,* easy to digest, a gift for the Buddha, letting him taste the bounty of her cows.

Ma craved the sweet-tart guavas of Bangladesh when she was pregnant with me, but there were no guavas in 1980s middle America, so she had to make do with applesauce. Three years later, pregnant with my sister, she worked part-time at a Houston movie theater, still learning English, as Baj finished up his postdoc at Rice University; the stress of keeping us afloat had him laid out, flattened on the floor in back pain. Ma developed a new craving, the baked terra-cotta tiles sold on the street of her village as a snack for pregnant women. The scent of *mati,* of rain-wetted clay heated by fire, tasted like earth chocolate.

One afternoon, so desperate for *mati* on her tongue, she ate a morsel of dirt from the landscaping outside of our apartment building. She spat it out. *How stupid,* she realized, trying to turn Texas Miracle-Gro into home.

Sanskrit means *artificial, refined* language, whereas the vernacular of everyday people was Prakrit, or *natural* language. The word *prakriti* means the feminine aspect, anything pertaining to women. Buddha delivered his teachings in a Prakrit language, Magadhi — to make it accessible to the people. By the thirteenth century, North Indian Prakrit evolved into Apabramśa, a transition between older tongues and the ones spoken today, and the word *Apabramśa* translates to *corrupt* in Sanskrit, indicating what the Brahmin Indo-Aryan male language speakers thought of folks in the east, where language flourished beyond its pale.

Bangla absorbed words from all the peoples who've lived and settled in the eastern reaches of the subcontinent, so Pali, Dravidian, Sanskrit, Persian, Arabic, and Turkish influenced its evolution. The Bengali words for pen and paper, *kalam* and *kagaj,* are Perso-Arabic, a reflection of a belief in Islam that the written word wielded divine power. Literacy increased among the rural people of East Bengal with the rise of Islam, as the erudite Vedic Brahmins had never formed enough of a stronghold to spread scripture among lower-caste, pre-literate, snake-goddess-worshipping farmers and fishermen. Some scholars have asserted Sanskrit as the Indo-Aryan ancestor of Prakrit languages that developed into the modern ones we speak now. Are we supposed to believe that men's artificial, refined language birthed the Indigenous peoples' tongues?

Baj left us to work in St. Louis. In the evenings, my sister and I snuggled on the couch with Ma after she finished her schoolwork, and sometimes, if I was lucky, she let me stay up to watch David Lynch's new show, *Twin Peaks.* I was too young, for sure, but she was too scared to watch alone. The mood of the show unnerved and comforted me, from the first three notes of the theme, a haunting overlay of synth and electric guitar, tides of ambient synthesizer, evergreens and wood mill machines. I'd never seen textures like that before on television, the eerie yearbook image of the girl murdered and found blue, washed ashore; Agent Cooper's cherry pie, Joan Chen's cherry lips, Audrey Horne's teenaged lust. *Who killed Laura Palmer?* I didn't realize then that the death of a young white woman, a single white woman, could captivate the attention of an entire country, more than the death of thousands, or millions, of Black, Indigenous, or brown ones.

Everyone in the town of Twin Peaks wore plaid, buffalo check, like the plaid *lungi* Baj changed into after work. Checks and plaids, *ghamsa,* like the word *gham,* sweat, were the textiles of everyday people in Bangladesh. I missed my dad's swapping out his work-drag for a cotton sarong in the comfort of his own home.

I miss Baj, I cried, weeping myself to sleep hours later, feeling the ache of my father's absence. One night, Ma began to phonetically spell different words in Bengali. I repeated each spelling after her, learning to string together the words I'd known first in life.

মা, বা, বাড়ি, বাংলা — Ma, Baj, House, Bangla — the first words I learned to spell and write in our language. Spelling and sounding out these words felt more intuitive than the Latin alphabet I knew to read and wrote little books and poems in — a revelation. Bangla is an abugida script — consonants are the primary letters. Vowels are indicated by diacritics (lines, dots, loops), and the line across the top of the word to connect the letters is called *matra,* the word for mother as in *matra bhasha,* mother tongue. *Matra* can mean mother, but also air and space, just like the vowels in a word.

As I learned the Bengali script, my Nanu tried to teach me Arabic, the language of our religion, but I found Arabic impossible, disconnected to real life. I found her transmission of Islam through stories much more fascinating. Sometimes they had a distinctly Bengali and Hindu feel to them. This had been the authors' syncretic intention, a way of binding Islam to a Hindu universe. My favorite of those stories involved the Prophet Muhammad being chased by Quraysh warriors through a forest — never mind that he lived in the deserts of Arabia — until a banyan tree opened up for him to hide inside. In another story, as the Prophet tried to escape from danger, he hid inside a cave, and a spider spun a web to seal its mouth.

This is why you should never kill a spider, Nanu would tell me.

I was more into the aesthetic of prayer. I wore a nightgown like a makeshift hijab; I rolled out a plush prayer rug, I whispered and bowed my head to the ground. When Ma prayed, I copied her prostrations. And when she wore makeup, I stood beside her, waiting for her to swipe cherry on my lips.

My handwriting in Bangla is childlike, block-lettered. I think about the origin of our letters, traced back to the unadorned glyphs, lines, loops, and circles of ancient Brahmi, the root script of nearly all writing systems in South and Southeast Asia, from Bangla to Tamil to Thai, which spread across the subcontinent around 300 BCE. Brahmi has been found as inscriptions on rock edicts, on punched coins and potteries. Both South Asian and Western scholars have debated Brahmi's origins, whether or not Brahmi is *indigenous* or *derived* from a Semitic script outside of South Asia. Western scholars prefer the latter explanation, anything to center themselves, rather than believe that the Indigenous Dravidian peoples of South Asia are the ones who created and spread the usage of Brahmi. Is naming the script Brahmi, the feminine form of Brahma, the divine Hindu masculine, a tacit acknowledgment that the way we come to know the language of our people, the language inside of us, how we learn to write and to speak our tongues, comes from our mothers?

Ma was born in 1957, ten years after the Partition of India — as a citizen of East Pakistan. Islam was our sole connection to West Pakistan, home of the central government. When it was proposed that Bangla be changed to an Arabic script like Urdu, violence erupted on February 21, 1952, inciting the Bhasha Andolan, the Language Movement. Students protested. They wore cotton saris, braided their hair with jasmine, sung songs by Rabindranath Tagore, love songs and devotional Hindu songs, asserting Bengali as their language, not Urdu. Nation — in this case, East Pakistan — could never be extricated from the poetry of the people. Students were murdered.

Our millennium-old language could never be colonized, Ma reiterated, and we had absolutely nothing else in common, not in looks or music or food or temperament, and, most importantly, not language, with Pakistanis. Over the years, on trips to Bangladesh, she purchased saris block-printed with the Bengali alphabet. I never wore them, they felt gauche, too on the nose — but whenever I have this thought, I feel guilty for betraying the students who spilled fresh blood for each of us who bears their memory, who refuse to let our language be erased.

We still say the Urdu word آب و هـوا — *ab-o-hawa*, water and wind — for weather. We'd never deny a beautiful phrase.

We say *pani,* as Bangladeshi Muslims, the word for water used throughout North India and Pakistan. West Bengali Indians use *jol* or *pani,* interchanging the words depending on whom they're speaking to. Bangladeshi Hindus will say *jol,* distinguishing themselves from the Muslim majority. Both words can be traced back to Sanskrit, *paniyam* the word for drinkable; *jala* the word for water. Language, down to a single word or phrase, might reveal whether we were Muslim or Hindu, starting with all our separate words for water, bathing, hello, goodbye.

SCIENCE FICTIONS

> For some time now, our masters have considered us akin to valuable ornaments. Our beloved jewelry, these are nothing but the badges of slavery.
>
> — Begum Rokeya Sakhawat Hossain, "Amader Abanati," "Our Downfall," 1904

As a geography student in Eden College, Ma lived in an all-women's dorm called Rokeya Hall, named after the writer Begum Rokeya Sakhawat Hossain, a Bengali Muslim writer from the early part of the twentieth century who started a Muslim women's school in Kolkata, India. She believed that women should wait until age twenty to marry. She wanted Muslim women to be as educated as their Hindu and Christian counterparts. She believed that living in *zenanas,* the inner sanctum of a home, secluded from society, not allowed to see anyone except family members, kept these women from their intellect and hurt Muslims as a community. She rejected men's interpretations of Islam, calling for education, jobs, and literacy among the women in her community.

"Sultana's Dream," her feminist utopian science fiction short story, is written in English, the fifth language she knew, after Bengali, Arabic, Farsi, and Urdu. She was born in Rangpur, East Bengal, in 1880, to a family of landowners, *zamindars.* Her father forbade education, but her sister, a poet named Karimunnesa Khanam, taught her Bengali. As a young girl, Rokeya grew up observing strict *purdah,* the word for curtain, veil, cover — and the practice of *purdah* forbade women from being seen by any men outside of the family. Muslim women wore burqa in public spaces, and mostly stayed inside their homes. Only her husband — no other man — could gaze at her body, her bare face.

Rokeya wrote "Sultana's Dream" in 1905, the year of the first Partition of Bengal, the first splitting of the Muslim-majority East from the Hindu-majority West.

The story opens, *One evening I was lounging in an easy chair in my bedroom and thinking lazily of the condition of Indian womanhood. I am not sure whether I dozed off or not.* So begins "Sultana's Dream." A Bengali woman named Sultana dreams that she's transported to Ladyland, a futurist utopia where women rule. The Queen — less royalty and more of a prime ministerial figurehead — deems that all women should be educated. The state religion is Truth and Love. The surviving population of men surrender their power and are sequestered away in *zenanas,* the inner quarters of the home, the same way women in India lived at the time.

In Rokeya's story, the women of Ladyland are free to be scientists, gardeners, free of veiling, and free to use their minds. They were no longer ghosts. Her work — revolutionary and ahead of its time — smashed the patramyth that women should believe in the innate superiority of men.

VEILS

After living in quarantine, I can a bit better imagine how it must have felt, spending your best years — rather, your whole life — sequestered away in a *zenana.* Did the separation and disappearance of women from the public and the practice of *purdah* begin with Muslim conquest? Too simplistic, since Hindu women were restricted from participating in men's rites and rituals before the *zenana,* and under the British, who categorized, divided, and criminalized women as prostitutes.

Who the hell wouldn't want to stay inside?

The pre-Islamic practice of veiling, *purdah,* and *hetaera* courtesan culture were adopted by Indic and Islamic cultures from the Greeks. Though Muslims and Hindus practiced *purdah,* they were not alike in their strictness. Whereas a Muslim woman wore burqa with any and all men who were not kin, a Hindu woman returning to her ancestral village might not necessarily cover her head with the end of her sari — and never in a burqa — reserving this modesty for instances where she interacted with elders in her husband's family. *Purdah* is how generations of South Asian women lived, how my great-grandmother lived, how my grandmother lived later in life, indoors, safe from strange men, burqa-clad when they ventured outside.

Rokeya didn't condemn the practice of *purdah,* but she didn't hide the cost of the practice to women. In *The Secluded Ones,* published in 1929, a few years before she died of a heart attack, she documented *purdah* deaths. Death by house fire, just to avoid a crowd of men throwing water to put out the flames. Death by heatstroke, in a horse-drawn carriage, windows covered in thick fabric. Death by tripping on train tracks, no stranger willing to help her get up — a man's touch dishonored modesty. Rokeya herself wore loose *purdah,* with the end of her sari around her head.

My grandmother wore burqa in public, but as a young woman, she knew freedom and fashion. She was stylish, the wife of a local government official. There are very few photos of her in a sari, showing a bit of skin, gold-bangled, smiling at a camera — things she'd never do after her husband and son died. Generations of women married when they were barely teenaged, to men twice their age. Given away by their families, taken not by force — but given. As if being a married nine-year-old were more respectable than choosing a mate in her own time. Mate is not what the family wanted, anyway; the Bengali word for husband, *swami,* means master.

My grandmother ended her schooling to marry, the only one of her sisters to not pursue university. Yet she was an avid reader in Bengali her whole life, reading translations of American classics like Alex Haley's *Roots.* Had Nanu read "Sultana's Dream"? She was born just after Rokeya died in 1932. She gave the middle name Sultana to her daughter, my Ma, who went to university, flaunted her beauty and body in a sari, hair uncovered, who married Baj, both of them in their twenties, a man she loved and chose for herself.

We ping-ponged around the Midwest and the South: Carbondale, Illinois, where I was born, on to Houston, Texas, where my sister was born, a short stint in Alabama, several years in Missouri, in Columbia and St. Louis. I remember each apartment, its layout, the outdoors, the smallness, sometimes overrun with roaches or termites that thrive in communal complexes, no matter how much Ma tried to keep our home spotless. For a spell, in the late '80s, we lived apart from Baj, when he got a gig as a chemistry adjunct at St. Louis University, crashing on a mattress at his friend's apartment, despite his fragile back. My sister and I lived with Ma as she finished her bachelor's degree in geography at the University of Missouri in Columbia, a continuation of her studies back home in Dhaka. As constantly stressed as they were about money, as tethered as she was caring for me and my sister, she loved how geography connected her to the vast world beyond our apartment. Our housing complex was populated by students or teachers from the university. All the neighborhood kids gathered in the playgrounds between buildings, each one with its own slightly different composition of jungle gyms, monkey bars, swings, and slides. I struck up friendships with other kids who lived in the three different complexes, learning hand games and hopscotch from Black girlfriends, like my perfectly named friend Jackie Berry, who'd learned from her older siblings, games that my parents had never played. Double Dutch, though, I could never seem to time my jump into those intimidating beaded ropes, which often smacked the glasses off my face.

One of my older friends, a girl whose name, Iram, sounded like her country, Iran, let us ride double on her bike after school.

Iram wore her curly brown hair in a messy ponytail, a cloud of bangs. Never saw her in a dress. Ma warned me not to double ride, it was way too dangerous, but it was the closest I'd get to riding a bike — we couldn't afford one. Iram made sure to ride us around the farthest complex from my house, just so my mother wouldn't worry. *Hold on tight,* she'd say, laughing when I dug my nails into her waist, because it tickled. I concentrated so hard on making sure to balance my feet off the ground that I never got to enjoy the rides.

Iram and I played with a trio of siblings whose parents had emigrated from Pakistan. Ghazala, the oldest daughter, was my age. She'd invite me over to their house for dinner. I relished their mother's Pakistani food, the saffron rice pulao with chicken, fragrant and exotic to my taste buds that had only known our Bangla home cooking: *daal,* white rice, mustard oil mashed potatoes, curried chicken and fish — something my people are known to love — but I hated. We had a pet fish and the idea of eating its kin bothered me. Ma never forbade me from hanging out with them, but she didn't want me over there for dinner too often, concerned they might think we were poor Bangladeshis.

As I write, I text my mother a lot, for details to sharpen my child memory. There's so much about her that I don't know. Those friends weren't Ma's first intimate encounter with a Pakistani family. Her first gig back in Illinois had been as a shop girl at a clothing boutique called International Fashion, owned by a Pakistani immigrant couple.

Did your bosses ever acknowledge the war?

No. There was no space for that. We were not especially close, what boss and employee are, really?

If she felt triggered by my closeness with my first Pakistani friends, I never knew. Something as soft as childhood friendships meant our parents all had to confront the violence, the military coups, the bloodshed, the birth of a homeland. Darkness they dare not feel, even when innocence stirred it up. More often than not, they swallowed their past. Worse yet, some families, like Iram's, were struck by tragedy, even after all the danger they'd escaped back home. We learned about what happened in the newspaper. One day, she and her father were riding their bikes through Columbia. As her father crossed the intersection, Iram, who was right behind him, was struck by a car and killed.

Our sense of scent has a limited vocabulary. Across known languages, anthropologists have found fewer words for our olfactory experience than any other sensation. So, we speak of our olfactory experience in similes and metaphors. We reach for language to describe smells in relation to our other senses. *Bright, green, metallic, smoky, floral, fecal, loud, round, sharp,* or *citrus* are words I might use, but these notes can be traced to objects, not the odors themselves. My favorite perfumes are slightly addictive, like the feeling of devouring a book.

Perfume language is purple, its prose comfortable for me, it's as if I revert to sensory language when I forget the performance of writing for a society (a country? a culture?) that loves a bare, spare sentence. I've been a devotee of purple anything since childhood: clothes, lipstick — a sentence. I admit that when I write in perfumed language, I feel truer as a writer, wilder and messier, anachronistic or mystic, I feel more embodied, when I write the physical materials I work with, encapsulating a story inside of a vessel. I perfume with materials distilled from the earth, but also aroma chemicals extracted from fossil fuels. This leaves me with more questions than answers, but perhaps that's how we know there is a future, when we continue seeking answers to eternal questions: What is real, what is false? What is natural, what is artificial? What is necessary, what must be thrown away?

SCENTS & SARIS

Ma, in typical Bangladeshi hustler fashion, held down a motley of part-time gigs: shop girl in a clothing boutique, movie theater concessions, preschool teaching assistant, and grocery bagger. No matter her gig of the moment, Nina Ricci L'Air du Temps stood exalted on her dresser. I'll never forget those iconic frosted glass doves on the perfume bottle, designed by French glass artist Marc Lalique, it seemed to mismatch the surroundings, just like my mother's 24K gold and saris hiding out in their dingy closet. The perfume's bouquet of gardenia, rose centifolia, iris, and jasmine is punctuated by the spiced clove notes of carnation, which dries down into a powdery base of musk, cedar, and sandalwood from Mysore. The online description of this post–World War II perfume tells us, *The war was over, and the world began to breathe, dream, and make plans.* Perfume, in this version of the new world, allowed the wearer to forget the fascism, the Holocaust, no whiff of the revolutionary uprisings stirring in the colonies Europe had thieved.

Drugstore beauty — L'Air du Temps, 99-cent store Jordana kajal, and Revlon red lipstick — afforded Ma the armor of beauty, even without much money to spare, a necessity in a society that judged her on first glance, at the first sound of her accent, at the way she smelled. When my baby teeth fell out and my new ones grew in huge and bucked, Ma cried a little, she told me years later, because of how teeth invite instant class judgment. I'd inherited my grandmother's teeth, and Ma was determined to get me braces. She tried whatever American diet was in vogue. Grapefruit and cottage cheese. Cocoa-flavored SlimFast. As a young bride at five foot two, Ma weighed a smooth eighty pounds. I imagine the pressure of wanting to maintain her lissome *notun bou* look, as a new bride and mother navigating the American beauty hegemony. No matter how our bodies looked, or what clothes we wore, any plain white woman would still walk through a door we'd held open out of a regular old kindness. Half the time she'd never bother to glance at us, or say thank you. She hadn't even seen us. It's still true.

Ma sewed dresses for me and my sister on a Singer sewing machine, adding her own touches to McCall's patterns, pretty cotton florals and ginghams, ruffled taffeta and silk, less expensive than store-bought, made to measure for bodies she'd borne of her own. We wore Bengali clothes for a Saturday *dawat,* weekends were when our double life emerged, when we retired our American selves to hang with our Bengali friends. Sometimes, I felt self-conscious about the difference between our apartment and our friends' sprawling midwestern ranch houses, their parents felt more settled, they'd made a home. I hated the roaches in our St. Louis apartment, the single queen bed I shared with my sister. I wanted my own space. Every *dawat* let us draw power from our Ma's inner sanctum of luxury, textiles and gold, a material culture much richer than any Target or Walmart clothes, "American" clothes — *made in Bangladesh* — that we wore to school.

Saris hold the history of men's power. Floral *jamdani* muslin saris are the modern-day version of Bengal's legendary Dhakai muslin — from Dhaka — called *bafta hawa,* woven air, beloved by the Mughal rulers of India. Weavers loomed this mythic fabric at an 1,800-thread count, so fine it could be tucked inside of a matchbox. It's commonly told that the art of weaving Dhakai died out because the British chopped off weavers' thumbs. Whether or not this is true has been debated and is considered apocrypha — we'll never know for sure if there was indeed a weaver who lost their thumbs. That the British East India Company leveraged disastrous taxes and tariffs on the weavers as the power of their Mughal patrons waned in India is an undeniable truth. As the British exploited Bengal for raw cotton used in their own textile factories, they sold this back to Bengal — slowly killing the art of Dhakai muslin, which became extinct, living in the afterworld of the museum, diaphanous as ghosts.

Today, artisans in Bangladesh are working to revive this lost ancestral technique.

Whereas *jamdani* and *katan* silk exude elegance, they aren't available to everyday people like the *taant* hand-loomed cotton sari, iconic Bengal, which become softer as they're washed and worn. Made from thread of recycled scraps, spun, cut, starched by women, *taant* saris are worn by poor and rich women alike, sturdy enough to last their lifetime. In Bangladesh, the district of Tangail is historically known for producing these saris. Women once folded these saris into strong and thick squares to filter waterborne diseases, like typhoid and cholera, but nowadays, since saris are made from a looser weave, imported American cotton, their *taant* saris can't offer this protection.

Vasanas are imprinted in textiles, traces of perfume and natural body oils and dirt locked in the weave of vintage silk, cotton, polyester. Holding the memories of the wearer. But what about the traces of the laborers embedded in the fabric? From farm to factory, the weavers, the spinners, the pickers of cotton bolls and silkworms, the fabric cutters and dyers, their sweat and blood pricked from a needle, *vasana* of touch. *To be touched is to be made and unmade in relationship to another, another's body, another's desire, another's trace,* according to scholar Poulomi Saha.

Ma's cache of finery held our secret self, our rich self, our dripping in 24K self, our ancient self — our Bangla self. Shadow self: war survivor who made sure her children ate every grain of rice on their plates, collected loose change in a jar, saved everything today because tomorrow was never guaranteed.

Some weeknights, when Ma worked concessions at the movie theater, she'd come home exhausted, but treat us to leftover popcorn or nachos, junk food we'd never dream of, unless it was free. My sister and I rubbed her swollen feet, scented like buttery popcorn and faded jasmine.

JASMINE

Jasmine summons our foremothers. Across the South Asian and Muslim diaspora, the most popular fragrances are showy and sexy, loaded with jasmine, rose, sandalwood, saffron, and oud, defying notions of modesty or respectability. What makes it unforgettable is what makes it dirty. Indole gives jasmine its intoxicating narcotic note, an aura of shit. Animalic not only in scent, but at sight, jasmine absolute is thick and viscous as menstrual blood. Absolutes are another incarnation of the flower, extracted by a solvent. When I work with this material in dilution, the dark red garnet hue turns the color of sunset, sheering the white floral notes to smell more like the living thing. I use jasmine absolute in one of the first perfumes I created, Night Blossom, a full bloom of white florals — jasmine, orange blossom, champak — voluptuous and rife with sultry associations.

I remember the first few times I encountered jasmine, it felt like it found me. My body rejected midwestern pollen and ragweed, I fell sick, often, riddled with bronchitis or pneumonia. We left one summer, for our first trip to New York, to visit Ma's oldest brother, and our grandmother who stayed with him that year. I arrived sick. I couldn't stop throwing up the bitter medicines, so Nanu dipped a pair of cotton balls in her jasmine attar — jasmine flowers steeped in sandalwood oil — and tucked them into my ears. I lay with my head on her lap, until the scent of the attar lulled me to sleep. In each breath, I experienced illness, relief, love, family, and history — that trip to New York, there in Nanu's lap, a serene new sense of home.

I strung jasmine into my braids for a dance performance choreographed by an auntie, me with three of my best Bengali friends, Paula, Fahmina, Tantralita. Afterward, I wanted to preserve the flowers as a perfume, so I soaked them in a bowl of water overnight. By the next morning, they'd browned rotten.

Snakes are drawn to narcotic flowers, *raat ki rani,* queen of the night, among their favorite places to hunt for food, flicking their tongues, sometimes spreading the tips wider than their heads, sensing the chemicals in their environment in three dimensions, navigating direction, pheromones, and prey, all at once. Speaking with a forked tongue is an American idiom, meaning to speak disingenuously, to doublespeak, to say one thing but mean another. By the 1700s the white settler patramyth attributed the phrase as derived from their enemies, Native American tribes they stole land from — this is still popularly claimed as the idiom's genesis on the Internet.

How can this be, if serpents are revered as sacred across tribes?

This misattribution tells us more about the settlers who reviled the serpent as the Devil lurking about in Eden, tempting Eve.

It tells us more about who has the tendency to lie.

Perhaps our memory, too, is a forked tongue, our version of what has happened versus whatever did happen. I read and loved books between the sentences, imagining myself in those characters because no book ever imagined me as the reader, as the descendant of its history.

REBELS

In this society where injustice and a law of the jungle prevail, rise like the tormented serpents in the image of the Destroyer. Respond to the call of your sister, by roaring like thunder, my sisters, as you flash like a streak of lightning!

— Masuda Rahman, in *Dhumketu,* 1922, a magazine
started by the poet and musician Nazrul Islam

Baj and I rehearsed the first multi-verse song he taught me for a night of music, dance, and theater performances in St. Louis, with our mixed community of families, Hindus and Muslims, from either side of the border, West Bengali Indians and Bangladeshis, together. That evening, I sang a Bengali song by my father's favorite artist, a *truly radical, secular person,* the poet and musician Kazi Nazrul Islam, born in a village, Churulia, West Bengal. So beloved is Nazrul (iconic as his wavy pageboy haircut), I'd always actually believed him to be born in Bangladesh. When his father died at a young age, Nazrul became the village imam, worked in a local bakery, and joined a band of performers.

In his body of work, more than three thousand songs, Nazrul braided Sufi and Hindu devotional motifs, composing in ghazal, bhajan, kirtan. While stationed in Karachi during World War I, he heard the Turkish folk song by Safiye Ayla, "Kâtibim Türküsü." Using this melody, he wrote two sets of lyrics, a secular version, "Anklets of Dried Leaves," and an Islamic version that I performed that night, "Beloved Muhammad of the Three Worlds."

One of the singers, a West Bengali auntie, fainted, struck by heat and hunger. She'd been so wrapped up in her performances, she hadn't taken a moment for herself. When she came to, she told me, *Ami tomar gan mone shunte peyechi, Ma. I heard your song in my heart.*

I felt the same way when she performed the version of the song about the dancer. I had wanted to learn hers, it felt more like me, but I learned to praise the Prophet instead.

In Nazrul's magazine *Dhumketu*, *The Comet*, he amplified the work of fiery Bangla Muslim women writers, like Masuda Rahman. His poem "Bidrohi," or "The Rebel," catapulted him to literary and political renown, and caught the attention of British colonial authorities. Alarmed by his incendiary calls for freedom in *Dhumketu*, they arrested him. In jail, Nazrul wrote hundreds of poems, and in court, he defiantly recited a poem in verse as his defense. He opposed Bengal's Partition and married a Hindu woman from East Bengal, Pramila Devi. When Rabindranath Tagore, his friend and supporter, died in 1941, a heartbroken Nazrul performed an elegy, "Rabihara," "The Loss of Rabi," on All India Radio. Devastatingly, a year later, Nazrul lost his ability to speak. He suffered for the next thirty-five years with an untreatable neurological disorder. How painful it must have been, rendered mute by illness, silence instead of his ecstatic kirtans, just as the India he had been writing and fighting for became free.

NEW YORK

In 1992, we saved enough money to spend a summer in Bangladesh. Monsoon air, thick and mud-scented, permeated our grandmother's Dhaka apartment. I broke out in a prickly heat rash from the endless sweat. Hair sprouted on my upper lip, my underarms, my pubes. My pits stank — violet talcum powder did nothing. Stupidly, on that trip I brought a single book with me, a Judy Blume paperback, *Just as Long as We're Together,* which prepared me for my period but not the squatter Turkish toilet. I went a week without shitting until my stomach split in pain from constipation. I'd have done anything for a fucking can of Pringles or a peanut butter and jelly sandwich. Or Friday nights, when we'd lay out a sleeping bag on the floor, order a five-dollar pizza from Little Caesar's, and rent videos from Blockbuster. My depression over junk food seemed spoiled to the family I'd met as a toddler — how could I be willing to spend twenty rickshaw rides' worth on some potato chips? They teased me about my buck teeth and glasses, joking that I looked like one of my uncles. Their honesty made me feel like shit. My aunt's new husband cheered me up with chocolate-dipped vanilla ice cream bars, spicy tomato shrimp-flavored chips, Bengali sweets, *chom choms* and *shondesh,* ice-cold glass bottles of Coke, made from cane sugar, not the high fructose from the cornfields we'd pass on those long midwestern drives that I'd never know again.

We were moving to New York.

My new home, a downstate suburban village called Pomona, without any of the charm of its sunny cousin in California. As soon as we got there, I felt I was home.

New York folks flaunted more style than my friends back in St. Louis. I was ten, in sixth grade, my tits sloped upward, my upper lip and legs were still hairy, my thick glasses announced me as a nerd. I was, reluctantly. I absorbed the different cliques. The Black and Puerto Rican girls impeccably coordinated their colors, a subtle pop of pink in the swoosh of their Nikes matched the flowers on their bodysuits. I loved their tight-fitting flared jeans, door-knocker earrings, their name-brand kicks — name-brand everything. Rich white Jewish girls dressed straight out of *My So-Called Life,* plaid flannels, wide-legged JNCOs, bell-bottoms, poet shirts, yin-yang chokers. Filipino girls dyed their hair platinum blond (or what often happens to us black-haired ones, an orangey brass), wore hazel contacts and baby tees, navel exposed. South Asians could go drastic in any direction — from fresh-off-the-boat sneakers and salwar suits, to fast-fashion trends scored at the mall for cheap, from Joyce Leslie, Mandee, Charlotte Russe — the aunties of Forever 21.

It's Looking Day, Ma warned us whenever we went shopping. "Cool clothes" became a battleground for us. If I wanted to wear clothes and shoes that weren't on sale at Marshall's or TJ Maxx, Target or Payless, Ma told me, *You have to buy your own clothes.* I took to covering my body, sporting oversize men's clothes, my father's corduroys and velour shirts, a vintage version of what people bought fresh. That first year in New York, I wanted clothes to elevate me. I felt visibly out of touch and still so midwestern that I became invisible, except for when I got picked for a random appearance on the kids' television show *Where in the World Is Carmen Sandiego?* The episode aired on Halloween, though, so no one watched.

My friend Alex, still a close friend and one of my top-five white people, will never let me live down the outfit I wore the first day we met in French class, but I doubt she knew how even wearing that crochet top and fitted green leggings took lots of shouting and every fiber of my being to wear.

I was among the last of the girls in school to shave my legs. Ma feared temptation — if I shaved, I'd want to wear miniskirts. I did. She even asked my pediatrician if I should shave. When my South Indian doctor shook her head no, my eyes could've killed Dr. Mallavarapu. I wore Ma down with my moody rages that ended with *You don't fucking understand anything. I hate you!* Ma insisted that she shave my legs for me. Mortified, I stood in the tub, staring up at the bruise of mold on the ceiling, staring down at my mother on her knees in front of me, as she slathered my legs in shaving cream and ran the razor upward. I survived the mortification. By the end of it, my legs smooth as silk. I wasn't allowed to show them, though.

Our New York Bengali community felt outright segregated — it was nearly all Muslims, except for Ma's best friend, Manju

Biswas, but she was Bangladeshi, married to a Muslim man. We had way fewer Indians from West Bengal among us. My parents socialized with people who were émigrés from the late '70s, after the war. Maybe mixing with Indian Hindus would make dinner parties complicated — vegetarians versus meat-eaters; prayer rooms without idols; political discussions on live-wire topics like 9/11, Narendra Modi, the mass migrations of Bangladeshis into West Bengal.

These borders between us dissolved on the national level, at massive cultural conventions like the annual Bongo Sammelan, where Bengalis the world over intermingled and watched performances — dances, plays, music — by artists across the Bengali diaspora. All of the teenagers would sneak away from the shows by sundown, to get drunk and high and hook up with each other at the after-parties. At one convention in Atlantic City, I greeted an auntie, both of us decked out in saris, both of us wearing a round *teep* on our foreheads.

As-salaam-alaikum, I said, *peace be unto you,* in Arabic, without thinking.

The auntie smiled, a bit uncomfortable, I realized. She shook her head. *Oh, I'm not —*

Oh. Sorry, I apologized, realizing she wasn't Muslim. *Namoshkar, auntie.*

No problem, she said, in Bengali.

If she'd responded, *wa-alaikum salaam,* I would've been pleasantly surprised, but I loved saying *Namoshkar,* it made me feel more Bengali, somehow, so it didn't bother me to say it to her, an Indian woman from West Bengal. *Namoshkar* connected us, just like *as-salaam-alaikum* connected me to a Muslim anywhere in the world. But her discomfort felt obvious, this auntie couldn't meet me at hello. The expectation to yield to the dominant culture's way is something that Hindu and Indigenous Bangladeshis, the minorities in Bangladesh, know all too well. Subjected to rudeness and mistreatment — or brutal violence or murder — because of their caste status in a Muslim-majority country.

This Indian auntie couldn't say *wa-alaikum salaam,* maybe because it felt too inauthentic as a Hindu — impure. Or perhaps she wanted to signal her power, for I belonged to the culture perceived as smaller, submissive. Without saying a word, with only an amused look, she let me correct myself and greet her in the proper Bengali — Hindu — way, *Namoshkar,* rather than commune with me as a Muslim.

SHYAMLA, BROWN-SKINNED BEAUTY

In the late '90s, white beauty hegemony looked like Calvin Klein heroin chic or any of the annoying actresses on *Friends,* devoid of voluptuousness, color, body, lips, or hips — irrelevant in my view. Any time I'd felt judged as a youth for how I looked, how I smelled, how my belly was too fat, or my legs were too skinny, it was either a white kid or an auntie from my own community who dished out a nasty comment or critique. We know the obsession with appearance — body hair and smell, skin color and texture, the size of lips and noses, the straightness of teeth, the shape of hips and butts, the amount of fat or wrinkles

— a discomfort rooted in eugenics and anti-Blackness and xenophobia, and self-hatred for not conforming to beauty ideals that harm them, too.

I never wanted to be white or light — Ma drilled enough brown self-love in us — but the possession of beauty and the desire for domination or erasure that it evoked in others terrified me.

Our noses sharpen at adolescence, as our hormones shift, as we emit new natural odors. Beauty and perfume, intertwined, to make us obsess over how we look, and how we smell, to soften the edge of our animal judgments of one another. Beauty called attention toward you, from everyone, another form of judgment, of our voluptuousness, color, body, lips, or hips. There seemed to be many Black or Indian or Filipino girls around me navigating beauty on their own terms outside of the specter of whiteness, but it seemed like South Asian girls did not register as hot or fuckable outside of South Asian relationships. I do remember thinking that my gorgeous Indian friend Shilu and her sisters — who wore glasses too, but shed them before me — were proof that I couldn't be ugly.

Whenever I stared in the mirror, I couldn't remember any of the old versions of myself. I saw my maroon square wire-rimmed Coke-bottles, ridges filled with dirt I could never seem to clean off. I saw the hairs between my brows, the fine mustache on my upper lip, my giant eyebrows, until I stared so much that I plucked them into uneven crescent moons. *Why don't you love yourself?* Ma asked me the next day, looking hurt that I'd done such a thing. Another night, I almost burned down our house heating up beeswax directly on the stove. I stupidly threw water on the flames, which became a tower of fire before it extinguished, along with my hopes of waxing myself instead of waiting for Ma to hook me up. I stared so hard that one day, somehow two small sties appeared on my eyes, probably when I rubbed them after crying. When I took off my glasses, I became blurry, I squinted, moving closer to the mirror until my nose touched it and I disappeared.

In eighth grade, a list went around of the ugliest girls in school, I heard about it in math class, from a white girl who looked like she was already in her thirties. I felt nauseated at the thought that I might be on the list; and in the moment, she seemed like she knew something but wouldn't tell me. A list of the ugliest girls was easy to write, but being cruel to an actual person was harder. That year, Missy, a short white girl with a bulbous nose, braces, and mouse-brown hair, would announce as she entered social studies, *Ugh, it's attack of the smellies!* about me and another girl who was bullied for being fat and the smell of her body. Strange, I'd gone to Missy's Bat Mitzvah — I thought we were friends? — and I religiously shampooed my hair every morning and spritzed with Victoria's Secret Enchanted Apple. Her nastiness seemed unfounded. Both the fat girl and I were quick-tempered, but we ignored this mean white-girl shit. We had dignity.

When we got to high school, the tides turned. We were no longer in the same classes. Now the Black, Filipino, and Puerto Rican girls were the babes; I shed the glasses and braces and

blossomed into a babe, too. I ran the literary magazine and published the writing of the other girl she'd bullied. I'd see Missy in
the hallway, but I never bothered to say hi. I pitied her.

Late at night, long after my parents went to bed exhausted from
work, one of the white boys in orchestra would call me up for
phone sex. We'd set a time — midnight — and I'd call a random
1-800 number so that the phone wouldn't ring when he called
me. He alleviated the edge of feeling dissociated from myself
and depressed. I heard him grunting as he jerked off. I kept
repeating, *Cum all over me, baby,* purring sighs that I'd never
revealed to anyone else, hardly myself, even, only when I made
myself cum. It sounded disgusting to my own ears, but I knew
what he wanted. I hadn't even watched porn at that point. I
had a good voice for phone sex, a bit husky, sweet in time for an
orgasm. I don't think I ever actually masturbated with him on
those phone calls, but I was super wet. Phone sex let the energy
pent up inside of me out, let me feel pretty. Let me feel sexual
and wanted. Wild — like the animals we were.

A few years ago, I took Ma out for lunch at an Indian restaurant
in Williamsburg, Brooklyn — a joint owned by Bangladeshis.
She got up to go to the bathroom, and as soon as she was out of
earshot, the Bangladeshi waiter asked me, curious, *Your mother
is so . . . beautiful and clean. How are you so . . . dirty?* The word
he used, *moila,* means dirty, but when used to describe the skin,
the beholder is letting you know they consider you too dark.
He seemed genuinely confused how my pale mother had such

a dark-skinned daughter. I wanted to reply that she liked her
men dark like chocolate, like him. But his rudeness shocked
me. When I told Ma what he said, she reddened with rage,
snarling, *Shaitaner haddi. Devil's bones.* I calmed her down —
not my usual response — but much worse than his comment:
a light-skinned middle-class woman raging on a dark-skinned
working-class man. Besides, it was the only Indian spot in the
neighborhood.

Ma is *forsha,* milk-skinned, moon-pale, a Bengali beauty ideal.
She witnessed the damage of this constant praise for her beauty
throughout childhood, praise that her sister, my aunt, more café
con leche, curly-haired, freckled — rarely heard. Dark-skinned
was considered *mishti,* sweet, at best, never *shundor,* beautiful.
When my sister was born, our mother prayed that we'd be the
same shade of brown. She didn't want us to experience the pain
of sibling skin difference. *We're all the same, brown is beautiful, brown is more beautiful,* she'd say, even though we knew Ma
insisting on our sameness was a soft lie, letting her affirm the
beauty of her children.

    I am *shyamla,* which I understood to mean brown-skinned,
bronzed, dusky, neither *forsha,* like Ma, nor *kalo,* black, like Baj.
Devoid of the reverence to the goddess, *kali, kala, kallu* are
words for black pitched upon the dark-skinned feminine body,
anti-Black, casting her as undesirable. Untouchable.

Ma tells me in a text: *Shyamla isn't brown, it means green.*

Ma suggests an etymological connection — *shyola* — moss. It doesn't occur to her that our ancestral Hindu holds a Sanskrit origin.

Our skin color, *shyamla,* green, blue-black, lotus-blue goddess Shyamala Devi, an incarnation of the much-beloved Tantric goddess Kali, the black-skinned One, who lay on a bed of snakes, the great goddess of cosmic time and destruction and rebirth, sometimes known as Shyama. Kali is the first Devi of the Mahavidya, the Great Wisdoms, each goddess a manifestation of the feminine divine power, *shakti.* The Mahavidya are the ten incarnations of the Divine Mother, the mountain goddess Parvati, sometimes known as Gauri, the white-skinned one, wife of Shiva. In parts of South India, Shyamala Devi is another name of the ninth Mahavidya Matangi, the goddess of inner knowledge, who is supposed to be born of a Dalit father, a Chandala, disposer of corpses. Green-skinned, third eye crescent-mooned, she is the goddess of pollution, half-eaten food, of the indigenous forest. Devotees proffer her everything that Brahmins consider highly impure. Putrid. Leftovers and rags of dried menstrual blood.

Kali, Parvati, Shyamala originated as Dravidian, Naga, non-Aryan goddesses, eventually renamed and admitted into the Hindu pantheon as the Brahmins expanded eastward across the subcontinent. *These renamings were yet another way of consolidating settlement in a new land, using a woman's body to bring under one map self-contained aboriginal settlements,* wrote Gayatri Spivak. Did the Brahmin patramyth name the fair-skinned Parvati as the origin of Shyamala and Kali to assert the superiority of the pale-skinned? Or is she just another *gauri* like Ma, a light-skinned woman who loves her brown-black-skinned man, their daughters, brown-skinned, facets of her feminine power?

Shyamala and Kali, in human flesh, become skin tones, brown and black, *shyamla* and *kali,* no longer a Devi to worship, but dark-skinned women to disregard. Destroy. Brown and Black women held as objects of desire. Hypersexed, enslaved, fucked, angry, unloved, unmarried. This fear of our darkness, our curves, our fat is an ancient hatred, but also an ancient lust of the bodied, the odorous. *Shyamla,* surreal green, as the rice paddy fields and mangrove forests that cover Bengal; *shyamla,* as the brown-skinned Bengal, where light and dark have mixed over eons. *Kali,* black as wet earth, the darkest hour before the blue light. Shyamla-Kali, women and femmes who labor in homes, in factories and fields, the seams that hold the world together. The ultimate project of caste: to dominate the people whose work brings them closer to Earth. Closer to the forests and farmlands and rivers and ocean, to the animals, to sex, to art made with their bodies, to shit and death — and more vulnerable to upper-caste violence.

Somewhere between the beauty of the Black and Puerto Rican and Filipino and Indian girls — and no doubt *the* brown-

skinned Bollywood babe of the '90s, Kajol — I inched closer
to my own aesthetic. I started to wear lipstick to school for the
first time ever. Ma encouraged it, sensing that I needed this social armor to face school. My favorites were gourmand shades
like Cinnamon Raisin and Frosted Brownie, outlined in dark
velvety brown. Nanu shook her head, mystified why I wanted
such moody colors for my lips, and suggested I try her personal
favorite, *tuk tuké lal,* bright-bright red, her tastes that of a young
Bengali village bride. Hot red would pop better on my *shyamla*
skin, it flattered everyone's skin.

Your lips are *tuk tuké lal,* I teased her, *because you eat paan.*
Nanu laughed, sweetly flashing her buck-toothed, dark red,
paan-stained smile. My sister wore black eyeliner first — all
praise due — but I pulled some bitchy older-sister shit and
told her people with pretty eyes didn't need to cover them up.
Maybe I didn't want to take beauty tips from her, not right
when I started to feel cute. She'd been cute her whole childhood, even her awkward phase seemed cute to me, though
she might disagree. I disavowed the rawness of our inherited
beauty culture of kohl-lined eyes, red lips, orange aurum bling
of 24K gold — I didn't want to be seen as gaudy, cheap, or too
much. Hard to believe that I ever rejected this South Asian
beauty staple, but that's how deep our need to erase ourselves
can go.

The last summer that I shared a room with my grandmother
and sister, our apartment became possessed. Black spots of
mold appeared on the bathroom ceiling, slowly spreading like

a dark galaxy, until meteoric chunks of drywall plummeted into the tub as we slept. At night, I heard the sound of snapping branches, and by morning, we discovered the beams of the wooden floors had split open as if we were living on a fault line. I named the sudden crumbling as the work of a malevolent spirit, a devil, the Shaitan that my grandma so feared. My whispery prayers to Al — h fell on deaf ears, as our apartment disintegrated more each day. It was easier to believe in a demon, I suppose, than to believe we lived in a home designed for poor people.

That summer, my parents announced that we'd be moving out of our broke-down apartment into an actual house, with an upstairs and a downstairs, a deck, a backyard — and, finally, a room of my own. My sister would still have to live in the same room as Nanu, but I was ready to be rid of communal quarters. A pine tree blocked light in my new tiny bedroom, and I despised the décor of this little American boy cave — the cobalt-blue carpet, the walls plastered with Ralph Lauren Polo teddy-bear print wallpaper, the tiny closet. After they'd put money down on our new home, there was no way I could ask my folks to replace the wallpaper or carpet. I improvised by papering my walls with celebrity collages and magazine ads — Salma Hayek and Keanu Reeves and Versace and Absolut Vodka — all the forbidden things: sex, bare skin, alcohol. On my dresser — Elizabeth Arden's Sunflowers, Victoria's Secret Enchanted Apple, a sample of my mother's Trésor. Perfumes held everything forbidden in one bottle. The disintegration of my Muslim-ness started soon after I moved into the new house. Finally, I felt free — of my sister, of my grandmother, of god.

Ma's career shapeshifted in New York, as she worked her way from bank teller to portfolio manager, while our father worked as a chemist in a private-sector pharmaceuticals company. Their newfound economic security meant our beauty and perfume tastes expanded, replacing L'Air du Temps with big-brand gems of the '90s: Trésor, Calvin Klein Eternity, Estée Lauder Pleasures. Ma bought beauty products from Clinique, scoring free gift sets with purchases of fifty dollars or more, meaning I got to try free luxury makeup and perfume samples for the first time. But most of the colors and foundations were too ashy. By the end of middle school, I ditched my thick glasses for contacts. She took me to the Macy's counter of the largest Black-owned beauty brand, Fashion Fair. *They'll be able to match your skin tone,* Ma told me. Better not to risk a painful experience at a makeup counter where I'd be told they didn't have my color. I remember being surprised at my own face; how strange it felt to no longer be obscured behind thick glass. For the first time, I saw something innate, inviolable about myself, something that whiteness or lightness could never possess or steal. It was mine. I was mine. In the mirror, my eyes looked watery and giant; I felt like an alien discovering a new life-form.

Idiots who'd forgotten I'd been right there began to notice me after that summer, some boys even forgot that I'd gone to middle school with them, that we'd ridden the bus together every morning and afternoon, that I'd been there the entire time. One of them, a skinny South Indian boy a few years older than me, with dark, brooding eyes, did remember me. *I liked you that way, too,* he told me.

o

A woman needs her own money, separate from her husband.
I don't want a husband.
You still need your own money.

Sick of hearing me complain about shopping at Marshalls, Ma told me I'd better get a job and buy my own damn cool clothes. I started working retail at Express, a shop girl like Ma, but fitted with a corny headset and low-stakes commissions for selling clothes. I flirted with the tall Filipino barber who did security on the side, sold tons of capri pants and Technicolor stretch jersey tops. I still can smell the staleness of the Nanuet Mall, the wafting odors of Cinnabon and Wendy's that called to me for my lunch break. For less than five dollars a day, I gained twenty pounds downing foods I constantly craved — French fries and chicken nuggets and Coke — but hardly got to eat since Ma cooked every night. Just before returning to the store for my shift, I'd peruse the perfume and beauty counter at Lord & Taylor, collecting vials as if sampling possible versions of myself. Each of those fragrances as full-sized bottles was roughly the equivalent of ten to twenty hours of work. Of all those fancy fragrances, I coveted the one destined for a drugstore: the amber-hue and rhinestone-encrusted bottle of Elizabeth

Taylor's White Diamonds, a composition of sparkling soapy aldehydes, oakmoss and musk and sandalwood; at its heart, the aura of decadence: violet, rose, and jasmine.

In my twenties, I worked as a youth organizer, teaching artist in the outer boroughs of the city, nonprofit manager, shop girl, and cashmere sales rep before landing a job as a brand manager at a hipster arts start-up. The space had a wood and metal shop and classes on anything a mid-aughts millennial hipster's heart desired: midcentury furniture reupholstery, oil painting, sewing, jewelry making, and perfumery. I loved all of that. I hated the *Bros Before Hoes* poster that stared at me all day while I designed the marketing newsletters at a communal table. I was used to working with queer women and young people, not bros. The only thing I got out of that job was a natural perfumery course with a teacher whose name I don't remember. She read parts from Mandy Aftel's *Essence and Alchemy* and Diane Ackerman's *A Natural History of the Senses*. I found both books intriguing, better than the class. After six months of working there, the megalomaniac founder ruined his company, greed had widened his eyes bigger than his bank account. I got laid off. I started collecting unemployment, four hundred bucks a week, and bought essential oils to experiment at home.

ZENANA

Don't sit on my bed, tui to napak, you're impure, Nanu scolded me whenever I had my period. My body became *napak,* unholy, sullied her bed, where she read from the Quran, whispered *dua* on her tasbih beads. Her hemophobia didn't faze me. I'd already been indoctrinated and shared her disgust. Mostly it was how I dealt with blood — tampons — made of bleached processed cotton and wrapped in plastic destined to become microplastic. I hated the way stagnant blood smelled: metallic, marine, fishy. Twenty-seven years after my first period, I've switched to a cup, a silicone chalice that holds my blood like sacramental wine. I pour it out in the shower. I shower afterward, every single time. Do I still feel impure, I wonder, even as I've long disavowed religious men's ideas of menstrual taboo? Do I wash myself because the idea of my bleeding body's impurity was written on me too long ago for me to forget? Is this when I first began to think of myself as separate from nature?

Abrahamic and Brahminic religion wages war over land and sacred animals, but when it comes to impurity, they share an accord: a belief that menstrual blood contaminates men's sacred spaces and holy books. As if a lifetime of moon cycles and releasing blood isn't a kind of ritual, no matter how much I've hated it each month. *Gunah,* modesty, purity — these fears pervaded the women in my family — my body seemed to be the site of so much power in how it was perceived. How I behaved determined whether or not I was sinful or filthy. How could a single drop of blood render me impure? *Tui to napak, but you're impure,* the opposite of *pak,* as in Pakistan, land of the pure, a country we eventually learned to think of as an enemy because of its military genocide of our people, its national flower none other than little stars of white jasmine.

Gunah hobe, my mother muttered, *sin will happen,* a warning I vaguely worried about; All — h had never felt more far away. *Gunah* whenever I stripped out of my jeans and T-shirts into the short skirts I wanted to wear, *gunah* for eating the after-school slice of pepperoni pizza, *gunah* for sipping Malibu and orange juice cocktails at my Trinidadian friend Camilla's house, *gunah* for never praying, *gunah* for letting a boy touch me, *gunah* for sneaking *The Joy of Sex* out of my parents' bedroom to look at the meticulous pencil drawings of sex positions. *Gunah* for learning to lie about everything. *Gunah* meant forbidden by Islam. The word *gunah* comes from Old Avestan, the Indo-Iranian sister language to Indo-Aryan, the language of the ancient Aryan nomadic pastoralists.

On the other hand, the phrase *gūn acche, you're skilled,* was praise. *Gūn* meant you were in possession of talent, intellectual prowess, versed in science and all manner of arts: playing the violin, singing Bengali music, writing poems and stories and plays, cooking, sewing, decorating a home with tasteful elegance, draping a sari with perfect pleats, knowing multiple languages or the quality of a substance — what kind of textile or gemstone. I blame this obsession with skill possession on the desire to be the impeccable colonial subject, holdovers from Victorian respectability politics, on classism and caste. But the idea of *gūna,* Sanskrit for quality, talent, gift, or skill — precedes the British. *Gūna* means a single thread, a strand — a recurrent concept in Yogic philosophy — *gūna* is the essence of all things, how nature is expressed in three inherent qualities that one might find in anything: *sattva,* goodness, preservation, harmony; *rajas,* creation, passion, ego; *tamas,* disorder, destruction, and death.

Gunah and *gūna* — sin and skill — false friends. How could we be so inundated with a fear of *gunah,* but somehow expected to possess *gūna,* be worldly, artistic, cultured, smart — as if that were fucking possible without committing a few sins?

Whereas Ma warned me, *gunah hobe,* Nanu scolded Ma, for wearing clingy American clothes without a hijab when she went to work at the bank. I suppose each generation wears less fabric and shows more and more skin. Our ancestors wore saris without blouses or petticoats underneath, just a single drape of fabric, until stitched blouses and petticoats came into vogue in the colonial era, because of the modesty-obsessed British, who scorned bare skin and bellies as savage.

Nanu wore a cotton sari under her burqa, which she still insisted on wearing anywhere she might be seen by men. The mall, the beach, a *dawat.* We wanted her to wear a periwinkle-colored burqa, that felt more grandmotherly — but to hell with that, she wore the jet-black burqa. Only her bespectacled eyes visible. I'm ashamed to admit now that as a youth I was ashamed of her choice, for her stubbornness about the burqa. Back then, I believed it made her a most visible target, because I believed she wanted to hide. What made her feel protected and safe made me feel exposed.

She didn't want to be invisible. She wanted to assert her right to move in her body, free, with ease.

If she had worn a sari, would it keep people from staring? She honored faith, herself above the judgment of others. When I think of it now, I'm floored at how brave and irreverent she remained about her modesty — she gave no fucks about the stares, she answered to All — h. Not bigots. She'd observed *purdah* in public, whether at home or in the States, until finally, the last decade of her life, she stopped going outside.

Whenever we got ready for *dawats,* Ma insisted on tying my sari — not that I could, anyway — in a meticulous, Bengali *nivi* drape, getting down on her hands and knees, duck safety pin in her teeth, scolding me when I hadn't tied my petticoat tight enough for her to tuck in the fabric. My mother takes great pride in tying her sari, never hitched too high, nor too low, just the right number of pleats and *anchal* draped at a length that let one appreciate the designs without tripping the person wearing the sari. In a simple act of *learning to drape the sari,* writes Poulomi Saha, *the muscle memory of a matrilineal world.*

It felt goofy to stand there, so I'd pop into a squat and pump my ass and hips, trying to scandalize Nanu. She laughed and laughed. *Tanu! Tor pasa ta tho shundor! Your butt is beautiful!* There, in the private corner of Ma's bedroom, we shed our American clothes and dressed in silk, and it never bothered Nanu when we flaunted ourselves, acted sexual, ridiculous, too much, too loud, and too revealing — we could be ourselves in that little suburban New York *zenana.*

Mati — Perfume Interlude

AN ODE TO MANASA

HEAD

Saffron

Timur Pepper

HEART

Jasmine Absolute

Betel Leaf

Champaca

Pink Lotus Wax

Indian Rose

BASE

Mitti Attar

Sylheti Oud

Bengal Patchouli

Sandalwood

Auranone

Hibiscus Ambrette

I'd learned Arabic prayer from the photocopied book *Tarteeb of Salaat,* but I preferred to sing mantras learned off Ravi Shankar's *Chants of India,* the words felt more familiar to me. I had no concept of caste — because of Islam — so it never occurred to me back then that I myself would be denied participation as a lower-caste Hindu if we rewound the narrative by several hundred years. I only knew what I felt in my body. Mantra slipped off my tongue easier than surah. My face, my body, eyes, the way I moved — how was I not a Hindu? If anything I felt closer to the aesthetics of the goddess, of ancient temple carvings that looked like me, I felt a closeness to rituals and traditions marked by fragrance and flowers and idols, more concrete than All — h, than the rules and restraint of an Islam that I'd been born as, born into, without ever being given a choice.

The Australian-Canadian writer of Bangladeshi descent Fariha Róisín was part of my reconnection to Islam, as I had been hers to our ancestral Hindu. She gifted me a terra-cotta pot, a perfect sphere with a hole that seemed made to hold scent strips I use to compose the first drafts of my perfumes. A single drop of each oil on the strip, divided into base, heart, head, gives me a sense of where I want to go. When I write, I look for signs everywhere, to assure me that I'm on the right path. Once, I pulled a Tarot card in the Wild Unknown deck, and I received the Daughter of Wands, depicted as a serpent the shape of an infinity symbol wrapped around a staff. When Fariha pulled a card in a Native American deck, I received a snake, again. I hoped the transformation and fertility did not mean pregnancy.

Serpents began appearing everywhere in my texts.

As a Muslim, I had not grown up knowing Manasa, the serpent goddess. In the summertime, people worshipped her to bring the monsoon but to keep away the snakes that came with the rains. The Aryan horsemen never quite penetrated the hinterlands of East Bengal, where snake-goddess worship thrived before they arrived. Like other Great Goddesses, they eventually absorbed Manasa into their pantheon, replacing an older, Indigenous Buddhist goddess called Janguli, the curer of snakebites. In order to assert *shakta,* hard, masculine power, Manasa emerged from a drop of Shiva's semen on a lotus petal, so turned on had he been by the pond's beauty. As Spivak reminds us: *There is no great goddess. When activated, each goddess is the great goddess. That is the secret of polytheism.*

I lace the perfume with objects used in *puja,* the *mati* clay pot, as the note of mitti attar, clay from the Ganga River distilled in India's perfume capital, Kannauj, gathered at the end of summer heat to smell like the monsoon rain on earth. The mélange of patchouli, sandalwood, musk, and oud evoke the stink of a pond, the plants of worship in the notes of jasmine, champaca, and rose, as they would be arranged on a betel leaf. Pink lotus wax, reminiscent of the god's cum. A few drops of saffron and Timur pepper, a cousin of the Szechuan, gives the perfume a bite, goddess vengeance sharp as snake venom. As a survivor, Fariha's work reminds us that mothers are complex, sometimes maleficent — and have the capacity to inflict great harm.

I wonder if Ma's fear of snakes is a subconscious fear of our Hindu ancestry, a wild divine feminine, a contradiction to All — h. Does knowing a goddess through a text make my connection to her inauthentic? No, I decide, since all the parts of myself that I found in books — perfume, writing, Islam — became practices I made my own.

Other Tongue

Perfume as Motherland

NOTES
Mati, or Rain on Earth

A corpse, sister, bathed

jasmine, blue —

— Tarfia Faizullah, *Seam*

Tikka Khan had issued a blanket order to set fire to the houses of Bengalis, kill them, rape their women, turn East Pakistan into a nation of slaves and concubines, as he did not want the people of Bengal, but the land of Bengal.

— from *Rifle, Roti, Aurat* by Anwar Pasha, novelist, murdered in the massacre of Bengali artists and intellectuals by the Pakistani Army on December 14, 1971

WAR

One day, we were traveling by train, the army stopped us on the platform, demanding to see our ID, to see if we were Hindu. I was so afraid. We knew they were capturing young women all over the country, raping them. These soldiers were very poor boys from Pakistan, barely educated, they didn't understand Bangla, we didn't understand them. A young solider poked me and demanded to see what I was reading. I showed him my magazine. I was so scared. But he smiled at me, when he saw the Pakistani actress Rani on the cover. Maybe it made him feel comfortable far from home. He left me alone.

Near the end of the war, I stayed behind in the village — I had just turned fourteen — your Nanu and Nana were afraid men might try to take me away. When the rest of the family returned to the house by the pond in Tongibari, they were shocked — the entire house had been looted — we had nothing. Did we think Indian soldiers took everything? No. Sometimes when the Mukti Bahini or the Indian Army rode through our village, all of us young girls cheered and clapped for them, they were so handsome, they were fighting for us. We thought of them as heroes. One day, young Mukti Bahini men showed up to the house, they'd heard that the family had a daughter — they demanded that one of their men marry me. *Bhagheesh chilamna,* fortunately I wasn't there, so they couldn't take me. No woman felt safe then. It's true, Bihari women were raped too.

— Ma reminiscing about 1971,
on a phone call, August 2020

The military is coming! The military is coming! Joydeb screamed, running back from town, breathless, rushing home to warn his sisters, Durga and Gauri, that they needed to hide. Quickly. The two sisters leapt into the pond, sinking into the green, low as they could, enough to cover their bodies under water hyacinths that bloomed on the surface. Invasive species. Their only protection from the ferocious invaders that descended the night of March 25, 1971 — Pakistani soldiers who everyone feared would kidnap and gang-rape young girls. Durga and Gauri waited out the soldiers, laying in absolute stillness, breathing from their nostrils that peeked out of pondwater. One night, Joydeb, Durga, and Gauri left, their family decided — as did millions of Hindu families — to risk everything and leave their homeland to cross the border into India.

My mother never saw her friends again.

Months later, when Ma stayed in her own ancestral village, around fourteen years old, word spread that the Pakistani military would be coming for girls in their village, so she ran and ran, ran about a mile to a secluded area, where there were only trees. When she finally caught her breath, she realized that she'd been running alone.

I heard a few scattered tales of Ma's life during the Liberation War of 1971, a year that holds Bangladeshis and our diaspora in a perpetual state of reckoning. Every family has their record of the war, their version of the story. Neither Ma nor Baj fought as guerillas in the Mukti Bahini — Ma too young, Baj pro-Liberation but his elderly father needed him at home, and violence never fit his disposition. We heard the numbers repeated like a mantra, the death toll of the war: three million murdered and one hundred thousand to four hundred thousand women raped by the Pakistani Army. All in the span of nine months — the gestation period of a baby nation. Chaos made quantifying death impossible. Among their friends, our aunties and uncles, some joined the Mukti Bahini as freedom fighters, but they would spend most of their lives building new families in the United States.

○

Being a woman, my body was considered to be dangerous to myself and others.

— Laila Ahmed, a freedom fighter who trained in the Gobra Camp, India, in an interview with Yasmin Saikia

When I was twenty-two, I worked at the organizing center Make the Road New York, named after the Spanish poet Antonio Machado's line: *we make the road by walking.* My Dominican friend Benny took me to get a tattoo for twenty bucks in a Bushwick basement. I handed the tattoo artist Bear — hirsute as his name implied — a tiny printout of a Bengali woman holding a bayonet, from a propaganda poster encouraging women to join the struggle for Liberation. Today, the black ink of my tattoo woman is greened, blurring the sharp edge of her weapon into an auntie's warning, wagging finger.

Did I — do I — have it in me *to kill* for freedom and nation? I imagine it would take extraordinary circumstances for me to fathom ending the life of another being. Would I do so if I were being attacked, threatened with rape? I think of all the people who were faced, in a moment, with inexplicable terror and had no time to take cover, protect themselves, and run as far away as fucking possible. Laila Ahmed, a freedom fighter, reminisced about her experiences in the war, training in the Gobra Camp, in Kolkata, India. The oppressive, male-dominated nature of warfare denied her the chance to fight, despite her height, strength, and desire to engage in armed battle — men considered her a liability. Many women freedom fighters worked in infirmaries and clinics, doing revolutionary work as caretakers and healers. Seeing death all around her, Laila remembered the moment that changed everything, that made her want to fight. *The dead bodies were wet, rotten and lying in muck and water, my father's barely covered with earth.*

How to stitch together the knowledges collected in thousands of books over the fifty years since Bangladesh's birth? At the end of this book, there will be a list of all the books I've read, whose pages are dog-eared, smeared with kajal from my eyes to my fingers after crying, books full of facts about survivors and perpetrators. As a writer, fiction is my preferred form of story-telling — the ground is softer for burying secrets — and telling the truth hurts in a way I had not expected it to. I close my eyes, breathe, let myself weep, pierced by the immensity of suffering, like shrapnel lodged in my heart. Ma and Baj rarely told us details of that year, perhaps wanting to spare my sister and me what wasn't ours, even though this history is ours, history we would have to learn someday, when it was time.

PIONEERS

The Ganga shifted course in the sixteenth century, as the rush of its flow displaced river silt and pushed the waters eastward, connecting the river to the Padma. Soon, the riverbeds in West Bengal dried up, and the isolated East Bengal hinterland transformed into a new center of trade and agriculture. The fertile delta experienced a surge in population, as the abundance of arable land along the rivers fed the people of the lowlands. For more than a hundred years, the Mughals made Dhaka their capital. They awarded land grants to Turkish Sufi adventurers charged to lead the people to clear the dense sal forests of the Bengal frontier. As they labored in the forests, cutting trees to make fields for wet rice cultivation, they absorbed Islamic teachings.

They built thatched bamboo shrines, dedicated to their *pir*, the Sufi mystic with whom they'd deforested their land. An emergent Sufi universe founded on a brotherhood of men, equals who labored together, ate and prayed together. Mughal authorities loathed fishermen, and never sought to convert the Indigenous people of the rural countryside to Islam. As the river changed course, so, too, did the religious identity of the masses. People had long worshipped mother goddesses, who offered them respite from harsh living conditions, like Sitala the goddess who protected from smallpox, or Manasa, the serpent goddess who protected from snakebites. As they faced the ferocious jungle wilderness, floods and monsoons, snakes and tigers, these men who labored sought guidance and authority, living wages, and, most importantly, a sense of brotherhood.

We each yearn for a story about the Cosmos.

As the Sufis brought their faith to these men, where were the women and femmes? From conquest to taming the land, Islam gradually changed the way Bengali women moved on their land, shifting their worlds deeper inside.

BOAT GIRLS

Vasanas of Bangladesh that I long for after I leave: the sound of *adhan* in the morning, calls to prayer harmonious across the city. Bathing myself with a hot water bucket, the languid streams massaging my scalp. Books scored in a Shahbag Aziz market smelled aquatic, like a wooden raft on water. Boat rides on a *haor,* vast, temporary seas of monsoon waters collected on the land, waters that will disappear by the dry season. Traces of that water in the radiant green fields that follow the rain.

I come across the phrase *nouka meye,* boat girls, as I look for lost femmes in eastern Bengal, and there they are, riding a boat, fifteen of them huddled close together. The year is 1875. They are Brahmin or Dalit, young widows, some passing as Hindu, though they are Muslim, girls riding all the way to a *ghat* in Sylhet to meet potential husbands. Hindu bachelors who can't afford a steep dowry arrange to meet these *nouka meye.* When the boat docks, the men circle the boatload of young women like vultures eyeing prey, assessing the girls' bodies from head to toe, tooth to nail. Each man chooses the girl he lusts after the most to be his wife. For those who aren't chosen by a man, they must work as a maid, a sex worker — or be enslaved without pay.

People worked themselves to death to pay off their landlords, the *zamindars*. Folks who defaulted on land payments were thrown into a pit of human shit as punishment, the stench and filth a way of dehumanizing them. Slave trade of young women and children on the Indian Ocean circuit, between the colonies run by the Dutch and British East India companies, increased during periods of famine, when families sold their young children to save them from starvation. European enslavers forced people's labor to harvest sugar and spice, building vast wealth they themselves would never see. For hundreds of years, our people have been deemed backwards, rural, illiterate, but why do we forget that those with power have pushed them back to assure their own ascendancy?

PARTITIONS

The people of the land now known as Bangladesh have known mass death for centuries, because of greedy, wealthy, land-grabbing, grain-withholding conquerors. People all along the eastern subcontinent died in the Bengal famines: ten million in 1770, one million in 1896, and three million in 1943. People died in the 1974 famine, from the steep price of rice and devastating flooding of the Brahmaputra River, lasting from March to December of that year, the length of the war, killing 1.5 million people. Deaths of our people like invisible scars imprinted on everyone who survived. But does the fresh blood spilled in war — from acts of intimate brutality — make death harder to bear?

Denuded land and exploited labor made Empire. Rice, jute, tea, cotton, silk, pearls, indigo, Dhakai muslin were extracted from Dalit and Muslim farmers and weavers and fishermen scorned by fellow men, the Brahmin *zamindars,* Mughal rulers, and British colonizers. For the smells and skills of labor, their way with language, their diet — our diet — fish, rice, *daal.* Their bodies, too brown, languid, lean, and for the climate of the East, humid, balmy, hot, and wet — the very conditions that made such fecundity possible.

The people have continually rebelled, asserting their right to freedom and independence over the last several centuries. The flourishing riverine rice cultivation in Bengal not only meant an increase in population, but a greater mass of rural people who organized powerful political coalitions. They demanded an end to British colonial rule during the Partition of 1905 when Lord Curzon cleaved Bengal in half to break the dominance of the province. They fought in favor of Pakistan during the Partition of 1947, sick and tired of being ignored by upper-caste Bengali Hindus who saw themselves at the forefront of India's national-ist movement and feared Muslim mass domination. Peasants and workers of East Bengal overwhelmingly voted for Muslim parties who directly spoke to their interests, and so, West Ben-gali Indian Hindu nationalists agitated for Partition in 1947, splitting East and West, once and for all.

When the Partition of 1947 separated India from its frontiers to the East and West, two faraway lands found themselves unified as Pakistan because of their shared religion, Islam. But Islam didn't stop West Pakistan from funneling money out of East Pakistan to develop its own infrastructure, an estimated 2.6 billion in 1971 dollars — equivalent to 16.8 billion dollars today. Money that could have built the roads, housing, schools, and hospitals in East Pakistan. East Pakistan's bounty of raw materials developed West Pakistan's flourishing new country. Children labored instead of going to school, swimming with their parents in water-logged jute and rice paddies, picking tea on hilly plantations, or working in textile factories, treated as machines.

In November 1970, the Bhola cyclone killed more than 500,000 people, devastating the coastal districts in the Bay of Bengal. Survivors were met with indifference and bare compensation for their extreme losses from the central government in West Pakistan. By December, when the elections came around, East Pakistan's Awami League won by a landslide, with more than twelve million votes. The future prime minister of Bangladesh, Sheikh Mujibur Rahman, was slated to be the next leader of Pakistan. Yet his rival, the Pakistan People's Party leader Zulfikar Ali Bhutto, refused to share power. Bhutto and Pakistan's President Yahya Khan feared rule by the "Hindu-like" Bengalis they despised, so they delayed the meeting of the National Assembly in Dhaka until March 1971.

Open rebellion erupted across East Pakistan. Students protested in the streets. They burned Pakistani flags. They stitched their own flag of Bangladesh, its colors the verdant paddies that the people labored, the blaze of a red sun rising high. They screamed: *Joy Bangla! Victory to Bengal!*

Riots broke out in the southern port city of Chittagong, between Bengalis and the Biharis, Urdu-speaking Muhajirs who'd migrated from India during Partition. They shared language with West Pakistanis, establishing trust and gaining them access to higher-paying jobs. Three hundred Bihari people were killed in that mob violence. Neighbors and friends, men, began attacking one another.

Each Partition deepened the wound, until it became a severing, permanently casting the East as the ancestral, rural, Bangla feminine, separate from the West, the modern, cosmopolitan Indian masculine. East Bengal came to represent the poetic past of all Bengalis, whereas West Bengal held the future. In every upheaval in East Bengal, whenever Hindus departed for India, a country where they would become refugees, they ate the soil to make *desh* a part of their bodies. *Mati* held the scent of their motherland, Purba Bengal, East Bengal, ancestral Bengal. When they tasted *mati* for the last time, they absorbed the essence of *desh,* a sacred, desperate act of holding on to motherland. They knew they might never return home again, so they settled for the memory of the earth, the rain-wetted dirt taste of *mati* on their tongues.

Our mother tongue, our saris, the *teep* on our foreheads, our *shyamla* and *kalo* skin, the music and poetry of Rabindranath Tagore or Nazrul Islam were seen by West Pakistan as impure, *napak*. Everything about Bengali culture made East Pakistanis un-Islamic, infidels, lazy, dark-skinned, and inferior — too Hindu. Syncretic culture was not only *gunah,* sin, but an unspoken allegiance to the enemy of the state, India. Lovers, spouses, artists, queers, colleagues, fellow students, and family friends, who lived between East and West Pakistan, who felt unified and moved by each other's art, music, language, and culture, would mourn the loss long afterward.

ARCHIVES

The record of the Liberation War of 1971 is immortalized in an archive of black-and-white photographs. That is how I first learned to see what happened to our people. Photographs of women freedom fighters, students, guerillas, holding rifles, hair braided, wearing classic *taant* saris, fierce, ready to fight for mother language, motherland. Photographs of slaughtered bodies, dismembered, frozen in pain, in gutters, ditches, mass graves of the massacred. Photographs of Sheikh Mujib speaking to a crowd of hundreds of thousands of people, a foreshadowing of him as the first prime minister of Bangladesh; of him releasing doves into the sky. Photographs of August 15, 1975. Celebrations of Independence Day for India and Pakistan, in Bangladesh, the death anniversary of Sheikh Mujib, a single photograph of him shotgunned to death, martyred in the early morning, along with most of his family. He appears asleep, still in his plaid *lungi,* just like my father wears to bed, black nebulae of blood on the fabric, eyes closed — betrayed in the end by his own men. His killers believed they had saved the country from a dictatorship.

Photograph of a rape survivor, a *birangona,* her hands are clutched like a heart, hidden by a veil of her long black hair.

I met the poet Tarfia Faizullah after I read an interview with her in the *Paris Review* in 2014, the year I founded my first perfume brand. She is the first Bangla woman I've found on the Internet who went on to become a best friend. That first day, we spent hours typing away on chat, both of us enamored by our instant bond. In 2010, Tarfia conducted interviews with *birangona* who survived harrowing and inhumane brutality and rape by Pakistani soldiers during the war. These interviews became the basis for her poetry collection, *Seam,* one of the first works I read about our people by a person of Bangladeshi descent, published by Southern Illinois University Press in Carbondale, the same town where I was born.

I read her poems while traveling in Bangladesh, seeing through her exacting details a sensorium of Bangladesh, a motherland we know as soon as we arrive. *Stitch-thin rickshawallah. Woman stepping lightly across green field into a green pond.* Tarfia's reckoning with these women's remembrances and the death of her own young sister became the first time that I held quiet, mournful space in my heart for the horror the *birangona* endured and survived. Their stories were never the narratives discussed in our parents' dinnertime conversations. In English, and in Bangla fragments, *Seam* taught me a new version of our origin stories. Tarfia and I met in real life soon after, in Brooklyn, where she was born. We sipped *cha,* smoked cigs, and painted our nails blue in my apartment. After holding space for our people's pain, for our own, these little pleasures felt so good.

○

> Shankhari Patti, a street in the old town, where the conch-shell craftsmen lived, was closed at both ends. Everyone was ordered to leave the houses. Hindus were separated from Muslims. And the Muslims were ordered to return to their houses. The Hindus were then machine-gunned to death.
>
> — *The Events in East Pakistan, 1971,*
> a Legal Study by the Secretariat of the International
> Commission of Jurists, Geneva, 1972

My last trip to Bangladesh came soon after that meeting with Tarfia. This would be the last time I saw my Nanu. I visited Dhakeshwari *mandir* — said to be named after the goddess of Dhaka — a Hindu temple in Old Dhaka. Dhakeshwari became the most important house of Hindu worship in Bangladesh after the destruction of the Kali temple by the Pakistan Army.

Anyone was allowed inside this open-air temple, and we left our shoes by the gate, paying a few *taka* to keep them safe. Four weddings were underway at the same time, separate huddles of families circled around *havan* fire, brides and grooms adorned in rose and carnation *malas,* receiving the incantations of the priest. Thousands of sticks of incense burned at the edge of the temple, and we gravitated toward the scent. A lone, elderly woman in a pink *taant* sari sat on the steps, curled into herself in prayer, rocking back and forth. My sisters and I lit sticks of incense, in silent prayer inside this sanctuary we — raised Muslims — felt as ours. Outside the temple gates, I bought a few *shankha* and *pola,* plastic bangles made to look like white conch shell and red coral — just as all the brides we'd seen had worn. Bracelets as an embodiment of the Matrika, the seven Indigenous Mother goddesses, inspired by the dark-skinned femmes who spoke foreign tongues and lived at the edges of the Brahmin imagination, swallowed into orthodox Hindu tradition. I was not yet married then. I wanted to have a piece of Old Dhaka with me, the peace of the unions and worship on the grounds where there had been so much bloodshed.

BLOOD

On the night of March 25, 1971, US Consul General Archer Blood heard the machine-gunfire from the rooftop of his Dhaka residence. Tracer bullets turned the sky magenta as the watermelons in season, fires burned orange, the university and Hindu neighborhoods in the city reddened by fresh blood. He sent the infamous Blood telegram, condemning the horrific acts of the Pakistan Army against Bengali people. The Pakistan Army had unleashed a massacre at Dhaka University and its surrounding neighborhoods. They rounded up and shot professors with machine guns. They massacred students at the forefront of protests. They destroyed Jagannath Hall, the Hindu dorm on campus.

Convinced that West Pakistan would win the war, Richard Nixon and Henry Kissinger ignored his message. They even deployed the USS *Enterprise*, a nuclear aircraft carrier, into the Bay of Bengal. They never believed that Bangladesh would become a reality. They were wrong.

I sit with the truth that the United States, this country of my birth, threatened nuclear warfare, opposed my people's Liberation. The Bangla Muslim part of me merged with the part of me that held Black art, beauty, feminism, movement, dance, freedom struggle, and consciousness as my blueprint for being. There was a sadness I felt as a youth at times, feeling shunned, alienated from the Black-white experience because of my embodiment. But I knew early on where I stood, whose struggle I wanted to fight for. I rejected the numbness and societal protection and lack of empathy that whiteness affords. This comes at too great a cost: hating myself. After a lifetime of absorbing the histories of this land — with endless gaps in knowledge — I know for me to imagine our collective future, to know true solidarity, I must reckon with my people's pasts.

From that first night of terror, over the next nine months, the Pakistani Army attacked village after village, aided by Al-Badr and Al-Shams, the paramilitary groups of Bengali and Bihari Muslim collaborators who believed in a unified Pakistan, men who are still referred to as *rajakars,* traitors. The Mukti Bahini, freedom fighters, were composed of military men who'd defected to form the Bangladesh Armed Forces, as well as young guerillas, who trained with the Indian Army in camps all along border towns between India and Bangladesh.

Between March and December of 1971, these men raped, tortured, looted, killed, and terrorized noncombatants on the land known as East Bengal, East Pakistan, and, ultimately, Bangladesh. The Mukti Bahini, the Bengali Liberation militia, and the soldiers in the Indian Army — the liberators and winners in history — are not absolved of these crimes. They, too, stole property, attacked, and killed innocent people, especially vulnerable minorities. No one was spared.

Women, children, the elderly, the disabled, queer and hijra femmes — from Bengali, Muslim, Hindu, Bihari, or Jumma Indigenous communities — were annihilated in the name of Nation; by calling the land their Mother, men absolved themselves from the fresh blood they spilled. Women were attacked by military men or trusted neighbors, colleagues, and friends. Young men were raped, too, but their stories never became public. Private admissions to interviewers from men who bore witness.

Bengali women survivors would be the only ones named, collectively: *birangona.* A brave, tenderhearted woman, a war heroine, a term the rape survivors never named themselves.

BIRANGONA

As a birangona neither can you wear it, nor can you take it off.

— Moyna, in *Ami Birangona Bolchi*, 1994, a book by
Nilima Ibrahim, based on the lives of seven Hindu and
Muslim *birangona* that Ibrahim met at rehabilitation
centers after the war. Moyna is a pseudonym.

Whereas historical events and male political actors who led the call for war are immortalized on the Record, the Bangladeshi archive of the *birangona* — rehabilitation center intake forms, counselor notes, mental hospital evaluations, job applications — is sparse. Even as there are films, novels, and art devoted to *birangona,* many of the actual records of the women's experiences in the war have been destroyed, lost in fires, eroded in boxes, and when they are discovered by a curious researcher who wants to tell the story of South Asia from the survivors' point of view, the notes are all written in pencil. Impermanent. Easy to erase. Most documented narratives of the *birangona* are anonymous, or they are named by pseudonyms, to protect their privacy and safety from more violence. Archiving the lost stories of the *birangona,* undertaken by artists, academics, and activists who preserve their memories, includes sensory details, though that isn't often their focus. I read the text for *vasanas* to build a sensorium of this history that I've inherited. Pieces of poetry, plays, films, and interviews with women whom I will never meet myself become the precious threads of a loom — a tantra — of their memories and stories of survival.

It is Eid today. We have not made any arrangements at home. No one has bought any new clothes. The curtains have not been washed. Cobwebs have not been dusted. No vial of attar rests on the table. Sharif, Jami have not gone to perform Eid prayers. But still I woke up early today and cooked *jorda* and *shemai*. Just in case some of Rumi's fellow freedom fighters come to visit. In case some guerilla fighter comes in the dark of the night, separated from his parents and siblings. To feed them, I have cooked *polao korma, kofta kabab*. I will serve them food with my own hands, should any of them show up. Even a bottle of attar awaits them, stowed away, to make their clothes fragrant with scent.

— from the diary of Jahanara Imam, November 20, 1971,
a little more than a year after the Bhola cyclone. Her son
Rumi was killed as a freedom fighter in the Mukti Bahini.

We did not know what we would find there. We did know the need. I would bring my old cotton saris and rip them to pieces. I could not offer them a whole sari, but I would wrap the pieces around them to cover their bodies as we took them out.

— activist and author Maleka Khan, in an interview with
Poulomi Saha, author of *An Empire of Touch*

During the war, women, young and old, Muslim, Hindu, Bihari, Buddhist, Christian, were raped in their homes — homes they would live in after the violation — some were raped in front of their family members. Some were abducted and taken off to Pakistani military cantonments. They were stripped naked of their saris, hair shorn so that they couldn't hang themselves with their own braids, as many women had. They witnessed each other being humiliated and tortured. Unborn babies cut out of wombs, heads bashed with brick and fist. They smelled the putrescence of infected wounds, the dead bodies of women who succumbed to beating.

When Maleka Khan found the women in the cantonments, she held their naked bodies in the embrace of a textile, the scrap of her sari soft as her touch, stirring the maternal muscle memory of once draping themselves in a *taant* sari. Sari, worn soft by the oils of another woman's sweat and skin, returned them to femininity, modesty, a wild relief after months naked and filthy in a living nightmare.

For the rest of their lives, simple, familiar things from the time before, like the taste of guava or hot rice, the scent of monsoon rain or fried eggs, the act of slicing fish or tying a sari, became daily triggers. Scents pulled them back to that moment when they felt the hot barrel of a rifle against their breast, where a burning heat would flare in that very spot forever. The moment they were knocked unconscious and awakened to the liquored breath of a man they'd known as a kind neighbor.

Trauma turns what we love against us.

Ma's nickname for Baj—Biru—shares the same root as *bi-rangona,* a portmanteau of the Sanskrit *vir* and *angana,* pronounced *bir* and *ongana,* in Bengali. *Bir* is hero; *ongana* is a beautiful woman. *Angana* can also mean an impurity of the mind, an empty space—again, we see how Sanskrit words hold multitudinous, discordant meanings. Nilima Ibrahim, the author of the book *Ami Birangona Bolchi, I Am Birangona Speaking,* said that Indian Prime Minister Indira Gandhi suggested the word *birangona* to Sheikh Mujib, inspired by a definition used in the literature, a brave, tenderhearted woman. Unfortunately, none of these powerful heads of State thought about the implications of this naming, the word *birangona* sounded so close to another word, *barangona*—prostitute.

Bara, as in outside, or in slang, penis—a woman who loves to be outside, a woman who loves the penis. Their euphemism made the rape survivor a hero, an erotic, beautiful woman; they mythologized her suffering to turn her into a national symbol. Naming survivors was a radical act, but what did it mean for these women, without reparations or mental health care? What use is being called a hero if you never feel held and loved? Even after being named as women to cherish and honor, as war heroines, this couldn't protect them from toxic gossip in their village communities, domestic violence, lack of job opportunities, from being seen as traitors, sexually promiscuous gold-diggers.

Birangona and *barangona,* both words for women who could be discarded, for they threatened masculine sexual prowess, pride, and power. One word named them a hero, within the breath of a vowel, another word named them a whore. *Birangona* became rendered as symbols in art and literature — illiterate, poor, madwoman, traitor, temptress. Sometimes, even within the same language, words betray us like a false friend.

Moyna took the cooked rice off the fire, pointed to the embers and said: "The fire that was there in that body had been put out, though the flames stayed under the ashes. That fire has been fanned, and now it has become a blaze whereby the whole village can see the forest fire from afar though they can't see the tears that burn inside me. I feel a burning sensation inside when I remember myself running, kicking, and struggling." She said anxiously, *Sometimes I feel like setting fire to my body's stories — how will I do it?*

— Nayanika Mookherjee in conversation with a *birangona* from her village in Enayetpur. Moyna is a pseudonym.

Fire, cyclone, flood are the *vasanas* imprinted in their bodies, reflecting the chaos they feel in their mind. Flood and cyclone, the equivalent of mass death. Fire, like a Hindu widow's *sati*, when a woman is burned to death on her husband's pyre. Was it ever a choice if your own family wanted you to die? *I am a corpse, I am sinner, I am spoiled, I am the loser of the world, I am broken,* they lament, as though they're the ones guilty of committing *gunah*. Words like *the violation, the story, the job* are used, but never the word *rape* — ধর্ষণ — *dhorshon*. When you utter the word *rape* in Bangla, your tongue pushes through your teeth. Though spelled differently, the word sounds similar to দর্শন — *darshan* — the sacred sighting of a deity, in a way, experiencing sexual violation imparts in us a survivor sight, one that warns us, protects us, teaches us new, tender ways of seeing.

Writing is an act of recording the silent specter of trauma within us, as a serpent crawls on its belly, close to the earth, tracking the sensorium it can hardly see or hear, its tongue its only guide, as language cannot undo genocide or enslavement, language, often fragmentary, reaches to bring the survivor, the descendant back to a stolen body. When I have created perfumes with survivors of domestic violence and incarceration, we discuss the *vasanas* of their life before and after their experiences of violence. Each fragrance is a composition of the scent memories amassed throughout their lifetime, notes from their childhood, of solace, of yearning. Only a thin boundary separates the scents of trauma and pleasure. When we work together to build a fragrance, I ask them to think of this act as a metaphor for their freedom. *Once you release a scent trapped inside a vessel onto your skin, into the air,* I tell them, *you are no longer the only one who has to hold this pain.*

The impure — *napak* — specter of the raped woman haunted the pure — *pak* — emergence of the nation. Pregnant women received expedited emergency abortions; the State had no intention of making room for children considered bastards. Being a modern Muslim nation meant women safely accessed birth control and abortion. Some women gave birth. They held their babies for a few moments, then gave them up for adoption by families in Europe or Australia. The State created a failed program promising men payment if they chose to marry *birangona*, as if this were a charitable act, even though in most cases, unsavory men with bad intentions married for the money and then abandoned the women after they received the funds. Some women were married off to first cousins, and some found acceptance and love from husbands, going on to raise families.

Some middle-class Hindu women, disowned by their families because they'd lost their caste, crossed the border into India. Some Muslim women left for Pakistan, perhaps choosing to marry soldiers, knowing they might be abandoned once they arrived. They knew they might have to become sex workers, thousands of miles away from home. Exile a better option than being eternally ostracized or, worse yet, causing unbearable shame to their parents. This common fear — that the men in our families will get sick or die or kill themselves if they know that their wives, daughters, or sisters have been raped — is something I've heard from many South Asian friends. We are taught to protect men from the harm they cause, as well as the harm caused by other men.

Some women committed suicide. What was Liberation if they would never feel free?

They started rubbing Vicks on my private parts, which you know, can be dangerous. They couldn't find soap, and they started cursing and swearing. These men were officers of the Pakistan Army, mostly captains. The others below the rank of captain were worse. There was an officer among them who helped me after the gang rape. His name was Altaf Kareem.

> — Ferdousi Priyabhashini, renowned sculptor and *biran-gona,* excerpts from a conversation with Yasmin Saikia

Ferdousi Priyabhashini faced belittlement and abuse from her community, including her own family, prolonging her trauma for years afterward. As a child she witnessed the constant beatings her father inflicted on her mother, and looming poverty plagued her own marriage — she knew rape culture long before and beyond the war. She demanded war tribunals for *rajakars* who'd raped and procured women like herself for the Pakistan Army. And yet, in an interview, she made the rare admission: she fell in love with a Pakistani officer who offered her protection, Altaf Kareem. She spoke poignant truth about life after the rape being just as bad, if not worse, because of the constant mental agony inflicted by others. Love of *desh* forbids loving the enemy, and her story disturbs the collective memory of the *birangona* as women without their own dreams and complex desires.

Her aesthetic was classic Bangla feminist-artist, moon-faced, kajal-eyed, red, round bindi between her brows. In an interview she said, *Everything I've used has been borrowed from nature, from my surroundings — a dead branch from a tree, a piece of tin from an old house, a discarded object lying around. I try not to cut away at the wood or change the materials I work with. The smallest object can be full of meaning.*

Survivor stories inhabit the silences in history. All the pain that has been erased. Their stories are considered the degraded material in the nation's archive, recorded in pencil, but in these memories, we uncover the evidence of grave violence unleashed on women, trans and queer people, as men fashioned the patramyth of Nation to protect themselves. Nation made it so that we attach ourselves to a race, an identity, or a people, at the cost of losing our interdependence with nature, our humanity, and ourselves. The silence that inhabits the survivor is not a void. It is in this absence of language that the body begins to repair itself from damage. As a writer, the task of undoing patramyths means listening to this silence. It means we must imagine a new language to name what has been endured. Perfume is a body language, one which reconstructs silence into sensuous experience, a new memory of pleasure that had been stripped away. Perfume floods the prisoner of war, the enslaved, the victim in the reviving spirits of pleasure.

When I remember, my being shatters. What have I lost, what have I gained. *I don't like this.* That Mozhair should've been caught. People should've seen how evil that bastard was. I've lost it all, he made me a widow, I lost my *sindoor.* Tie his hands behind him. Shoot him in front of me. Can you do it? If I don't witness this, the burning within will never cease. He was a killer. He killed my children in front of me. What else?

— survivor Gurudashi Mondal to filmmaker Yasmine Kabir in the 2005 documentary *A Certain Liberation*

After a young Hindu woman, Gurudashi Mondal, witnessed the murder of her husband and children — including her nursing infant — by *rajakars,* she was kidnapped and kept in sexual bondage until neighbors finally were able to save her life. Her mind and heart were shattered after the experience. Her friends took her to the only mental health institution in Pabna, my father's hometown, but she escaped so many times that she was released. In the first few minutes of the documentary *A Certain Liberation,* we witness her yelling at men, swinging her *lathi,* a long bamboo rod, at their asses. She loves all of the young children, she even nurses infants whose mothers can't. Most of her teeth have fallen out, stained red with *paan* residue, but her smile is sweet, mischievous. One of her close friends, a Muslim woman, notes how her family stopped eating meat so Gurudashi could eat her vegetarian meals with them. *Call me Ma,* Gurudashi says, weeping, *or I'll kill myself.* She worships at the Kali temple, lays down blood-red hibiscus blooms as offerings to the goddess. She wants to be buried not cremated, so that people can leave gifts and prayers upon her grave. Losing her identity as a wife and mother, losing the red vermilion mark on her forehead, stole her desire to live. The unhealable wound of the war. I wept witnessing Gurudashi's visceral pain, sensing her despair and madness as an intricate performance to survive the unimaginable. I wept for the deep love and ease these women in Khulna knew between themselves, how Hindu and Muslim were not fixed, masculine, separate identities but fluid, feminine, and shared.

During a rally for Prime Minister Sheikh Hasina, daughter of the slain Sheikh Mujib, Gurudashi is forbidden entry, unrecognized by the State as a *birangona*. A local newspaper printed a photograph of her crying, locked behind a gate, with a few of the details of her story — but not the details of what she endured in captivity. Her world ended as soon as her captors murdered her family. She never says more. The State's word *birangona* acknowledges that women were raped — by the Pakistani Army and *rajakars* — but the women become a mythic anonymous. Did a woman's madness without public admission of rape make her a more authentic survivor? The hushed secret of Gurudashi's history acknowledged that she suffered, but without the naming and subsequent shaming that so many *birangona* faced in their villages. Gurudashi is tenderly protected and accepted as a Mother to all, Mother of Bengal, a woman utterly *swadhin* — free — to say and do whatever she pleases. Men cannot harm or control her. And yet, her village cremated her body after her death, despite her wishes — no doubt the men decided cremation was the only acceptable rite for a born Hindu — they scattered her ashes into the river. *Liberation.*

I stare at the great bamboo tree at my parents' house, a backdrop of a man-made pond, the Florida swamp water hides alligators and snakes in the murk. Ma has shorn this bamboo of the wild foliage that grew at its base. Hacking away all the green that attracts snakes to hide. Her fear of snakes is shared among most humans, an evolutionary ancestral memory of their venom. Some snakes play dead in the face of danger, rolling on their backs, mouths open, tongues out. Some snakes may even give off a rancid stench to deter predators. But what we humans fear is the strike of death, even knowing they are more afraid of us than we are afraid of them. What protects them kills us. How far will each of us go to protect ourselves?

There are things not to be spoken about, they are not describable. Don't ask me about those days, my blood begins to boil. Don't ask me about my daughter. There was a river of blood and slaughtered heads of people were strewn all over. My sons and brothers were killed in front of me; I saw them with my own eyes. I don't want to talk about these things.

— Nurjahan, a Bihari woman refugee in Camp Geneva,
in a conversation with Yasmin Saikia

STRANDED PAKISTANIS RELIEF CAMPS reads the sign at one of the camps where 300,000 Urdu-speaking Bihari people live as permanent refugees in Bangladesh. They have been abandoned by Pakistan and are still considered traitors in Bangladesh. Generations of children have been born in the absolute squalor of the camps, which are prone to flooding and overflowing toilets that are shared by thousands of people. In photographs of suffocating dwellings, eight-by-eight-foot homes separated by only a couple of feet, whole families are crammed between walls mold-dappled, painted mint green.

The Bihari are stateless, ineligible for citizenship. Despite a law that grants citizenship to children who were young during the war or born afterward — often who rightfully consider themselves Bangladeshi — when they apply for papers, they often face bitter rage, distrust, and discrimination by Bengalis. Among the dwellers in the camp are women survivors of rape by Bengali men, in the name of revenge. Beloved to one man, Enemy to another, so any feminine or vulnerable body can be destroyed — in the name of *desh*.

Ma and I are asked to donate money for medical supplies that will be distributed by a Bangladeshi health care organization. We learned that one of the Bihari camps would receive funds, provoking a reaction in my mother. *Why are they still flying the flag of Pakistan in the camps, when they'll never go back there? Why won't they accept Bangladesh? Then Bangladesh will accept them.* I know that not having lived through the war offers me an empathy for people considered the betrayers. This empathy for the enemy — even though many of the women and children in the camps did not inflict violence — is hard for survivors to feel. Even all these years later, they feel bitterness. The memory of venom. I don't know the answers to her questions. So I ask her, *Do you think that All — h would want us to help people, so that healing is possible, so that people no longer suffer?*

PATRAMYTHS

On December 14, 1971, Bengali intellectuals were abducted from their homes, killed, their bodies ditched in mass graves. The massacre of *buddhijibi* — those who live a life of thought — included artists, professors, doctors, scientists, journalists. I am shaken by the cruelty of inducing a nation's stillbirth. There are a few women's names I come across — Selina Parvin was a poet and journalist — killed by two bayonet wounds, one to the eye, one to the stomach, and two bullet wounds. These people were murdered by the Pakistani military and Al-Badr, pro-Pakistani Bengali men. Liberation's light extinguished at the eleventh hour. Everywhere, everywhere: the stench of rotting corpses and blood.

Two days later, Victory Day, at an unfathomable cost. The iconic moment captured in a photograph of two Punjabi men: one, a Pakistani, General Amir Niazi, in a beret, surrendering to the other, an Indian, Lieutenant General Jagjit Singh Arora, in a turban. They settled the scores between India and Pakistan over a newborn Bangladesh. There has never been admission of the looting committed by Indian soldiers. They stole radios, watches, televisions, as if Bangladesh were a new colony. So often, the Liberation War is called the Indo-Pak War of 1971, a battle of masculine and powerful states, a patramyth that erases Bangladeshis, as if they had nothing to do with their own freedom.

RANGAMATI

On a night bus to southern Bangladesh, my sister and I grimaced at our unspoken fear of being two femmes surrounded by men. We were traveling with an uncle, but we could not help but think of Jyoti Singh Pandey's fatal rape in Delhi, on December 16, 2012, how she, too, had been with a friend. Five years earlier, I'd lived in that harsh, gorgeous, and intense city, as an NGO volunteer in the middle-class Punjabi neighborhood Lajpat Nagar. At dusk, the bustling marketplace died down, only men and dogs roamed free, out and about. I'd hail a taxi or auto and ride the bus, often alone. Dark thoughts seeped into my half-dreams that night; we kept one eye open, flinching every time the bus driver swerved back and forth between lanes, honking the entire ride on the highway, a macabre chorale punctuated by blaring white high beams.

We reached the lush hinterland of Rangamati — *red earth* — capital city of the Chittagong Hill Tracts. We stayed at the government hostel, near the suspension bridge that led to Kap-tai Lake. Chakma women wove colorful lanyard bags all along the path. Rangamati is the largest district by land, and home to the Indigenous Jumma people, named after the word for slash-and-burn cultivation, *jhum*. After the creation of the state of Bangladesh, a new armed struggle arose. The Indigenous peo-ple's Shanti Bahini fought for autonomy against the Bengali Army and migrant settlers. For the Jumma, the coercion of the Bangladesh Army and Bengali settlers is indistinguishable from the Pakistan Army and armed Bihari and Bengali collaborators during 1971. The Chakma are the largest of the eleven Jumma peoples living in these hills, different from Bengali folk in their East Asian features, faith, language, and textiles. It's undeniable though, that our peoples have always mixed, the imprint of these encounters written in our faces.

Kaptai Lake is known as the Pahari people's tears, our uncle told us during our languid ride on the man-made lake, which displaced hundreds and thousands of Chakma, drowned their palace, forced them to live high in the hills, where the land is not as arable. Water hyacinth islands covered the surface, an invasive species that deprives the lake's flora and fauna of sun-light. Bright textiles swayed like flags on the hills. I asked our boatman to dock. We walked up stairs carved into the hillside, entering a village. We heard a Chakma woman call to us. *Asho, bhai, bon, asho. Come, brother and sisters, come.*

Her name was Puspumaya. Slim as bamboo, weathered as bark, a cigarette dangled out of her mouth. She gestured that we come inside to see more of the textiles like the freshly dyed shawls that hung from a clothesline. Latticed palm leaves woven into her little blue hut. Spare, joyous details everywhere — a Buddhist altar of candles and flowers, a tiny television, a world map — and we sat in plastic lawn chairs. Puspumaya offered us tea, along with a tray of cookies and cigarettes. We spoke in Bangla, not her mother tongue, both of us stilted in a language we felt less like ourselves in, we were minorities in the countries we'd been born. Our people had colonized her people's land, ever since she was a girl, but still she showed us warmth. We smoked and sipped our tea, chose a few of her woven pieces — black, white, color-blocked shawls. The smoke, incense, textiles, and tea — everything that made a home feel true. The way I decorated my own home in Brooklyn.

We lived where the lake is, until I was five, Puspumaya told us, exhaling a smoke ring up to the ceiling. *There used to be tigers, snakes, elephants, lots of animals.* She shook her head wistfully. *Nowadays, there are only humans.*

In 1997, the Shanti Bahini signed a peace accord with the Bangladeshi government, but the abductions, disappearances, rapes, and murders of young Jumma women by the Bengali settlers and the army have continued. In 2018, the Chakma queen Rani Yan was attacked at Rangamati Sadar Hospital, when she stood in solidarity with two young Marma women who had been sexually assaulted by Bengali men. Most women remain unnamed, unknown. Say their names: *Kalpana Chakma, Sabita Chakma, Sang Khai Marma, Sangnu Marma.*

INSANIYAT, OR HUMANITY

On the opposite side of the room, is a map of the subcontinent in black stone. The borders of what was Pakistan, East and West, are lined in silver. Our cities are marked with small turquoise pins: Larkana, Karachi, Quetta, Dacca and Chittagong. But India itself is dark. Its periphery does not shine with metal; its cities are not remembered with gemstones. The map bears no remembrance to the partition of Pakistan, no snuffing out of its Eastern parts, that would come later. Just like we broke India, so too would Bangladesh break us.

— Fatima Bhutto, "My Grandfather's Library,
Relic of a Freer Pakistan," in Literary Hub

Throughout my life, among Indian and Pakistani friends and acquaintances, I have mostly found either total ignorance or silent shame about this war. Those who've read and learned the history share the same sense of haunting that I've felt. Whereas the Pakistan Army's atrocities are preserved in Bangladeshi memory, in museums and thousands of books and works of art, the Liberation War is near-absent from Pakistan's collective memory, written off as a bitter loss of a unified Pakistan.

In her essay about her grandfather Zulfikar Ali Bhutto's library, the novelist Fatima Bhutto unwittingly reveals a dominant patramyth that lives on in Pakistan. *So too would Bangladesh break us.* Her grandfather's library holds syncretic texts that any writer would dream of getting lost inside: books on tantra, Simone de Beauvoir, World War II, Lenin, and thousands of his letters, directives, and musings about the state of affairs in Pakistan. There are figures of Buddha in every room. Buried in this treasure of ancient and modern texts, there is no record of a military laying waste to poorer, darker, lower-caste people in East Pakistan, people who labored to make the West more abundant. Freedom will never be found in that library.

In 1979, five years after Sheikh Mujibur Rahman's assassination, Zulfikar Ali Bhutto, the man who refused to let Rahman ascend as leader of Pakistan, would himself be hanged to death — murdered by the military. He'd persecuted ethnic minorities in Pakistan, the Ahmadi and Baloch people. Zulfikar Ali Bhutto chose his own power — as short-lived and fraught as this would be — forsaking the lives of young, poor, illiterate, and rural Pakistani soldiers who'd be left haunted by the violence they inflicted on innocent people. After surrender, these soldiers would become prisoners of war in India, held in camps for two years. Two hard years to reflect and regret what they'd done. Since then, a few of the soldiers have found All — h and want to atone for their *gunah,* the sin of harming women, for killing people who simply loved their land and language. They have had to face their own loss of انسانیت — *insaniyat* — humanity. In Urdu, there is no word for rape, there are ways around it: to humiliate, to disrespect, to harm. I wonder, then, if a true apology or admission of rape is possible, if the act cannot be named in the perpetrator's tongue?

Survivors of rape, the women and femmes upon whose bodies the war for *desh* was waged, Bengali, *birangona,* Bihari, or Chakma, like Puspumaya, are the ones who have been landless, stateless, left without *desh.* Even named *birangona,* by and large, they have not been cherished, loved, healed, and heard in their truth — the women themselves have been forced to hold it inside. There is much to learn when we unravel silence. They are the living archive of the land. They have been hurt in the worst way, in the name of the most violent patramyth: that woman, nation, and *desh* are versions of the same essence, bound not only to each other, but to the honor of men.

MADE IN BANGLADESH

When I'm in Bangladesh, my family and I will take a shopping trip to Aarong, a lifestyle retailer of all Bangladeshi-made textiles and artisanal goods. We stock up on *nakshi katha* rugs and pillow covers and curtains, hand-loomed saris and terra-cotta *mati* potteries, nose rings, all manner of motherland talismans, a memory until the next visit. Building Resources Across Communities, the prolific, now-worldwide nonprofit, more commonly known as BRAC, was founded by Sir Fazle Hasan Abed after the war in 1972, with the goal to set up small-scale relief projects for refugees. In 1978, Ayesha Abed, wife of Sir Fazle, established Aarong, a marketplace devoted to Bengali handicrafts, a few years before her death during childbirth. They sourced goods made by women's collectives composed of survivors of sexual violence. In rehabilitation centers, *birangona* learned sewing and traditional embroidery, *nakshi katha,* the same techniques Nanu used to upcycle her old saris into *kantha* quilts. They threaded their own familial practices into the textiles, their art a meditation, a distraction from pain, embedded with traces of sweat, blood pearled on a needle-pricked finger, tears interwoven into a new country's healing. Some would never be accepted by their families, could never return home, even as they made wares to adorn everyday life for their people. Holding these textiles lets us feel their touch, a place beyond language, where survivors sutured together a nation as raw as stitched skin.

Around 2 a.m., I found a couple embracing each other in the rubble. The lower parts of their bodies were buried under the concrete. The blood from the eyes of the man ran like a tear. When I saw the couple, I couldn't believe it. I felt like I knew them — they felt very close to me. I looked at who they were in their last moments as they stood together and tried to save each other — to save their beloved lives.

— Taslima Akhter, "A Final Embrace: The Most Haunting Photograph from Bangladesh," *Time*

The tag *Made in Bangladesh* beckons us to remember the tragic human cost of a country fashioning its global exports economy by exploiting vulnerable labor. Taslima Akhter's photograph of a couple found dead in the rubble, holding each other in a heartbreaking last embrace, is the tragic, iconic image of the Rana Plaza factory collapse on April 24, 2013. The collapse claimed the lives of 1,134 Bangladeshi garment workers, and 2,500 were injured, in the deadliest garment industry disaster in history since the Triangle Shirtwaist Factory fire in New York City, which happened on March 25, 1911, sixty years before Bangladesh's Liberation. In that tragedy, immigrant women and children died from smoke inhalation, and many leapt to their deaths, trying to escape. Mass death, once more, in the name of modernity. Women, the shattered backbone of the global economy under capitalist exploitation.

Since Liberation, the Singer sewing machine became a powerful sumbol of women's independence and modernity. In villages, in cities, in my mother's first apartment in Illinois — the sewing machine offered a means to make a living and clothe one's own family. Bangladesh's economic growth and development have been measured by women's lives: their literacy and life expectancy, their reproductive health and production as laborers. Such numbers indicate that women's lives are less tenuous than in India or Pakistan, without accounting for the sexual violence that persists.

On that last trip to Bangladesh, my sister and I visited a garment factory in the Badda neighborhood of Dhaka. Workers dressed in brilliantly colored salwar kameez and saris — florals, polka dots, batik — stitching garments that neither they nor we would ever wear. On the ninth floor, men filmed a few workers spraying a hose mindlessly out of the window. They were filming a compliance video, our guide told us, to assure the retailer that adequate fire safety measures were in place, to prevent another tragedy like the Tazreen Fashions fire in 2012, where more than a hundred people were burned alive. There were no sprinklers in the factory. If there was a fire, that dinky hose would do nothing.

Fast fashion is a myth. The phrase is a classist condemnation of trendy clothes that low-income people can actually afford — the clothes I grew up wearing. Fast fashion erases the meticulous touch and humanity of the workers — mostly young women — who support their families. In the factory we visited in 2014, workers made 11,000 taka, which as of 2020 is $129 per month, at 11 hours a day — 42 cents an hour. For a single garment, there is the worker who runs a bolt of fabric through a machine to catch any irregularities or tears. There is the worker who cuts the pattern. The worker who hems the shirt's edge, lays down the pockets, the worker who pricks a shirt collar to make sure it's pointy. Our guide walks us through the labor behind a single sleeveless button-down shirt in a flamingo print, gifted to us at the end. "I feel proud when I see this," he says, smiling. "This is made in Bangladesh." We, too, were moved by how our people made these garments in order to better live.

I wear fast and slow fashion, high and low, new and old. After Rana Plaza, I found myself collecting vintage clothing and textiles, a connection to my people's pasts. A way to wrest back clothes worn by rich white women of yesterday, their Orientalist leisurewear, their cosmopolitan taste and world travels. When I wear flowing, psychedelic print kaftans and colorfully embroidered, mirrored dresses — *Made in India, Made in Pakistan* — I wear them because they look better worn by us, and now I can afford them. Ma never wanted me to wear vintage — to her, shopping at Goodwill signaled that we were poor, that we couldn't afford new clothes, even though some of these vintage pieces are still priced way beyond our means growing up. If the collar tag reads *Made in Pakistan,* and it is a *ghamsa* plaid or gingham or block print, I wonder whether it was made before 1971, in East Pakistan — I'll never know for sure. None of them will ever say *Made in Bangladesh.*

Ma's career shapeshifted once more, after she left banking forever to tend to my grandmother's cancer, twice. As a Bengali medical interpreter, she translates crucial information for Bangladeshi patients dealing with life and death: cancer, heart disease, diabetes, suicidal ideation, post-traumatic stress, injuries sustained while crossing the Mexican border, the violent separation of children from their parents. As an interpreter, she hears about young men from Bangladesh who fly into Mexico in order to migrate to the US. As climate change floods the landscape of Bangladesh's coastal communities, young men have been forced to find their livelihoods in other countries. They survive harsh conditions in jungles, deserts, mountains, just to reach a border for their chance. Bangladeshis are hyperlocal ghosts, perhaps a local outlet in Texas will report their existence, but in the news about the migrant caravan, Bangladeshis disappear. They survive violence on their route to the US, and when they speak to my mother, they've been worn down as far as a person can go without dying. They trust her voice in Bangla, a familiar feeling of home, against the stark coolness of a doctor's English. She feels connected to her people, a momentary comfort for new immigrants as she'd been forty years earlier.

আমি দুঃখিত. *I am sorry, sister.* They hang up the phone, they will never speak again. She will never know if they made it through.

The families of the victims of Rana Plaza quilted a *kantha* in memoriam for the loved ones they lost, stitching together layers of saris embedded with photographs of their dead. Nanu, too, sewed textiles with her hands, her *kantha* quilts made of old saris she didn't wear anymore, in colors like turquoise or bubblegum pink. I regret never quilting with my grandmother. I still don't have the patience or a sense of straightness for most needlework, I fail to thread a bobbin properly on a sewing machine, I can't do much more than sew a button back on. But I don't know if communal quilting interested my grandmother. What is left of Nanu is in my memory and material archive. The photographs she never wanted taken. The scent of *jorda* in her *paan* tin — she and I shared a penchant for the sweetness of tobacco to take the edge off — her *kanthas* were her works of art, the bright lines of her running stitches her meditative practice, a way to bind her memory into a textile, to still her mind, to momentarily forget her pain. When she died in May 2020, I draped myself in one of these blankets, one side a terra-cotta color like *mati,* the other side chartreuse. Color combinations I felt were off as a child, when I wanted to blend into this strange country she never got used to. Feeling the softness on my skin, I wished that I had gotten to see her, to ask her about the stories I've had to find on my own, in language that will always reach for her. When Nanu died, I hadn't seen her in nearly seven years. When I visit her again, her remnants will have returned to Earth. Ma asked her family to plant a *raat ki rani* tree near her plot, to let its sweet fragrance summon her mother's spirit. *Begum Jahanara,* queen of the night.

Mala — Perfume Interlude

HEAD
Saffron
Clary Sage

HEART
Turkish Rose
Turmeric Root
Carnation
Coriander
Cardamom
Henna Attar
Nag Champa Accord

BASE
Tobacco Absolute
Marigold Absolute
Choya Nakh
Sandalwood

She is enraptured by her own pain.

— Fariha Róisín, as we pass a joint between us

I left for New Delhi to escape New York, to escape the longing I felt for V, to escape a depression that had settled somewhere in me, so deep I couldn't extract it myself. Self-medicated
with weed, liquor, and sex, but nothing works when you can't
feel yourself, and that year, I unraveled, I walked around sup-
pressed and enraged in the same way I imagine millions of Indian people around me felt. I had never felt so riveted and so
alone in a city. Beauty and misery within steps through the market, the same place I bought my nag champa gold incense and
nose rings, a man with atrophied arms and legs tied up behind
his back lived on a makeshift skateboard. Shopkeepers took
care of him, I hoped; he lay as close to the ground as I'd ever
seen an adult, a little cup beside him to collect rupees. At night,
the market closed, and only dogs and security men with lathis
strode the dark grounds. I crossed the dead expanse to hail an
auto, to meet friends for drinks at a hotel, or to meet a lover I
knew I'd be leaving in less than a year.

When I returned to New York, I missed my old haunts and scents of the little Gold Leaf cigarettes I smoked, tea, spices, garlands of rose, carnation, and marigold dangling from the wedding shops, so I re-created that place in this perfume, Mala, as in a garland of flowers, beads, and stories, and in Spanish: a bad woman. I use a single drop of *scent of a loose woman* — choya nakh oil — to fix the perfume so that it lingers. Drops of turmeric are in the heart of this perfume, not enough to discern its smell. This is a secret *vasana,* embedded in this incense, the remnants of flowers and memories made to burn. Reborn as fragrant smoke.

Mala

Perfume as Transmutation

NOTES
Remnants of Flowers

Turmeric oil is a deep orange-yellow liquid with a blue fluorescence, like a candle flame. The plant is a cultigen, meaning it cannot be traced to a single ancestor or found in the wild. It cannot fruit on its own and is a hybrid of wild curcumas selected and cultivated by humans for thousands of years, older than its naming in the *Atharvaveda*. *Curcuma* comes from the Babylonian *Kur-kun-a,* or the Semitic *kurkum,* like the Sanskrit *kumkum,* for saffron, for the dark reddening of turmeric when it is mixed with lime, a paste for Kali, a substitute for saffron filaments plucked from crocus sativa flowers in the valleys of Kashmir, misnamed *safran des Indes* by the French, wrong as they were about Vietnam, where turmeric traces its origins, as the golden root shaped like swollen palms of the migrants and monks who traveled, passing these roots between each other, to heal wounds, the traveler's shits, and eventually it became Indian, its origin another patramyth. Named for its brilliant yellow hue, *holud, haldi, manjal,* yellow for the earth, for pre-Aryan, pre-Vedic rituals sealing marriage and death. Sanskrit texts name this plant by fifty names, names that disagree, names that require this root to be everything, names that fashion an impossible feminine, as unnatural as this root, a man-made hybrid fantasy — chaste, fair, fertile, fat-free, dark, beautiful as night, as the moon, as a perfume, holy, a harlot, a whore.

Now, turmeric is a trend. It is a health and wellness super ingredient, an all-purpose, anti-inflammatory, healing spice, touted by Ayurveda practitioners and influencers alike, used in everything from lattes to face serums. Shades of turmeric, curry, marigold, and mustard, the golden colors my mother always wanted me to wear, are everywhere. Curry is having *a moment*.

For me, this note is the longest score my body kept.

For years, the scent of curry felt thick with an association I'd rather forget. Besides when I ate my Ma's food, I'd never cook curry. I didn't really mess with home cooking, the shame itself felt like a damn shame, since curry is the note that defines home for our diaspora. Whenever I walked into my parents' house, I disassociated, always ready to go back to my own apartment in the city. Memory is fragmentary, fractured in its nature, triggered by everyday sense experiences in the middle of regular life.

Every single thing that I've ever tried to hide about myself is in the public discourse. We are reckoning with our bodies and our traumas, their thickness, their hairiness, their gender expressions, and their violations. There's relief, living through this opening of an aperture in a culture that no longer regards me as alien. Each utterance of *me too* is to acknowledge what happened. Massive anti-rape protests have erupted in Bangladesh in response to the rape and murder of a young girl by her boyfriend, the long shadow of the war, the hidden archive of the *birangona,* unleashed by collective rage.

I call him Savage, my name for him for whenever I've written about him in poems or plays; Savage, for his temperament and the brutish look in his eyes; Savage, for his obsession with me, my first brush with noxious, destructive, stalking, vampiric masculine desire. Savage appeared one day, after school, aggressively popping a Snapple cap right up to my ear, the kind that had some questionable trivia inside of it. I remember feeling thrilled by his attention. No one had ever expressed desire for me up to that point, my crushes all deep secret, unrequited, unresolved. I knew, as cynical as it seems to me now, that flexing my intelligence to answer the inane trivia on that cap, being the nerd I was, would make me less pretty. I just laughed.

Our relationship bloomed in secret. Our parents, mine Bangladeshi Muslims, his Indian, Malayalee Christians, would undoubtedly try to destroy our relationship, based on the grounds that our love was doomed. No teenager wants to concede the obvious to their parents. We cut class and snuck out to the movies, we hooked up under the stairwell at school, my house, his house, the park. We marked each other, with hickeys and bites, each ravenous encounter I later revived with my fingers. I became a punch line among him and his friends: *You better Bang-your-gal-eee, son!* It bothered me, but sexual objectification felt like being desired, which I had never felt before.

Sometimes, Savage wore my clothes, bending his slim body from masculine to feminine, an androgyny I found riveting —

it softened him, it made him more like me. He looked good when he wore my clothes. Femme, but like everything else, this gender play is our secret. I admitted to him that I would masturbate and think about women who looked like men, and he anointed me with the term *bi-curious*. It fit for a while, until *bisexual* defined me better, until later, in college, *queer* felt right. He had a temper that he flashed when he felt deprived of pleasure or my time; he was angry about his grades at school, his father's rage, and his future prospects. He had a plan, though, to get his citizenship and to get the fuck out of his parents' house: he'd join the Marines.

No matter how many candles we lit or air fresheners we sprayed at home, the sizzle of spices infused our skin, our hair. Savage slathered himself in cologne, Issey Miyake, rather impressive taste for our dream-dead suburbs. I spent money I made working at the mall on clothes, cigarettes, and a rotation of fruity Victoria's Secret body splashes: Love Spell, Pear Glacé, Enchanted Apple. Sometimes at night, my bedroom became a portal where the forbidden permeated the walls. As my parents slept, exhausted from their long days at work, he would show up after work or a football game, climbing up the shaky pine tree into my room. We were fervent, scared of being caught, sticky with evergreen sap and sweat. He left me by dawn. I lit a cigarette and exhaled menthol smoke out my window; soon, daylight would steal this freedom.

I started calling myself Indian, trying out an ethnicity that Americans actually recognized, unlike Bangladeshi. He gifted me a cross. I reveled in the power of wearing the cross — what was more American than a nice Christian girl? I wondered why we hadn't thought of this as our cover story during the Gulf War, but omitting our faith from the conversation was different than an outright conversion. It felt like a victimless lie, a minor adulteration of the truth. One day, Ma noticed the glint of infidel metal on my neck, immediately. *What are you wearing? Take that thing off. You're a Muslim!* Where I saw love, my mother saw *gunah*. I refused to play the part of a good girl, *bhalo meye;* the bad girl, *baje meye,* knew so much more about life, even if it came at a cost.

There is a scattering of visuals from that winter afternoon that shimmer in my mind. He squeezes my cheek, hard. Cinnamon gum on our breath. His cologne, a force field around me, masculine and bitter bergamot and sage, blue lotus aquatic dried down into the musk of our sweat. In the golden-hour light, in his bed, a painting of the Virgin Mary staring at me, the cool platinum cross pricking my tongue, Savage's eyes crossed with pleasure, oblivious to me. My — defeat. It was February. I was fourteen.

When my mother found out I'd been lying about everything, she flipped out, grounding me forever. I broke off the relationship. Distraught, Savage started using cocaine. One night, during one of his binges, he carved my name into his arm with a razor blade cauterized by candle fire. He'd faltered after the W, my name stopped short at the height of his pain. Sometimes, he'd stalk me, waiting for me down the block from my house, sitting in his car. He barely graduated and by summer's end he left for boot camp, ready to become a Marine. He would kill people and learn to survive them trying to kill him. By the end of his service, he would become an American citizen.

Around this time, I started stealing from other stores during shopping trips to the mall. At first, I slipped small items, like underwear, into my purse, eventually graduating to larger items like trench coats or shoes that I walked out wearing. My retail job reiterated the nothingness of things — all of the tags revealed origins in *Made in Mexico, Vietnam, Bangladesh.* I stole it back from the corporation that treated its workers like shit, I told myself. But mostly I wanted to know that I could get away with it. I wanted the thrill of committing a crime, getting away with it, bleeding the line within me that partitioned good from bad.

I didn't name what happened, not right away, but one night, months later, during a family road trip to Washington, DC, the realization settled on me like dusk. My sister and I were in a guest bedroom on sleeping bags, and I wept without sound.

Are you okay, Apu?

I — I think I was raped.

What do you mean? How do you know?

My sister was ten years old, too young to know what to say, her small voice heavy with worry.

In college, I started working with survivors of domestic violence in the Poughkeepsie Family Court, through the Battered Women's Services, a term I hated because it denied their agency and their dignity as survivors. I advocated for women during custody trials with their abusers, and wrote orders of protection for both survivors and perpetrators. Since then, I have documented and recorded the stories of survivors around the world, realizing that when people recall their trauma, scent is inextricable from the story. The scent of a torturer's perfume just before she electrified their genitals. The scent of clean laundry, cotton linens, a haven far, far away from a father's sexual abuse. The scent of fresh blood, after they witnessed the murder of a rapist.

In each of these stories, there is a *vasana* that recalls the violation of a boundary. Perfume disrupts the present moment, unearthing an unforgotten, unforgiven act, and new scents become a sanctuary, a place where a new memory forms.

Savage and I reunited after I graduated college and he returned home from Iraq. We ate Indian food cooked by Bangladeshis that afternoon, in Curry Hill, surrounded by Indian tech and finance bros, a comical juxtaposition to Savage's military regalia. His imperialist garb to recruit Black and brown high school students to possibly die in war disgusted me. We made it through the mediocre food and painful conversation, where he acknowledged what happened.

I had written him a one-line email: *Rape is too real.*

When it hit me, when I realized you were right, I was sitting at my base in Iraq, I realized what I had done to you. I swear, I almost took my rifle to myself that night. I'm sorry.

Back at the hotel, where we started kissing, first we lay on top of the covers, under them, undressed, without skipping a beat. A beast, reawakened. The hotel felt familiar like in high school, when we would skip school to day party at the Ramada Inn. The past dissolved into this present, the room smelled stale, our breath tinged with curry, he slipped inside of me, my body betrayed my mind, I started cumming uncontrollably, orgasmically, my cunt riveted by pleasure I did not want to feel. I still hated him. I hated myself. I had not been restored by justice, his confession made me feel electrified by sorrow. *I still love you, I'm so sorry. I still love you.* I did not say the words back. We passed out. I woke up a couple of hours later. I had a million text messages from my best friend Ngozi, she had been worried sick that something had happened to me. I had no words. I showered him off me, sitting in the tub, hot water and tears poured over and out of me. I still hated myself. I left him there, a beast asleep.

We never spoke again.

To survive is to slowly recollect your senses, after having been estranged from your body, we lose sight of ourselves, we lose our appetite or seem to never feel full enough; we cannot bear the sound of certain voices or tones; we cannot be touched, or we fuck strangers with desperate abandon. I neither forgave nor forgot after our confrontation. Both outcomes were too unsatisfying, forgiving and forgetting is a concept that buries the harm perpetrators have caused. I chose confrontation, a messy encounter, a severance — the final word. No survivor is required to forgive their abuser. Some people reject this word — *survivor* — to describe their experience. We spend our lives seeking solace, and through the retelling of our trauma we make space for others, each utterance deepens our compassion for those who, too, have survived. Since Savage, I have been scratched, licked, fingered, punched, slapped, dick-smacked, straddled, fondled, and flashed without my consent. It did not matter if I felt sophisticated and strong, or naïve and weak — violation happened. A line crossed within seconds. Which is harder — trying to forget assault and degradation, or disentangling an endless spool of shame?

My confrontation with Savage was the corridor between trauma and survivorship, influencing my decisions with men from the diaspora. I would date Indian and Bangladeshi men after Savage, and just like with him, I remained their secret, their shame as strong as their desire for me. I would never meet their parents; I would never be their great love or their future wife. If I were to fight for one of them, want them to possess me, to call me theirs, I wonder, would you be reading this now? Would you ever know my name?

During our Gaye Holud, a ceremonial rite where about-to-be-wed lovers are smeared with turmeric paste on the eve of their wedding, there is an anointing of love, a sacred bond, an inundation, a re-flooding with a new, perfect memory to displace trauma's backwaters. This tradition is found wherever hands passed turmeric, South Asia to the South Pacific, for there is no one point of origin, just like the henna on our hands is a gift we trace back to ancient Egypt. We are adorned with garlands of flowers plucked from Hawaiian land — white ginger, rose, carnation, marigold — painted clay *diyas* lit around us in a circle. For the ceremony, Ma has squeezed a bottle of turmeric paste into a stone bowl, I would've much preferred raw turmeric, sandalwood, and rosewater, you know, on that authentic tip, but she trusts what's in a package, says it won't stain my skin too yellow and won't smell too much. Alice Coltrane's *Journey in Satchidananda* plays, as Mojo and I sit on a quilted blanket. One by one, our friends and family dip their fingers in the bowl, and smear our faces with turmeric, and bless us, make us laugh, each smearing is the act of remembering. In Bangla, the word for love is *bhalobasha,* or good home.

On the day of our love ceremony, everyone waited on a catamaran for us to arrive. I took a few deep breaths; Mojo took a piss. Our nerves stilled us into silence. We kissed and whispered, *I love you,* and made our way to the boat. We rode quietly on a lake to a secret island, taking in the verdant green peaks that touched the clouds, with a small group of forty Beloveds. I never understood why Bengali brides wept on their wedding day, why they kept their eyes low. Why sorrow on what should be a joyous day? *Because they're leaving their family,* Ma would tell me. In that moment, I understood what it felt like to have everyone's eyes take you in, how electric ritual felt. That day, Mojo wore a sherwani suit, the high-collar Nehru jacket and pants, but made in a tan Irish linen, perfect for the balmy mid-August Hawai'i weather. I wore a tiered lilac gown that I had made by a queer design duo in Manhattan, I forsook the color red, the color of tradition, for my spirit color. Twenty-four-karat gold dripped on my ears, nose, neck, fingers, all purchased in Jackson Heights, Queens. Yet this wasn't a wedding. We had been lovers for seven years. I wouldn't be given away by my father, there would be no imam or priest offering religious validation. Just the two of us.

Our guests left us on the boat to journey to the ceremony site. They would walk under a giant dome of a banyan tree, dappled by sunlight through the honeycombed branches. We wanted the vibe to feel like a portal. I wish I had been able to see everyone trace the steps we'd arranged with our ceremony planner, a former Miss Hawai'i and a Kānaka Maoli who knew this land and had done this so many times. Overcast sky radiated the way Mojo and I felt together — moody and dreamy and diffused. Azikiwe played our cue music, "Ganesha," by Alice Coltrane, a cosmic duet between her harp and Sita Coltrane's tamboura, a drone held the space between their sounds. We walked the short trail between the chairs to our ceremony guide, our best friend

Contessa, who stood smiling, her silk dress pink and smooth as a tongue, her eyes wet. She read the words she'd written the day before, summoning the eclipse, Venus and Mars, the celestial bodies visible each night. Mojo and I spoke our vows, his written, mine spoken from my heart. My sisters, Promiti and Boshudha, carried over our lei — Mojo's made of wispy maile leaves, mine orchid, jasmine, and tuberose. Heady, narcotic notes, by the end of the night, they'd undoubtedly heightened our mood for fucking. Contessa invited our friends and family in a call-and-response. *We promise to stand by your love. May you accept each other in every way, shape, and form.*

I now pronounce you lovers for life. No soon as Contessa uttered these words, the sky parted and anointed us with a sprinkle of rain.

When I looked up at everyone, their tears flowed freely, our lips and fingers trembled as we walked amidst these people we loved. I looked at the men I had loved before V and Max, the two who'd been present on that first night Mojo and I met, when I had fallen flat on my face in the middle of a party. We had no idea then how much our lives would change from that day. We had no idea how much pain awaited the world. How heartbroken I would feel by reckoning with my personal and my ancestral trauma, by all the histories that are laced into this book. How being enraptured by my own pain would break me, and break me apart from people who I loved as much as I have ever known how to love.

Ngozi — Perfume Interlude

HEAD

White Grapefruit
Fir Needle

HEART

Ylang Ylang
Milk of Jasmine
Tahitian Gardenia
Cannabis Flower

BASE

Somalian Myrrh
White Musk
Black Frankincense
Madagascar Vanilla

When I first set my eyes on Ngozi, I knew we'd be friends. But I had her all wrong. I'd grown up in New York, she looked Dominicana to me, and from the accent I heard in her voice, she sounded like a southerner. Turned out she was half-Nigerian, half-white, from Portland, Oregon. We lived in the women and femmes dorm at Vassar, aptly named Strong House. That first year of college, we would hit up parties together in rowdier dorms. She flashed her gorgeous smile, her oval face haloed by a bountiful Afro. Our Black and Bangla duo drew people toward us, immediately. We had a few tipsy make-outs, but being lovers wasn't in our cards. We didn't have money like our rich friends to spend on drugs or liquor; we stuck to drinking forties or smoking someone else's weed. When it came to getting laid by men on a mostly white campus, everything that made us beautiful made us intimidating.

One night, I showed up at Ngozi's dorm room, sobbing. I'd nearly been assaulted by a man on campus who'd been visiting some friends, but I'd managed to chase him out of my room. She held me in her arms, her touch soft, perceptive, strong, and soothing, the hands of a healer. We spent the rest of the night talking endlessly about everything, about growing up Mormon and Muslim, the guilt of expressing our sexuality, crushes and racism on campus, being survivors. We stayed up until dawn. We looked out the window and gasped. *Oh my gosh, girl,* she said, careful to never utter *god* in vain. It was the middle of May, and it had started to snow.

Since that night, Ngozi and I have lived in Brooklyn as roommates, traveled through Mexico, India, Venezuela, driven down the Pacific Coast Highway, hiked in the desert. We've held each other through heartbreak, emergencies, the pain of hustling to live as artists and youth educators. Astrology is our love language. We believe we're born with a map of the stars at birth — Ngozi and I share a Taurus moon. We find healing in nature. The steady and grounding aspects of the Bull are exalted in this placement. Distilling a sisterhood into a perfume is daunting, but when I lived in Oregon for a monthlong residency, we made a prototype using a simple palette of oils she'd bought online.

I want something femme, she told me, *something that makes me feel sexy.*

The erotic offers a well of replenishing and provocative force, to the woman who does not fear its revelation, wrote Audre Lorde. Channeling the erotic is a site of liberation for all femmes who've been hypersexualized, criminalized, and brutalized, extracted for their nurturing and wisdom, and discarded by the patriarchy. We have spent our lives unlearning the fear of our own sexuality and erotic power. Our Black and Bangla sisterhood is bound in each other's liberation, a living practice of revolutionary Black feminist texts we have returned to over and over again in the last twenty years. Transcending the narratives imposed on our bodies is one of the most powerful aspects of perfuming. The more we've learned about the horrors of our people's histories, both in this country and in Africa and South Asia, the more determined we've become to assert our pleasure and joy. Sexy notes in a perfume need to have that addictive quality, a scent that you can't smell enough. A leather-and-lace accord of all-naturals, an intoxication: vanilla absolute, deep and sweet, diluted into white musk, the holy duo of frankincense and myrrh, a blessing, the meaning of her name in Igbo, her father tongue. Milky tropical flowers and a touch of cannabis for all of our good times are the heart of Ngozi's perfume. I wanted the invitation to feel bright and light, white grapefruit and fir needle, like a walk in the morning forest, the soft, radiant energy we want to exude when we call new lovers into us.

How You Love — Perfume Interlude

HEAD

Grapefruit

HEART

Cardamom Absolute
Jasmine Absolute India
Rose Oil Morocco
Honeycomb

BASE

Beeswax Absolute
Sandalwood
Musk

Dana El Masri's How You Love is a perfume that I've worn during multiple psychedelic experiences. She suggests wearing the perfume and listening to the song "It's Only Love That Gets You Through" by the singer Sade on her 2000 album *Lovers Rock*. Dana imprints this upon her perfumes, a synesthetic duet of what she describes as earthy and sensual beeswax absolute. It evokes Sade's *humble, low-octave voice, its ability to drip like honey. It's all in the private moments, what I create is full of intention, hopefully the person, and the skin that receives it, knows what I meant,* Dana says to me.

I met Dana at a fragrance trade show, a weekend that had damn near broken me as I tried to prepare my wares to showcase. After a disastrous printing of perfume boxes, I feared that all of my perfumes would be judged for the shoddy packaging, a kiss of death in an industry built on the opulence a brand projects. I was among the few perfumers of color at the show. Despite my lack of pretty boxes, I did end up signing a handful of accounts with shops owned by women across the country. They were drawn to my maximalism, the painted watercolor botanicals on the labels. Most brands around me flexed luxury with austere minimalism. I remember a duo of French fragrance evaluators, a blonde and a brunette, who seemed shocked when I told them I'd never gone to perfume school; the brunette exclaimed, *You should have been a perfumer!*

Dana smelled each of my perfumes, thoughtfully taking in each one. When I learned Dana was classically trained at the Grasse Institute in France, I instantly felt intimidated. Fuck, here was a classically trained perfumer smelling my shit, me, a writer in perfumer's drag. She smiled and commented on how Mala, my ode to New Delhi, nailed the scent of South Asian groceries she loved as a child in Dubai.

That evening, after the show wrapped up, she needed to drop off her perfumes at a shop in Flatiron, so I decided to walk with her to the train. We decided to keep walking, summer lingered in the air, and we talked about everything — the Middle Eastern–Arab–South Asian–Muslim milieus that inspired us, how the first perfumer in the world was a woman in the Middle East, Tapputi, a chemist in Babylonian Mesopotamia, how the erasure of these histories from the dominant culture valued the noses of white men, how we faced snobbery and struggled to make the outsides of our brands, the packaging, match the quality of our scents, with money we hadn't inherited.

One block became sixty, until we reached our destination.

I remember the date, September 17, 2016, because two blocks from where we stood, a Muslim man bombed a dumpster in Chelsea.

"There's this feeling of social caste when it comes to this industry," said Dana, in a conversation we record for her podcast, *On the Nose,* "when you talk about me being classically trained versus you not being trained. I almost envy self-taught perfumers sometimes; you have no restrictions . . . . When I met you, I had an intuition — I smelled your work, and I could smell the soul in your work. That soul is to me what makes a perfumer."

When I smell Dana's work, I feel her resistance to narratives of dominance. I smell the oases of North Africa, the ancient, the family genealogy, the mornings full of jasmines. *I wanted to remove this bullshit notion that Egypt only smells like roses and amber,* she said, and we laughed. Rejecting the constant classification and categorization of Western perfumery and all forms of knowledge means we might be deemed Angry Women, but we're after something beyond mastery — liberation.

o

O mother I burned
in a flameless fire

O mother I suffered
a bloodless wound

mother I tossed
without a pleasure:

Loving my lord white as jasmine
I wandered through unlikely worlds.

— Mahādēviyakka, twelfth century, Vacana 69,
translated by A. K. Ramanujan in *Speaking of Śiva*

Mukti, my first play I wrote while in college at Vassar, is the story of a young poet named Mukti who committed suicide after her rape. Her friends narrate the story of her life while she appears in flashback. In the tragic climax, I choreographed the two actors in freeze-frames reenacting the rape, the only sound the organ hymnal of Sade's "It's Only Love That Gets You Through." Threaded throughout the narrative are the poems of Mahādēviyakka, a twelfth-century Indian *bhakti* poet from Karnataka. She remains one of the most beloved of the Lingayat *bhakti* poets, who renounced caste and worshipped Shiva, the most indigenous of the gods. Mahādēviyakka swore off men, her own family, and even her clothes. She strode nude across the country and uttered poems to Shiva, or as she referred to him, her Lord White as Jasmine. *Bhakti,* devotional love to the Divine, electrifies her *vacanas,* which translates to a *saying, a thing said,* a near-homophone to *vasana,* the karmic memory of a perfume across lifetimes. Words leave their imprint, as each perfume speaks a perfumer's story. During this passionate *bhakti* period in Kannada literature, poets broke from formal Sanskrit traditions, the religious texts described as *shruti,* what is heard, and *smriti,* what is remembered. *Vacanas,* to the contrary, were uttered in the moment, a canon of now, spoken in her mother language, Kannada. In the years after my assault, death would be on my mind, often, uncontrolled thoughts, a drone of suicidal ideation. I kept them at bay with art, organizing, and protest. Theater let me work through that unresolved pain, by speaking it through characters and choreographing the movement of bodies onstage. Mahādēviyakka's words, nearly a thousand years old, threaded the play with ecstatic love in the face of debilitating self-hate. Her words were thick with the love I longed to feel from another. Longed to feel for myself.

Years later, at a writer's residency in Northern California, I had a faraway view of the Pacific Ocean, a mere strip of water. Each day, I watched the sunset and moonrise. One afternoon, I looked at the sky, and there was a rainbow, not the arc of one, but a little square-shaped tab in the sky, the rest of its body hidden in the clouds. Message received. I sprayed myself with Dana's perfume, placed a tab of acid under my tongue, and played the Sade song. I decided to walk into the woods for the sunset, I wanted to find the snakeskin a friend told me she'd seen on the path. I walked through the redwood forest uphill from my cabin, smelling How You Love, the evergreen notes of redwood and sweet California bay laurel, the balsam resins of a tree in harmony with the musk on my skin. I never found the snakeskin, but I watched the sun drop into the band of sea. Darkness would come quick, the forest pitch-black until the moonrise hours later. My heart raced with fear, even as a sublime rose-gold light filtered through the trees. I smelled my friend's love poem, this *vacana* I wore on my wrist, I felt safe, I felt protected, her perfume grounded me to my body.

III

HEAD NOTES

Pilgrimage

Ancients

Psychedelia

Soliflore

Soliflore

Pilgrimage —
Perfume Interlude

HEAD

Nutmeg

Saffron

Juniper Leaf

HEART

Genda Attar, Marigold

Gulab Attar, Rose

Carnation

Cardamom

Indolene

BASE

Mysore Sandalwood

Dark Patchouli

Seaweed Absolute

Buddha Wood

Mitti Attar

Saltwater Accord

Pyre Ash

The original heart-thread of this book was supposed to be a pilgrimage. I planned to travel routes on three Great Rivers and compose perfumes to re-create an olfactory record of the journey. The Ganges — Ganga — snakes across India, until the river splits and enters Bangladesh, where it is renamed the Padma, until it splits again and becomes the Meghna, the widest river in the country, before it pours out into the sea through its many mouths at the Bay of Bengal. Rivers, like a perfume, are borderless, sites of rituals, pollutants, trade routes, civilizations, mythic passages from Earth to the Underworld.

The Great Trip is a well-worn patramyth, one that I've read more times than I can count, a literary canonical tradition that is masculine, Western, wealthy, tilted toward conquest. But I wanted to document this as a Muslim femme — how many of us had written about passages on these waters?

My pilgrimage was designed backwards, perhaps, from the perspective of a Hindu or Jain pilgrim, but for me, the beginning of this journey lay at the end of the disappearing Gangetic Delta. I planned to document a sensorium — the sounds, sights, labors, and smells — first at Cox's Bazar, where the beach stretches unbroken for more than one hundred kilometers. Native Bangladeshi coastal communities reckon with deadly climate change and the trauma of living on the treacherous edge between land and sea, a burden they have shared for years with Rohingya refugees trying to rebuild their lives in the aftermath of their loved ones' massacre by the military in Myanmar. From there, I would travel north, to my paternal ancestral home Pabna, until I crossed the border into India. My route in India — the cremation *ghats* of Varanasi, the evergreen foothills of Rishikesh, the *attar* perfume capital of Kannauj, all the way to the source at Gomukh, a melting Himalayan glacier named after a cow's mouth — would shift from the profane to the sacred back to the profane.

The omnipresent danger of the virus made a pilgrimage impossible, as people fought for their lives — for every precious breath. My grandmother died as the world went into lockdown. The virus attacked my body, too. So, I sought the stories of Bangladeshi women who had journeyed to sites of pilgrimage, pushing new frontiers, while upending the patramyths of identity and nation.

I interviewed Fariba Salma Alam, an American artist, about the Bay of Bengal and her visits to the Rohingya refugee camp, where she works on storytelling and mural art projects. For the mountainous notes, I spoke to Wasfia Nazreen, a mountaineer and the first Bangladeshi to climb the seven highest summits on each continent. On the peaks of Everest, known in Tibet as Chomolungma, Goddess Mother of the World, or Sagarmatha, Goddess of the Sky, in Nepal, she describes the alpine sensorium that comes before the harsh glacial landscape. On my writing desk, I keep ammonite fossils found in the Himalayan river-beds, a remembrance that these colossal mountains emerged from an ancient collision in the sea. As Earth gets hotter, and more polluted, the glaciers melt at a rapid pace, and inevitably the lowlands of Bangladesh are inundated with floods.

Losing my sense of smell terrified me, threatening my livelihood and what brought me so much pleasure. When I regained my strength and nose, I went to my perfume studio to work on a commissioned fragrance. Bay of Bengal saltwater accord, dirtied drop by drop with the murky notes of patchouli, seaweed absolute, and red Buddha wood, reminiscent of river pollution, pyre ashes, aquatic funk. Mitti attar accord sourced from Kannauj, remnants of worship flowers, carnation, rose, and marigold, bright and spicy florals punctuated by cardamom and the nutmeg at its heart. Perfume would be my pilgrimage.

BAY OF BENGAL —
FARIBA SALMA ALAM

The first trip, it was barren, dry, hot, no greenery. Only red-brown dirt and huts, like a *mala,* actually, it was actually kind of beautiful, these hills dotted with huts. Inside, it's a maze, at the time there wasn't clean, running water. Everybody is fed through this voucher system, there are lines to collect food during the day. There are widows, so many widows, so many men were killed, so the camps are predominantly women and children. They live in bamboo structures, but there are no permanent structures. Those aren't allowed. There can't be any signs of permanence. Bangladesh wants the Rohingya to understand that this is a temporary, transient place. You can see how it would be a dangerous place at night, like a souk city, just trails and trails you can get lost inside. All the aid workers leave before sunset. All the violence occurs at night.

On the other hand, there's a lot of liveliness, too. People falling in love in the camps, babies born in the camps, goats having babies in the camps, people growing their own plants. There's a lot more greenery. There are little shops where they sell gold or attar perfumes, with both Bangladeshi and Rohingya shopkeepers. So, there's a recovery, even when they don't know where they're going to go, and now they're being moved to these little islands in the Bay of Bengal, which we know are going to go underwater. There's a trauma in having the story only being about their trauma. The daily joys of life are stripped out of the storytelling, and they become even more dehumanized, they take on the appearance of a monolith — The Rohingya Refugee. There are sewing circles, pottery workshops, but the goal of our work is to surface it up more, to the global community, to not forget about these people in the biggest refugee camp in the world. I want to weave in their stories with the stories of Bangladeshis living there, the beach pollution, the climate, the elephants disappeared, rainwater-harvesting projects.

Loss came with our birth, Bangladesh was born out of genocide, our own country was liberated through deep trauma, deep violence, and my personal loss, the death of my father, plugged me into a collective grief at a young age. Our parents left their land, everything they knew, to pursue the unknown. Stringing threads of stories of loss that have not yet been told is a sort of frontier-building, a new frontier that is not only physical — but psychic.

CHOMOLUNGMA —
WASFIA NAZREEN

I was told Wasfia means friend of the Divine, *fia* means spiritual travel, and Nazreen means to sacrifice. I believe in *karma,* I believe there are reasons I took birth in Bangladesh, but I've had many lives in the Tibetan world, the Vajrayana Buddhist world. Bangladesh and Tibet have a huge connection. Some of the Indigenous peoples in Bangladesh are of Sino-Tibetan descent, they have lived there longer than Bengalis. I myself didn't know about it, not until I lived in Dharamshala, India, when I met His Holiness the Dalai Lama, someone I have been blessed to have as a mentor and close friend since my early twenties. He said to me, *You're from Atisha's land.* Vajrayana is rooted in balancing masculine and feminine energies, had we held on to this, the status of women would be much better.

Everything in the Himalayas and other mountains has a musky hue to it: juniper, rhododendron, frankincense and sage, and fossilized amber from pine resin that I crush into powder and put behind my ears. In the monasteries, at dawn, they burn incense made of juniper, frankincense, and rhododendron.

On Chomolungma, before anyone climbs that mountain, there's a *puja.* The experience was a humbling surrender for me. At base camp, hundreds of people come together, doesn't matter what race you are, what gender you are, you take part in the prayer ceremony. The backdrop is the highest mountains in the world, you're in a vibration that cannot be compared to anywhere else in the world. It's one of the most interconnected events I've ever felt. You make an altar for Miyosanglangma, the Goddess that resides in the mountain. It's moderated by the Tibetan and Nepali people, who reside on either side, who often bring Lamas from nearby monasteries to initiate the prayer. They read a centuries-old script, over and over again: *I seek forgiveness, I seek forgiveness, please make ways for myself, my team.* Then Sherpa people look for signs that Chomolungma made the passage clear and it was the right time to go up.

Afterward, there are celebrations, traditional dancing with food and alcohol, *chang,* a barley drink. During my last summit push, while I started from basecamp, a Sherpa brother of mine lit a candle for me in the altar and kept it lit the whole time I was on my way to the summit and returned back to basecamp. In their belief, if the light goes off, the flame goes off — then I go off the mountain. When I returned from the summit, it was the most heart-touching reckoning that this elderly man did a *puja* every single day on a rock altar. He made sure that light didn't go off, even during high winds and storms.

When you're in higher altitude, in lower oxygen,

every second can feel like an eternity. You're so far from worldly gains. You have a total orbital perspective, like you're watching from outer space. You don't have energy to talk. Going to the toilet hurts. Eating food hurts. Your body's not functioning. In the death zone, which is above twenty-six thousand feet, there are dead bodies scattered in places. It's a surreal experience — when you're looking up at the highest mountains on the planet, for a mountaineer it's heaven, but then you look down around you, and first it looks as if it's trash, then you look closely and realize, *oh, it's a headless corpse.* On the last summit push night — we climb in the dark to avoid avalanches — I crossed seven corpses of mountaineers. I knew five of them personally. They perished on the way down. The summit is only half the way, we need to conserve energy and mental clarity for the way down, which is the hardest. The majority of the world may look at it as conquering Mount Everest, but for me, mountaineering is always a pilgrimage, each stay on the mountain is a prayer.

Ancients — *Perfume Interlude*

HEAD

Kashmiri Lavender

Cypress

Fir Cone

Alpha Pinene

HEART

Geranium Absolute

Balsam Fir

English Ivy

BASE

Wild Vetiver

Tonka Bean

Forest Moss

Fossilized Amber

There is an ancient conversation going on between mosses and rocks, poetry to be sure.

— Robin Wall Kimmerer, *Gathering Moss: A Natural and Cultural History of Mosses*

On the night I met Mojo, I'd been dancing in my friend and college love Max's apartment, feeling a twinge of maybe I still loved him, or that probably I would always love him (I do). We decided to go to a party where V would be spinning records. I was curious to see how I'd feel around him — our last epic goodbye had left us both weeping on a park bench.

Within a few minutes of arriving at a party called *The Lake*, Max ditched me to dance with V's ex, while V spun his records, paying me no mind. *Well, this is the worst party of my life,* I thought. No use hiding since I already felt invisible. As I left the dance floor to grab my coat, I ran into the curly-haired Turkish man I'd seen at the door.

Do you possibly want to smoke a cigarette? I asked.

Sure, he said, smiling. *Let's go outside.*

We climbed out onto the fire escape, and I asked him about his name.

I'm Algerian and Irish, my name is Mustapha Joseph, and no soon as he said the name Mustapha, it stirred that Muslim part of me. He'd studied mathematics and computer science, minored in physics, played bass, his quietude and eyes, shy, tilted upward, infinite blue — in that moment, we understood — we needed to know each other.

As we climbed back into the party to dance and drink some Red Stripes, I missed a step and face-planted in front of everyone, including Max and V. What a way to get their attention. Mojo picked me up off the ground, didn't laugh at me, at least not until hours later. We started dancing and kissing to a lovers rock song. Eventually, after watching us from his DJ table, V pulled me aside. *This is strange,* he told me. And for once since I'd met him, I realized that I didn't care what he thought of me.

Mojo and I left the party and hailed a cab back to his place. He played Marvin Gaye's "I Want You" on vinyl and made us cups of chamomile tea. By four in the morning, after talking and talking, I asked him, *Can we take our clothes off now?* We fucked from dawn's blue until daylight. I lay on his chest, my body brown against his pale, listening to his heartbeat, inhaling the damp masc funk of his underarms, a sharp odor that felt so foreign to my own. The morning sun grew brighter through the curtains, and the entire room glowed rose.

Perfuming the body of my Beloved is an act of transposing earth smells onto his skin. In nature and embodiment, Mojo and I are as different as two people can be — watery/dry, pale/dark, mellow/passionate — so a composition that he wants to smell on me is not one he wants to smell on himself. Whereas I prefer warm woods, amber, and spice, he prefers the scent of lavender, evergreens, and ocean. The *vasanas* of our hikes through the redwoods in California became Ancients, a *bhumigandha,* an earth perfume. Walking among the ancients, we remember how binary systems dissolve in nature. Towering redwoods and low-lying ferns reproduce, sexually and asexually, underneath our feet, a vast network of mycelium with thousands of sexes terraforms the earth, providing nutrients to the forest to ensure their own survival. In my perfume, head notes of evergreens, fir, cypress, pine — oils that evaporate quickly off the skin — represent thousands of years of knowledge imprinted in our consciousness that lay just beyond our grasp.

Psychedelia

Perfume as Psychedelic Experience

NOTES

Evergreens

In a psychedelic experience, our awareness of the interconnectedness of all beings becomes acute. Natural trips and highs on plant medicine like mushrooms and cannabis lend themselves to communion with nature, friends, artistic endeavors. My most intense psychedelic trips have transpired in the artificial refuge of MDMA and LSD. While they lack the perfumed smell of naturals, they mimic how synthetic aroma chemicals let the perfumer re-create nature's palette. Even as we know we're destined to miss the mark, we attempt to create a perfume that heightens the original experience of nature. Seven minutes to heaven — after one hit of a DMT pen, our living room shapeshifted into a disco ball, hennaed patterns swirled on my legs, my sister's hair black as squid ink — then back down to Earth.

Psychedelic experience dissolves the boundaries of the body, a flooding of the past, present, and future, from moment to moment, an erasure of our egos, a universal Oneness unbound by time and flesh, a sense of peace with our trauma, as we acknowledge ancestral trauma and suffering in the world. Fear marked my first acid trip. We tripped in the summertime, I remember the date, July 17. It was one day after the bloody, brutal Holey Artisan Bakery massacre in Dhaka, in which five young Islamic militant men took diners hostage at an eatery overlooking a lake in the posh Gulshan neighborhood and murdered twenty-nine people — and three months after the gruesome murder of queer Bangladeshi magazine publisher Xulhaz Mannan and the actor Mahbub Rabbi Tonoy. I sobbed in Mojo's arms, broken with sorrow at the horror men unleashed in the name of religion. I prayed for the eternal peace of everyone who lost their lives. During that trip, in our own way, we both experienced an ego death, unsettling everything we knew ourselves to be. Psychedelics illuminate eternal truths. Nothing is original, pure, sacred, nothing matters, but love, we are descendants from every path, every lineage, something that eons of queer and trans ancestors have known: the patramyth of the male-female dyad is dead, our genders and sexualities are as infinite as nature.

THE LAST NIGHT

My friends Sandhya, Sumit, and I meet at Elsewhere, a massive music venue in Bushwick, to see our friend Zain, also known as Humeysha, perform with his band. This was my first one-on-one hang with Sandhya, even though I'd seen her around for years at different shows or writer parties, we never connected until we shared a mutual friend, Ajay. Sometimes powerful femme energy intimidates, and you want to run from what arises in its presence. Zain dressed in a white kurta pyjama, his voice serene and yearning, the veins of Sufi qawwali reach for the frontier of spirit and language, a place where Urdu and English merge.

Sandhya's friend joined us, baby-faced and turnt up by the lines of cocaine I'd just declined.

As they started playing one of my favorite Humeysha tunes, "Nusrat on the Beach," I said, *Love this song. He looks so beautiful, doesn't he?*

Is he Muslim? He looks Muslim, doesn't he? Can't bring him home to my parents if he's Muslim! she said loudly, laughing as if I were in on the joke, too. We were both Bengali, but she was Indian and Brahmin.

I'm Muslim too. I narrowed my eyes at her, but I doubt she saw me in the dark venue. I hated this pretty, stupid girl, for so thoughtlessly stealing my joy.

I couldn't bring you home, either! She laughed again. Sandhya missed the whole conversation and came up to me, offering me some of this girl's molly. *Sure, why not,* I said, slipping the powder into my drink.

Sometimes drugs help make the intensity bearable. Where there is anxiety, MDMA floods the body with love and connection. My disdain transformed into empathy, however short-lived. I saw how destabilized a recent layoff from a tech company had made her, not an easy place as a woman among bros, I saw how the way I moved in my body, dancing, feeling the joy of the MDMA and not the edge of coke, stirred something in her — jealousy. I knew this well, from women like her, Indian upper-caste women who wanted us to be the same. We were kindred, yes, as *desis.* But I would never say anything like *I could never bring you home.*

When Zain finished his set, he joined us, and we started dancing in the vestibule; lit by an electric purple light, Sandhya and I took photos of ourselves, eyes and tongues, Bangla women channeling Kali, realizing that we had craved this connection between East and West, a longing that we would not have known until that night. That psychedelic experience touched a part of us that holds the wounds of our families and inflicts that pain upon ourselves. Sandhya had lost her father, and for the first time in a long time, she let herself feel abandon and joy. I had a vial of my Beloved perfume, which I slipped to Sumit, who layered the rose and saltwater perfume on top of the Hermès he wore. We danced until dawn. Within a week, each of us would be locked inside our apartments, we would mourn the passing of Sumit's father and my Nanu, and as Sandhya said months later — *it's like we knew.*

A FOREST OF SUFIS

Henna and I met at Prospect Park for a few hours to celebrate, a few hours where we pretended that the world would be a better place, that the new president of the united states wouldn't drop bombs on the Middle East or forsake Palestine. The collective ecstasy in the streets intoxicated us; we had to peel ourselves away from the city to make our way to the Berkshires for Ajay's birthday. I met Henna through him, and we had bonded instantly. She was a public defender dancing to hip-hop in an Adidas track suit, how was I not supposed to fall in love? Our Indian friend Ajay the bridge between us two, a Pakistani-Kashmiri and Bangladeshi. On our ride up, we listened to '90s music and talked about our crushes. We saw a white owl in the trees, a good omen, right, a sign of transformation and wisdom.

The next day, our crew of friends, including Zain and Sandhya, decide to do mushrooms. I took a half-tab of acid. I didn't want mushroom shits on my hike. We drove over to the woods for a sunset hike. Most of the leaves had fallen by November. Autumn's last breath: the pink dogwood leaves that matched my monochromatic satin skirt, Reeboks, and sweater. One of Ajay's friends commented on how refreshing our city aesthetics felt against the local garb of Patagonia-L.L.Bean. I started tripping. Prancing in the forest as the sunset hit our brown skin, I became overwhelmed by the moment, the realization that these were friendships our parents had never sustained, loving communion across country, caste, religion, all of our lineages blurring the borders between Hindu, Muslim, Indian, Bangladeshi, Pakistani, Kashmiri.

What do you call a group of Sufis? A forest.

I thought about how the war kept me from holding a single Pakistani person close, kept me from knowing them as my kindred for more than thirty years, kept them from knowing the pain of my people, how our land built theirs. We stood there, Henna held me as I wept, then Zain held us both, our bodies dissolving boundaries that never should have been, a warmth as radiant as that pink *dargah,* a shrine of trees unready to shed their leaves.

POND HOUSE

In the morning, tenderness. I practice yoga. Me in the living room, Mojo in his bedroom, both of us on our computers. It's always a mental game trying to get into my body for yoga, the rolls of my stomach suffocate me when I raise my hips to *sarvangasana,* shoulder stand, then all the way back into *halasana,* plow, the little hump at the base of my neck strained when I bend backwards in *urdhva dhanurasana,* the wheel. When we lay silent in *shavasana,* I start to cry, for fourteen-year-old me, remembering that afternoon with Savage, twenty-four years ago. At some point I began to commemorate the day by acknowledging it through ritual, making the time for a yoga practice, a massage, a written reflection of who I've become since. The doorbell rings, a delivery for a giant vase bursting with flowers. A note from my sister Promiti reads: *You are a cosmic force.* Mojo takes a photo of me hugging the flowers, while I'm still in my yoga clothes. Within a few hours, my youngest sister Boshudha arrives, and we walk to the river to meet Promiti. Staring at the water calms our nerves before their first trip. *I wept all morning,* says my sister, *thinking about how young you were, and then that photo of you hugging the flowers, looking like a baby, I just lost it.*

We head back to the house before the sun disappears, not wanting to be in total darkness at the start of the trip. Sadly, the best sunlight in our apartment is the mere reflection of the sun in the windows on the $2.5 million townhouses across the street. Mojo would be our sitter, ready to offer soothing words and sitar music, order us Chinese food and roll joints, pour glasses of lime seltzer. We slip the tabs under our tongues. I decide to string a beaded mala of red jade and purple kunzite stone for Boshudha. *To open that Kundalini energy, baby, raising that coiled serpent in your root chakra to your crown,* I tell her. *I'm into it,* she says, and we laugh. Within thirty minutes, though, I feel wavy and the necklace slips out of my hands, beads rolling all around me. I want to empty my body. I leave them in the living room to take a shit and shower. I keep the light off to see the tessellations of color, neon damask tapestry patterns cover the tile, twirling like a mandala. I remember that afternoon again, standing in the shower like this, forced on my knees, how good it feels to stand here, loving myself, naked, free.

When I return to sit with my sisters and Mojo, I feel deeply that I am safe, they are a living record of my survival, my growth after trauma, which they, too, each know in their own way. They have their own stories to tell. *I was so disassociated when you were born,* I say to Boshudha. She'd arrived in May, just a few months after what happened with Savage. I barely remembered her infancy. I'd forgotten so many things, trauma has a way of dislodging memories into lost corners of our mind. I'd forgotten a beach trip to Long Island with infant Boshudha, as a family, with our grandmother. I'd forgotten how the ocean felt forbidden to me, I had never entered the water in a swimsuit until I could drive to the beach liberated from my parents' gaze.

Everything is teeming with life in here, Promiti exclaims, noticing a section of the wall pockmarked by a civilization of carpenter ants. She and I had lived here for years, until she moved to Harlem. *Everything is a bit grimier now,* I say, laughing, *it's a pukur house!* She leans back, sinking into our couch with cushions so downy they feel like beanbags. She stares around at the turquoise walls, the silk lotus flower perched on the wall altar. *Oh my god, you're right, it is a pond house!* Her voice falters. *That makes me think of Nanu. I can't believe we never got to see her again.* Green ponds were our grandmother's private chambers. I imagine Nanu's lissome body on a lone swim, her languid backstroke in a sari, face submerged under floating strands of water hyacinth — bodied and fluid — sensuality I never witnessed in real life. I only knew her as an old woman, her sorrow as tender as her smile.

Soliflore

Perfume as Beyond the Binary

NOTES

Lotus & Water Lily

Our names and the names of others around us are our
own shrines to which we ought to make pilgrimage.

— Kazim Ali, Day Twenty-Five, *Fasting for Ramadan*

From the very start of my life, my name announced my gender and religion. Tanwi Nandini Islam is a name corseted
tight with meanings. When my parents named me, they wanted
to express their syncretic, intercultural, *adhunik,* or modern,
beliefs by honoring both the Hindu and Muslim traditions that
run through our country, like rivers that flow from the mountains in India through the plains of Bangladesh. Tanwi, in Sanskrit, means the epitome of femininity, a youthful intention
that my parents drew from a line of poetry, or a blade of grass
in Pali, the language of Buddhist texts. Nandini is a name for
the goddess Durga, a daughter, or a holy cow. And Islam means
submission, or peace.

Tanaïs, the name I have given myself, is a portmanteau of
the first two letters of my three names. There is no splitting me
apart. This renaming liberates me from patrilineage, gender,
and religion in a single utterance.

As language evolved through poetry and song, Bengali lost its gendered pronouns in an era known as Abahatta, or Meaningless Sounds, the period when Old Bengali crystallized into a distinct language. We kept our gender-neutral language — a vital remnant of our pre-Aryan ancestral tongue that survived the relentless Brahminical expansion into the eastern frontier of Bengal. Meaningless sounds, an arcane name that reveals the resentment of the literate Sanskrit-speaking upper caste about their holy language's bastardization by everyday people.

I trace the absence of grammatical gender in my mother language to why I don't identify as a woman in an inherent way. When I learned English, I learned to inhabit a painful gender binary. I learned to think of others as *she* or *he,* rather than *they* or *them.* The name Tanaïs is a genderless repossession of my personal proto-language before English stole this part of me. In Bengali, *Ó* refers to he or she, no matter the person's gender. The word *they* is *tara,* the word for star. I imagine my ancestors gesturing at a person or at the stars in the sky, until the words merged into one.

o

Here are the sacred places,
I have not seen a place of pilgrimage
and abode of bliss like my body.

— Dohakosa, *The Rhyming Couplets of Sarahapada,*
sometime in the ninth century

Between the eighth and twelfth centuries, Tantric Buddhist scholars who rejected caste and senseless binaries wrote mystic songs of realization, known as the *Charyapada*. One of these sages, Saraha, or the One Who Shoots the Arrow, is said to have been initiated by the Wisdom-Arrow Dakini, a low-caste, brown-skinned woman from East Bengal who told him, *Buddha may be known through symbols and actions, not through words and books.* Liberation is beyond words; it must be lived, practiced, acted upon. The symbol of the arrow — that which pierces the consciousness — illuminated the Mahamudra, or Great Seal, to Saraha. All beings can attain realization of emptiness in their own lifetime, with their own innate way of being, what was called the easy path, or *sahaja*. For the men who had been raised within the strict confines of caste, loving, fucking, learning from the women of the lowest castes became a way of realizing their consciousness. What did those femmes receive in return? Protection?

At the time, a revival of Brahmin social supremacy led to vicious attacks on Buddhist monasteries. Monks, nuns, and followers of Buddhist practice were tortured and exiled. Some crossed the treacherous terrain to seek refuge in the Land of Snow, Tibet. The *Charyapada* were written in *sandhya bhasha*, or twilight language, lush with metaphors and hidden meanings to protect this sacred poetry and the poets from being destroyed.

All beings have been my mother. In this endless cycle of *samsara*, every animal, plant, and person, no matter how far away or evil, has been our mother in one of our lifetimes. Meditating on this thought offered comfort apart from the rage I felt living in a neighborhood rife with microaggressions. Even the white woman who'd walked her dog so aggressively that I fell down on the sidewalk, battered my knees bloody while she hardly even glanced my way — both the woman and her dog had once been my mother. What a strange, beautiful thought that Buddhists have meditated upon for a few thousand years. A way to dislodge hatred — of ourselves, of others — that builds up after living under supremacy, in the States, white heterosexist capitalist patriarchy, our entire lives.

During the hardest parts of writing this book, as I immersed myself in the voices of rape survivors in Bangladesh, as I healed from the virus, I felt myself retreating to a nihilistic place, what was the fucking point of being alive when humanity proved itself to be so terrible, over and over again?

Mojo and I mothered each other during the past decade we've been together. The way we both inhabit the masculine and feminine, our queerness, is hidden by our external embodiment. He's shared a mantra with me — *Om Tare Tuttare Ture Svaha* — to help me relax and breathe. A new Mother: Tara. This *shyamla,* green-hued, Mother Goddess born of yoginis in Bengal. Some say Tara worship began with an ancient star cult, worshipped by seafarers who read the sky to find their way home across perilous waters. Though Tara worship would disappear from its birthplace, the goddess flourished in Tibet, spread by the Buddhist Bengali scholar and monk, Atisa Dipankar, who reformed Buddhism in the Land of Snows. Atisa, like Saraha before him, learned teachings from the femme yoginis in the *bon,* the forests of Bengal. Patramyth remembers only the great scholars who wrote their teachings down.

Mojo and I meet at a cultural confluence, as part of the Muslim diaspora, but his internal spiritual path of yoga and meditation practice draws from syncretic Buddhist traditions more than Islam or Christianity. The memory of a Buddhist or Hindu past has vanished in my family, but as a distant descendant, I wanted more information. Western practioners never discussed the radical vision Buddhism offered, as a way out of Brahmini-cal patriarchy for people of oppressed castes, women, and sex workers in South Asia. I tried to find spaces of meditation or dharma talks in New York City, curious to learn more about the different schools of Buddhist thought. I had always resisted the idea of renunciation of pleasure, drugs, or the enjoyment of the senses — it felt too serious. In the Theravada lineage, the most orthodox and oldest teachings recorded in the Pali language, the *arhat,* one who is worthy, sought to break free from the cycle of *samsara* to reach *nirvana,* liberation from rebirth. This strand of Buddhism lives on in Sri Lanka and Myanmar — both coun-tries with very recent histories of genocide. The Brahminical roots of this tradition persist. Mahayana traditions rejected the *arhat* as the ultimate expression of Enlightenment, moving to-ward a practice available to a *bodhisattva,* anyone who yearned to be a Buddha. Their path of selfless realization centered on *karuna,* compassion for all beings, and *sunyata,* emptiness, the Void where nothing exists–everything exists. Out of the Mahayana tradition, which expanded across East Asia through exchanges on the Silk Road, the Vajrayana tradition evolved, traveling from eastern India to Tibet. *Vajra,* thunderbolt or diamond, symbolized how this path led to faster realization. Still centered on love and compassion, from this lineage Tantric practices evolved. One had to be initiated by a guru into the secret Tantric rites, involving meditations, mantras, visualizations of mandalas. For the Tantric, the Divine existed in all beings, in *sunyata,* emptiness; all binaries — masculine and feminine, self and other, pure or polluted — fell away. In that perfect state of emptiness: sacredness.

In the *Lotus Sutra,* one of the most venerated texts in Mahayana Buddhism, there is a telling scene. A young Naga girl, the daughter of the Naga king of the ocean, Sagara, was said to have attained Enlightenment.

I cannot believe that this girl in a space of an instant could actually achieve correct enlightenment, said one of the Buddha's followers in assembly. Another said, *This is difficult to believe. Why? Because a woman's body is soiled and defiled, not a Vessel for the Law.*

Clearly, the Buddha's message had not undone their prejudices.

In response, the Naga girl produced *a precious jewel worth as much as the thousand-million-fold world,* and presented this to the Buddha, who accepted the gift. *Watch me,* she said, transforming herself into a man, unleashing all of the practices of a *bodhisattva,* reciting the Law for all living and heavenly beings, everywhere. The Naga sat upon a jeweled lotus, and the men believed. At that point of transformation — transition — they emerge beyond the gender binary, which was, and has always been, immaterial to consciousness. They rendered the patramyth that only men were the ones who could attain Liberation irrelevant.

o

Oh friend,
I tried to dive into the river of unconditional love.
I tried and tried in my heart, but could not immerse
    myself due to the fear of death.

— Baul song, composer unknown,
taught by Kanai Das Baul

We would not be able to journey on rivers as we planned, but we found a way to return to the Baul-Fakir mystic musicians of Bengal, in an online workshop hosted by Parvathy Baul, a renowned Baul musician whose family hailed from East Bengal but migrated west after Partition. She had heard a Baul musician sing and renounced her middle-class life to be initiated as a Baul. Her voice pierces the heart, as she plucks her one-string *ektara*, her dreadlocks so long they sweep the floor. We would learn songs by Bauls themselves, a taste of their *sadhana*, practices, which have evolved over a thousand years at the confluence of three Tantric rivers of South Asian thought: Sahaja Buddhism — a path of *sahaja* made self-liberation possible for each person; Vaishnava *bhakti* — devotion to the Divine in the form of Radha and Krishna; and Sufi Islam, where the worshipper is the Lover who seeks dissolution into All — h, their Beloved. No caste or religious dogma could ever contain a human being. None of that Brahminical obsession with purity and pollution; all of our profane fluids — shit, blood, piss, tears, semen, vaginal fluid, menstrual blood — were sacred as the tides, the rivers, floods, and the moon. Whether by their music or lovemaking, Bauls seek Realization, transcendence rooted in the body, a yoga to experience Oneness.

We tuned into the workshop in India near midnight, and our first teacher, Kanai Das Baul, taught us a song about the river of unconditional love. He appeared to be in his sixties, dressed in saffron-orange clothes, with a long white beard. After surviving smallpox as an infant, he lost his sight. When a Baul heard him singing, struck by his melancholy and sweet voice, he asked the ten-year-old Kanai Das Baul's parents, who were poor laborers, if he could initiate the boy as Baul.

After the death of this guru, Kanai Das Baul and his wife moved to the sacred Tantric Hindu crematorium at Tarapith, a temple devoted to a fearsome aspect of the Goddess Tara, her taste for blood akin to Kali.

That evening, we learned the lyrics to his song, which he sang three times, and each time we got to the end — *two died in one death, who else can die like that?* — I felt flooded with emotion. At the end of each session, they bowed down to each other, devotion to the guru at the center of their *sadhana,* they touched their forehead to the ground, and Mojo and I held our hands in prayer and bowed down, too.

Soliflore — Perfume Outro

HEAD
North African Neroli

HEART
Sri Lankan Blue Water Lily
Indian White Lotus
Indian Pink Lotus
Saltwater Accord

BASE
Mitti Attar
Bandarban Sandalwood
Leather Accord

I wanted to make a fragrance that both Mojo and I could wear, smell on each other, wear as we meditated in the morning, or practiced yoga in the evening, something delicate and ethereal, to ease this period of solitude so far from everyone. When the sacred blue water lily and white lotus oils arrive in the mail, I know I want to create a lotus-water lily soliflore, water florals blooming out of a pond, out of our pits and stink, sandalwood and mitti attar from the Ganges River, salted by the Bay of Bengal at its mouths, base notes of the pilgrimage I never went on, all of these eternal metaphors for beauty emerging out of shit. Perfume as fluid as language, as lineage, as rivers of sweat; men try to load flowers like guns, turning lotuses and water lilies into symbols of fascists and nations, and our bodies resist such meanings, so we make love in the afternoon as though we've got all the time in the world. We breathe and lick and kiss, and I can't help but think about everything, how we will lose everyone we love, we will lose each other, nothing can prepare us for this inevitable, so we begin, with what is easiest for us to let go — our breath.

Acknowledgments

I could not have written this book without the following loved ones, thank you—

Ma and Baj, Habiba and Ashraf, for your gifts of language and art, the love of everything Bangla, your stories and prayers under a full moon.

Promiti and Boshudha, for your profound brilliance and beauty, for each moment of beachside healing that brought us closer to the Divine.

My late Nanu, Begum Jahanara Rais, and my Dadu, Lutfunessa, your dreams bloom inside me.

My team: PJ Mark, for so tenderly believing in this work and seeing my vision in all its forms. Pilar Garcia-Brown, for reading my work with piercing insight, as well as Jenny Xu and the team at HarperCollins.

Writer and artist comrades, for witnessing and holding my work with love: Jenny Zhang, Ngozi Olemgbe, Talysha

Moneé, Chioma Ebinama, Imani Perry, Kiese Laymon, Nadxi Nieto, Julia de Quadros, Max Cohen, Victor Axelrod, Dana El Masri, Calvin Dutton, Priscilla Dobler-Dzul, Laila Lalami and Akwaeke Emezi.

MacDowell, Tin House, Djerassi, for retreats to write, fall apart, commune with artists.

My diasporic, syncretic inner heart: Ajay Madiwale, Samhita Mukhopadhyay, Zain Alam, Himanshu Suri, Anik Khan, Henna Khan, Bilal Qureshi and Vijay Iyer, for conversations, joy and reckoning with history through our union.

Bangla femme pioneers whose visions permeate my own, for your art and courage—Fariba Salma Alam, Tarfia Faizullah, Fariha Róisín and Wasfia Nasreen.

Mojo Talantikite, my love, we made it through one of the hardest years of our lives. You held me through it all. Our love is ocean. Infinite.

And finally, this book holds in its heart all of the forgotten femmes and queers whose art, writings, heartaches, joys, lives and deaths have been erased by the patramyth, to the survivors, the *birangona* of Bangladesh, to those who perished in the name of Liberation, to those who lived to build a nation, to those who scattered across the world, my people: this is for us.

Works Cited

BOOKS

Akhtar, Shaheen. *Women in Concert: An Anthology of Bengali Muslim Women's Writings, 1904–1938*. Kolkata: Street, 2008.

Ali, Kazim. *Fasting for Ramadan*. North Adams, MA: Tupelo Press, 2011.

Ambedkar, B. R. *Annihilation of Caste: The Annotated Critical Edition*. London: Verso, 2014.

———. *The Untouchables: Who Were They and Why They Became Untouchables*, 1948.

Anzaldúa, Gloria. *Borderlands, La Frontera: The New Mestiza*. San Francisco: Aunt Lute Books, 1999.

Arctander, Steffen. *Perfume and Flavour Materials of Natural Origin*. Elizabeth, NJ: printed by the author, 1960.

Bahadur, Gaiutra. *Coolie Woman: The Odyssey of Indenture*. London: C. Hurst, 2016.

Bald, Vivek. *Bengali Harlem and the Lost Histories of South Asian America*. Cambridge, MA: Harvard University Press, 2015.

Barthes, Roland. *A Lover's Discourse: Fragments*. New York: Hill and Wang, 1977.

Bass, Gary Jonathan. *The Blood Telegram: India's Secret War in East Pakistan*. Noida, Uttar Pradesh: Random House India, 2013.

Dehlvi, Sadia. *Sufism: The Heart of Islam*. New Delhi: HarperCollins Publishers India, 2010.

Denton, John M. *A Sanskrit Dictionary: A Concise Sanskrit Dictionary of Words from Principal Traditional Scriptures, Major Philosophical Works, Dhatu Pathah and Various Grammar Texts. Transliterated in English Script and Alphabetical Order and including Many Monier-Williams References*. DFT, 2015.

Diaz, Natalie. *Postcolonial Love Poem: Poems*. Minneapolis: Graywolf Press, 2020.

Dimock, Edward Cameron, Jr. *The Place of the Hidden Moon: Erotic Mysticism in the Vaisnava-sahajiyā Cult of Bengal*. Chicago: University of Chicago Press, 1966.

Doniger, Wendy. *The Hindus: An Alternative History*. New York: Penguin, 2009.

———. *The Rig Veda*. London: Penguin, 2005.

Eaton, Richard Maxwell. *Rise of Islam and the Bengal Frontier, 1204–1760*. Berkeley: University of California Press, 1996.

Faizullah, Tarfia. *Seam*. Carbondale, IL: Crab Orchard Review & Southern Illinois University Press, 2014.

Fanon, Frantz. *A Dying Colonialism*. Translated by Haakon Chevalier. New York: Grove Press, 1982.

Foucault, Michel. *The History of Sexuality*. New York: Vintage, 1990.

Guhaṭhākuratā, Meghanā, and Willem van Schendel, eds. *The Bangladesh Reader: History, Culture, Politics*. Durham, NC: Duke University Press, 2013.

Hallisey, Charles. *Therigatha: Poems of the First Buddhist Women*. Cambridge, MA: Harvard University Press, 2015.

Hartman, Saidiya. *Lose Your Mother: A Journey Along the Atlantic Slave Route*. New York: Farrar, Straus & Giroux, 2008.

———. *Wayward Lives, Beautiful Experiments: Intimate Histories of Social Upheaval*. New York: Norton, 2019.

Hossain, Begum Rokeya Sakhawat. *Sultana's Dream: A Feminist Utopia; and Selections from* The Secluded Ones. Edited and translated by Roushan Jahan. New York: Feminist Press, 1988.

Ibrahim, Nilima, and Fayeza S. Hasanat. *As a War Heroine, I Speak*. Dhaka: Bangla Academy, 2017.

Kettler, Andrew. *The Smell of Slavery: Olfactory Racism and the Atlantic World*. Cambridge: Cambridge University Press, 2020.

Knight, Lisa I. *Contradictory Lives: Baul Women in India and Bangladesh*. New York: Oxford University Press, 2014.

Lorde, Audre. *Sister Outsider: Essays and Speeches*. Berkeley: Ten Speed Press, 2016.

Marx, Karl. *Capital: A Critique of Political Economy*. Translated by Ben Fowkes. New York: Vintage, 1981.

McHugh, James. *Sandalwood and Carrion: Smell in Premodern Indian Religion and Culture*. New York: Oxford University Press, 2012.

Mitra, Durba. *Indian Sex Life: Sexuality and the Colonial Origins of Modern Social Thought*. Princeton, NJ: Princeton University Press, 2020.

Mookherjee, Nayanika. *The Spectral Wound: Sexual Violence, Public Memories, and the Bangladesh War of 1971*. New Delhi: Zubaan, 2016.

Morrison, Toni. *The Source of Self-Regard: Selected Essays, Speeches, and Meditations*. New York: Knopf, 2019.

Olivelle, Patrick. *Upanishads*. Oxford: Oxford University Press, 1998.

Prashad, Vijay. *The Karma of Brown Folk*. Minneapolis: University of Minnesota Press, 2007.

Ramanujan, A. K. *Speaking of Śiva*. Harmondsworth, UK: Penguin, 1973.

Reinarz, Jonathan, and Leonard D. Schwarz. *Medicine and the Workhouse*. Rochester, NY: University of Rochester Press, 2013.

Roy, Arundhati. *The End of Imagination*. Chicago: Haymarket Books, 2016.

Roy, Asim. *Islamic Syncretistic Tradition in Bengal*. Princeton, NJ: Princeton University Press, 2016.

Saha, Poulomi. *An Empire of Touch: Women's Political Labor and the Fabrication of East Bengal*. New York: Columbia University Press, 2019.

Saikia, Yasmin. *Women, War, and the Making of Bangladesh: Remembering 1971*. Durham, NC: Duke University Press, 2011.

Sarkar, Mahua. *Visible Histories, Disappearing Women: Producing Muslim Womanhood in Late Colonial Bengal*. Durham, NC: Duke University Press, 2010.

Sarkar, Sumit, Neeladri Bhattacharya, and Dipesh Chakrabarty. *The Swadeshi Movement in Bengal, 1903–1908*. Ranikhet: Permanent Black, 2010.

Shaw, Miranda. *Passionate Enlightenment*. Princeton, NJ: Princeton University Press, 1994.

Watson, Burton. *The Lotus Sutra*. Delhi: Sri Satguru, 1999.

Williams, Julie Stewart, and Suelyn Ching Tune. *Kamehameha II: Liholiho and the Impact of Change*. Honolulu: Kamehameha Schools Press, 2001.

Zakaria, Anam. *1971: A People's History from Bangladesh, Pakistan and India.* Haryana, India: Vintage, 2019.

ARTICLES

Ahmadi, Amir. "Two Chthonic Features of the *Daēva* Cult in Historical Evidence." *History of Religions* 54, no. 3 (2015): 346–70.

Ahmed, Shahab. "Ibn Taymiyyah and the Satanic Verses." *Studia Islamica*, no. 87 (1998): 67–124.

Allen, Richard B. "Satisfying the 'Want for Labouring People': European Slave Trading in the Indian Ocean, 1500–1850." *Journal of World History* 21, no. 1 (2010): 45–73.

Bano, Shadab. "Women Slaves in Medieval India." *Proceedings of the Indian History Congress* 65 (2004): 314–23.

Bhattacharji, Sukumari. "Prostitution in Ancient India." *Social Scientist* 15, no. 2 (1987): 32–61.

Boyill, E. W. "Empire Production of Essential Oils for Perfumery." *Journal of the Royal Society of Arts* 83, no. 4283 (1934): 123–40.

Briot, Eugénie. "From Industry to Luxury: French Perfume in the Nineteenth Century." *Business History Review* 85, no. 2 (2011): 273–94.

Chakrabarti, Kunal. "A History of Intolerance: The Representation of Buddhists in the Bengal Purāṇas." *Social Scientist* 44, nos. 5/6 (2016): 11–27.

Chaman. "The Voice of Nazr-ul-Islam." *Indian Literature* 20, no. 4 (1977): 109–18.

Chatterjee, Indrani. "Monastic Governmentality, Colonial Misogyny, and Postcolonial Amnesia in South Asia." *History of the Present* 3, no. 1 (2013): 57–98.

Chaudhuri, K. N. "India's Foreign Trade and the Cessation of the East India Company's Trading Activities, 1828–40." *Economic History Review* 19, no. 2 (1966): 345–63.

Dalrymple, William. "Rush Hour for the Gods." *National Interest*, no. 107 (2010): 28–37.

Dasgupta, Atis. "The Bauls and Their Heretic Tradition." *Social Scientist* 22, nos. 5/6 (1994): 70–83.

———. "Islam in Bengal: Formative Period." *Social Scientist* 32, nos. 3/4 (2004): 30–41.

Diouf, Sylviane A. "American Slaves Who Were Readers and Writers." *Journal of Blacks in Higher Education*, no. 24 (1999): 124–25.

Dubey, Muchkund. "The Sadhana of Lalan Fakir." *India International Centre Quarterly* 24, nos. 2/3 (1997): 139–50.

Eliade, Mircea. "Spirit, Light, and Seed." *History of Religions* 11, no. 1 (1971): 1–30.

Gautam, Sanjay K. "The Courtesan and the Birth of *Ars Erotica* in the *Kāmasūtra*: A History of Erotics in the Wake of Foucault." *Journal of the History of Sexuality* 23, no. 1 (2014): 1–20.

Gode, P. K. "History of Ambergris in India between about A.D. 700 and 1900." *Chymia* 2 (1949): 51–56.

———. "Studies in the History of Indian Plants: History of Mendī or Henna (between B.C. 2000 and A.D. 1850)." *Annals of the Bhandarkar Oriental Research Institute* 28, nos. 1/2 (1947): 14–25.

Gupta, Karunakana. "The Nāgas and the Naga Cult in Ancient Indian History." *Proceedings of the Indian History Congress* 3 (1939): 214–29.

Hatley, Shaman. "Mapping the Esoteric Body in the Islamic Yoga of Bengal." *History of Religions* 46, no. 4 (2007): 351–68.

Herzenberg, Caroline L. "Women in Science during Antiquity and the Middle Ages." *Journal of College Science Teaching* 17, no. 2 (1987): 124–27.

Howes, David. "Can These Dry Bones Live? An Anthropological Approach to the History of the Senses." *Journal of American History* 95, no. 2 (2008): 442–51.

Iqbal, Iftekhar. "The Space between Nation and Empire: The Making and Unmaking of Eastern Bengal and Assam Province, 1905–1911." *Journal of Asian Studies* 74, no. 1 (2015): 69–84.

Jash, Pranabananda. "The Cult of Manasa in Bengal." *Proceedings of the Indian History Congress* 47 (1986): 169–77.

Jung, Dinah. "The Cultural Biography of Agarwood: Perfumery in Eastern Asia and the Asian Neighbourhood." *Journal of the Royal Asiatic Society*, 3rd ser., vol. 23, no. 1 (2013): 103–25.

Karim, Anwarul. "Shamanism in Bangladesh." *Asian Folklore Studies* 47, no. 2 (1988): 277–309.

Khan, Muin-ud-Din Ahmad. "Economic Conditions of the Muslims of Bengal under the East India Company, 1737–1860." *Islamic Studies* 6, no. 3 (1967): 277–88.

Khan, Zillur R. "March Movement of Bangladesh: Bengali Struggle for Political Power." *Indian Journal of Political Science* 33, no. 3 (1972): 291–322.

Kim, Jinah. "Local Visions, Transcendental Practices: Iconographic Innovations of Indian Esoteric Buddhism." *History of Religions* 54, no. 1 (2014): 34–68.

Kim, Jinah. "Unheard Voices: Women's Roles in Medieval Buddhist Artistic Production and Religious Practices in South Asia." *Journal of the American Academy of Religion* 80, no. 1 (2012): 200–232.

King, Anya. "The Importance of Imported Aromatics in Arabic Culture: Illustrations from Pre-Islamic and Early Islamic Poetry." *Journal of Near Eastern Studies* 67, no. 3 (2008): 175–89.

———. "The New *Materia Medica* of the Islamicate Tradition: The Pre-Islamic Context." *Journal of the American Oriental Society* 135, no. 3 (2015): 499–528.

Krakauer, Benjamin. "The Ennobling of a 'Folk Tradition' and the Disempowerment of the Performers: Celebrations and Appropriations of Bāul-Fakir Identity in West Bengal." *Ethnomusicology* 59, no. 3 (2015): 355–79.

Lal, Ruby. "Historicizing the Harem: The Challenge of a Princess's Memoir." *Feminist Studies* 30, no. 3 (2004): 590–616.

Le Maguer, Sterenn. "The Incense Trade during the Islamic Period." *Proceedings of the Seminar for Arabian Studies* 45 (2015): 175–83.

Ludden, David. "The Politics of Independence in Bangladesh." *Economic and Political Weekly* 46, no. 35 (2011): 79–85.

McDaniel, June. "The Embodiment of God among the Bāuls of Bengal." *Journal of Feminist Studies in Religion* 8, no. 2 (1992): 27–39.

McHugh, James. "*Blattes de Byzance* in India: Mollusk Opercula and the History of Perfumery." *Journal of the Royal Asiatic Society* 23, no. 1 (2013): 53–67.

———. "The Classification of Smells and the Order of the Senses in Indian Religious Traditions." *Numen* 54, no. 4 (2007): 374–419.

———. "The Disputed Civets and the Complexion of the God: Secretions and History in India." *Journal of the American Oriental Society* 132, no. 2 (2012): 245–73.

———. "Seeing Scents: Methodological Reflections on the Intersensory Perception of Aromatics in South Asian Religions." *History of Religions* 51, no. 2 (2011): 156–77.

Meghelli, Samir. "From Harlem to Algiers: Transnational Solidarities between the African American Freedom Movement and Algeria, 1962–1978." In *Black*

Routes to Islam, edited by Manning Marable and Hishaam D. Aidi, 99–119. New York: Palgrave Macmillan, 2009.

Mohaiemen, Naeem. "Flying Blind: Waiting for a Real Reckoning on 1971." *Economic & Political Weekly*, 2011.

Morrison, Toni, et al. "Guest Column: Roundtable on the Future of the Humanities in a Fragmented World." *PMLA* 120, no. 3 (2005): 715–23.

Mukhopadhyay, Bhaskar. "Writing Home, Writing Travel: The Poetics and Politics of Dwelling in Bengali Modernity." *Comparative Studies in Society and History* 44, no. 2 (2002): 293–318.

Nath, Vijay. "From 'Brahmanism' to 'Hinduism': Negotiating the Myth of the Great Tradition." *Social Scientist* 29, nos. 3/4 (2001): 19–50.

Newcomb, Robert M. "Botanical Source-Areas for Some Oriental Spices." *Economic Botany* 17, no. 2 (1963): 127–32.

Parry, John W. "The Story of Spices." *Economic Botany* 9, no. 2 (1955): 190–207.

Pawde, Kumud. "The Story of My Sanskrit." In *Subject to Change: Teaching Literature in the Nineties*, edited by Susie J. Tharu. London: Sangam, 1998.

Puri, Jyoti. "Concerning *Kamasutra*s: Challenging Narratives of History and Sexuality." *Signs* 27, no. 3 (2002): 603–39.

Ram, H. Y. Mohan. "A Leaf from Nature." *India International Centre Quarterly* 38, nos. 3/4 (2011): 344–53.

Ratul, Tanvir. "Introduction to Charyapada." https://www.academia.edu/40886990/Introduction_to_Charyapada.

Ray, Himanshu Prabha. "The Archaeology of Bengal: Trading Networks, Cultural Identities." *Journal of the Economic and Social History of the Orient* 49, no. 1 (2006): 68–95.

Rotter, Andrew J. "Empires of the Senses: How Seeing, Hearing, Smelling, Tasting, and Touching Shaped Imperial Encounters." *Diplomatic History* 35, no. 1 (2011): 2–19.

Said, Edward W. "Orientalism." *Georgia Review* 31, no. 1 (1977): 162–206.

Sen, Amartya. "Poetry and Reason: Why Rabindranath Tagore Still Matters." *New Republic*, June 8, 2011. https://newrepublic.com/article/89649/rabindranath-tagore.

Sen, Tansen. "The Intricacies of Premodern Asian Connections." *Journal of Asian Studies* 69, no. 4 (2010): 991–99.

Sengupta, Mekhala. "Courtesan Culture in India: The Transition from the Devdasi to the Tawaif or Boijee." *India International Centre Quarterly* 41, no. 1 (2014): 124–40.

Shah, Shalini. "Engendering the Material Body: A Study of Sanskrit Literature." *Social Scientist* 47, nos. 7/8 (2019): 31–52.

Shulman, David. "The Scent of Memory in Hindu South India." *RES: Anthropology and Aesthetics*, no. 13 (1987): 122–33.

Singh, Anand. "'Destruction' and 'Decline' of Nālandā Mahāvihāra: Prejudices and Praxis." *Journal of the Royal Asiatic Society of Sri Lanka*, n.s., vol. 58, no. 1 (2013): 23–49.

Sopher, David E. "Indigenous Uses of Turmeric (*Curcuma domestica*) in Asia and Oceania." *Anthropos* 59, nos. 1/2 (1964): 93–127.

Spivak, Gayatri Chakravorty. "Moving Devi." *Cultural Critique*, no. 47 (2001): 120–63.

——. "Translating in a World of Languages." *Profession* (2010): 35–43.

Spruill, Larry H. "Slave Patrols, 'Packs of Negro Dogs' and Policing Black Communities." *Phylon* 53, no. 1 (2016): 42–66.

WEBSITES

Aftelier Perfumes, by natural perfumer Mandy Aftel. https://www.aftelier.com/.

Federal Writers' Project: Slave Narrative Project, Vol. 4, Georgia, Part 2, Garey Jones. 1937. Manuscript/Mixed Material. https://www.loc.gov/item/mesn042/.